Earthquake in Haiti:

The Pornography of Poverty and the Politics of Development

Books by Julian Vigo

Performative Bodies, Hybrid Tongues:
Race, Gender and Modernity in Latin America and the Maghreb

Earthquake in Haiti:
The Pornography of Poverty and the Politics of Development

JULIAN VIGO

Baobab Tree Books

London - New York

Published in Great Britain

ISBN: 0-9928354-0-2
ISBN-13: 978-0-9928354-0-8

Earthquake in Haiti:
The pornography of poverty and the politics of development / Julian Vigo
Includes bibliographical references and index.

Published by
Baobab Tree Books
www.baobabtreebooks.com

*This book is dedicated to my father, Surendra Mankodi,
who filled my childhood with love, the moral lessons
of Gandhi and Martin Luther King, Jr and
who taught me to answer lies with truth.*

Contents

Acknowledgments

This book advocates, among other things, rethinking the way we currently think about international development and humanitarian relief. This text chronicles my experiences from February through July 2010 when I went to Haiti to lend my hand to the relief efforts. As someone who came from academia although having experienced the NGO world in Nicaragua, Guatemala, Peru and Bolivia, I was still naïve about certain practices in the world of humanitarian aid that were outside my experience. I went to Haiti thinking that these institutions must have some effect on helping people if they continue to exist year after year, disaster after disaster. My ideas about most NGOs and UN agencies were vastly changed as my experience taught me to believe what I saw, not what I wanted to believe about these organizations. My work in Haiti served as a crash course in certain types of fieldwork with which I had not been familiar, but it also functioned as that experience when I went from being a person who actually believed that humanitarian aid works, to having my eyes opened as to how it truly functions. Or, as a colleague of mine in Haiti remarked, "If the UN were a business, they would be bankrupt since at the end of the quarter the balance sheets would not prove that anything had been produced and these agencies would be in the red perpetually."

The research and writing of this book would not have been possible without every single person mentioned herein, most notably the Haitian people whose devastating conditions and personal narratives I took to heart and incorporated within my struggle to make sense of my presence in this beautiful country. I especially owe a debt of recognition to those Haitians at UN Log Base who patiently stood by watching so many foreigners, so-called "experts," invade their country in order to enact a humanitarian carnage I hope never again to witness. These Haitians were an immense wealth of information for this manuscript and they assisted me in learning Creole, learning about their country and they allowed me to use computers, Internet connection or an electrical outlet to recharge my iPhone from which most of this manuscript was written.

I am also thankful to the many United Nations and NGO workers whose professionalism and perspicuousness in their missions and their own critiques of the systems helped me to understand what we were all immersed in. Having recently left a rather toxic situation at a Canadian university for which John Waters might have written that particular scenario of cruelty and comedy, these young specialists showed me the meaning of professionalism and collaboration. Likewise these individuals demonstrated incredible strength in their belief of a system which they knew was flawed and which they critiqued, all the while attempting to advance projects they believed that would help the people of Haiti. I am most especially thankful to some of the central actors in this text from the United Nations whose ability to withstand incredible abuse at the hands of these structures is commendable given their efforts to ameliorate the system from inside. While this text critiques the structures within which these individuals worked, this publication is simply not a critique of these individuals as most every UN staff member under the age of forty I met in Haiti maintained core ideals and professional practices which would be commendable outside of the theatre of development. However, this manuscript does not appraise these values, but rather takes to task the actions of development and relief efforts. Ultimately I try to strike a balance between these workers' impossible tasks in the field and the even more fantastic institutionalizations of "development," intelligible only as an extension of colonialism. Some of these staff members' names have been changed in this text given the possible repercussions on their livelihood even after having left these organizations.

It should be noted that I attempted to reach the UN offices in New York and Geneva from August 2010 through December 2012. I was promised calls in return. I never received any communication in return. Specifically, I asked to meet with UNICEF's Chief of Child Protection, Susan Bissell, but I ended up speaking with another administrator who claimed that no complaints by any UNICEF or NGO workers were lodged. I personally know of two individuals who made complaints with UNICEF for the unethical practices they witnessed and experienced while in Haiti. Their stories are contained herein.

I am grateful to Amy Dahl who read through this manuscript and who gave me incredibly detailed feedback. I must also thank Rodrigo Silva, another volunteer in Haiti, who taught me valuable lessons in permaculture and pedagogy. When the situations were not mind-boggling, they were enriching and often fun with you. Also of great importance while tidying up the redaction of this manuscript I must thank the good people at iPlanet, Mysore who were generous to allow me to utilize their computers since mine died upon arriving to the country.

I also wish to reach out to those who lent me support in my decision to leave Montreal. I owe a great deal of gratitude to my colleagues Terry Cochran, Philippe Despoix and Tonglin Lu who sustained me during a most surreal time and whose interpretation of events helped me to act quickly. It is deplorable, yet not surprising, how the professional misconduct of a few individuals, the equally pathetic silence of another few, can render an academic institution so perilously close to a fascist state.

It is also alarming how common academic mobbing is today and I hope that this book can, in part, serve to highlight some of the lessons that those of us in academia should be learning from the younger generations of individuals who understand teamwork and collaboration.

In this vein, I am deeply moved to my students, Hugo, Aurélie, Eloi, Nicolas, and Philippe whose good humor, music and wisdom lent me great strength in a time of bizarre politics. Your solidarity and actions meant the world to me and although I never had so much fun leaving a place which I disliked so much, it is in this spirit that I have "taken" you all with me. Thank you for the most amazing lessons of a sort of love that many academics tend to dispel.

I would also like to thank Véronique Cnockaert, Todd Porterfield, Vincent Crapanzano, and Angela Harutyunyan with whom I conversed about various aspects of the material contained within this manuscript. These dialogues assisted me in putting into perspective the immense depths at which Foucauldian constructs of power and panopticism operate and permeate what seem to be every functional aspect of our societies today. Through these interactions I gained new insights into Agamben's notion of "whatever singularity" and biopower and likewise a newfound appreciation for Nancy's "inoperative community" which renders community as that which is neither a hypostasized communal matter, nor a collection of separate individuals. In many respects this text is a culmination of my work in and on community which reveals its truth not as the product of social production or a "being-in-common," but rather as the absence of such "being-together."

This text chronicles a journey into the world of development and its interrelated political theaters. This book's aim is two-fold: to tell the story of the world of humanitarian and development work and to incite people to think beyond the traditional and normative structures of "good will." This book critiques the institutional and societal norms that inform the ways in which humanitarian aid and the practices of development are structured and exercised. Within the criticisms of the institution lies a parallel critique of the individual subject who writes out checks to UNICEF at Christmas or who watches the latest natural disaster on television to see the proof of her donations as Red Cross logos appear on the newly installed tents.

As someone who came from academia, I was naïve about certain practices in the world of humanitarian aid. I went to Haiti thinking that these institutions must have some effect on helping people if they continue to exist year after year and if their work undergoes internal and media scrutiny from time to time. My ideas about most NGOs and UN agencies have been vastly changed as my experience taught me to believe what I saw, not what I wanted to believe about these organizations. My work in Haiti served both as a crash course in certain types of fieldwork with which I had not been familiar and as a moment when I went from being a person who actually believed in humanitarian aid to someone whose eyes were opened to how it functions as a badly run business. As a colleague of mine said in Haiti, "If the UN were a business, they would be bankrupt since at the end of the quarter the balance sheets would not prove that anything had been produced as these agencies would be in the red perpetually."

While this book is not meant to single out certain agencies, it does focus upon those organizations with whom I worked and where I saw the most egregious forms of abuse towards their mandate, their staff and towards the very people they were ostensibly "helping." What I did notice within most NGOs and UN agencies was this: anyone under forty years of age was generally honest, hard-working and even idealistic about their role in the betterment of the world, specifically in helping out the earthquake victims in Haiti. However, those over forty were often corrupted by the system that in many cases paid them salaries in excess of $10,000 per month, tax free in many cases. One UN worker told me that the system attracts the best and the brightest, but only the most corrupt stay in: "Those who don't leave are usually the least talented and the most corrupt. They are paid to make it look like something is getting done but upon the termination of our contracts, senior staff often undo what we have done, only to give the very same tasks to our replacement." I heard this very sentiment from another dozen aid workers. There is hope that things can improve; yet there is cynicism towards the structures that are ostensibly offering hope to the victims of disaster, such as the Haitians.

While this book offers a critique of the structures of NGOs and UN agencies, it is also a call for every subject in richer nations—including you reading this book—to reassess your role in supporting these structures. If there is one result I would like to see from the publication of this book, it is this: that everyone can make a difference by demanding that these agencies change the way in which humanitarian aid is currently being exercised. This involves a philosophical rethinking of what it means to "help" another group of people who are vulnerable and whose economies have more often than not already weakened by the financial hegemony of the very nations coming to "help" them. There are problems in how monetary donations are handled and more seriously there are basic questions regarding why local professionals are excluded from discussions of their expertise in their own country. The UN and most every NGO has flown highly paid foreign professionals into Haiti at great expense—foreign experts who can do exactly what local experts can do. To walk into the United Nations Log Base in Port-au-Prince is a veritable scene from any colonial film wherein the lighter-skinned people are running around taking care of their projects while the Haitians are refilling the coffee machine, the hot water dispenser, driving UN workers around. There were very few exceptions to this scene. Meanwhile Haitian unemployment, what should have been the first priority, was all but ignored by every single agency on the ground.

I owe a debt of recognition to those Haitians at UN Log Base who patiently stood by watching so many foreigners, so-called "experts," invade their country in order to enact a humanitarian carnage I hope never again to witness. These Haitians were an immense wealth of information for this manuscript and they assisted me in learning Creole, inform me about their country and they allowed me to use computers, Internet connection and electrical outlets to recharge my iPhone from which 80% of this manuscript was written.

That UNICEF put in charge of its child protection unit a person who undermined her child protection officers' actions gives fodder to the critics of humanitarian aid. UNICEF's choice of Caroline Bakker ensured that the most vulnerable in post-earthquake Haiti were left in the hands of an individual who was incapable of realizing her responsibilities demonstrating complete lack of willingness to take on this matter. Worse, this person confirmed that she did not care to fulfill her duties when her subordinates brought certain urgent situations to her attention. For example, early in 2010 UNICEF had knowledge of one of the prime child traffickers who to this day operates at a very high level within the Haitian government. This head of UNICEF in Haiti refused to make an official statement on this issue in order to protect UNICEF' place within the political topography of the country and to foment their continued financial support within the community of international donors.

My experience in Haiti has taught me that doing something—doing anything irrespective of said action's residual effects—is often not the best solution to a problem. In terms of humanitarian aid there are many individuals—both Haitians and NGO workers—who maintain that Haiti would have been better off without any foreign intervention. Haitians needed jobs and few were created for them. Instead, they spent the past four years watching foreigners come to take jobs that were specifically tailored for someone commanding a salary of anywhere between 100 and 1,000 times a Haitian salary for the same position.

Fundamentally, there needs to be a change in ethos from within the humanitarian sector beginning with an evaluation of how foreign aid, development projects and disaster relief today maintain an extremely neo-colonial attitude towards those whom these projects ostensibly serve. For the days of the Viceroy being sent from abroad the manage the natives is not so distant. We are living it now in these sites of "disaster relief." For what one sees in Haiti, as one remarks in other places of "development," is that there is an unspoken collusion between foreign governments, private capital, NGOs and these official bodies such as the UN and USAID which enter into long and short-term projects of "development" whose end result looks nothing like advancement or development. To the contrary what is left on the ground are the ruins of a laboratory of social experimentation replete with unfinished projects, meetings about previous meetings, highly paid experts who are powerless because they are not familiar with the site-specific terrain (with most not speaking one word of the local language), incompetent senior managers who are out to earmark their careers with this "once in a lifetime opportunity" of disaster, and a plethora of well-meaning albeit well-paid individuals who have come to "gain experience" in this test drive of humanity. Meanwhile half a million Haitians still live in tents.

There is a noteworthy difference between compassion and pity. Pity feeds into the neo-colonial rhetoric and political structures which ensure that any light-skinned person flown across the planet will automatically be assumed to know more about a given situation and the means to change it. Compassion implicates the ability to work *with* those humans from their sites of destruction in order to create a better world *through their terms* of development and betterment.

Ready, Get Set, Go

I am about to go to Haiti in a few days to take part in the very human project of sharing, mourning, dialoguing and constructing. There is a disaster that has not taken us by surprise with January's earthquake. Deaths in Haiti are not new and were certainly not created by the earthquake alone. The deaths prior to the January 2010 earthquake simply did not make the headlines because in North America we are bombarded by images of terrorism, violence which has killed far fewer people in any given year than poverty kills daily. In 2003 it was estimated that 25,000 people die each day from starvation around the world. Today that number is significantly higher with the United Nations estimating that 100,000 people die each day from hunger and thirst. Yet our governments focus upon perceived threats in the Middle East and the never-ending "war on terror" as if to turn consciously our attention from the issues of social and economic inequality which are more pressing and more relevant to the earth's people. In turn, many of us allow our attention to be turned to topics of the "evil other," mostly fictions and fear-mongering. Such diversions keep us busy wondering what building will be next to tumble, if that vapor coming from the road is indeed vapor or might it be a dangerous gas, all the while our fatality from the violence committed in New York on 11 September, 2001, represents approximately 3% of the deaths that day due to thirst and starvation and less than 1% of the total number of deaths compared to those of Haiti's earthquake of 12 January, 2010. This begs the question: why, for so many is terrorism somehow "worse" than death by disease, starvation or natural disaster? How is it that we see free will behind acts of terror but we do not when it comes to understanding the relationship between our society's and body's excesses? Tangentially, why do we and our media focus upon terrorism as a political act originating in hatred, rather than to focus upon terrorism' root causes, namely the neo-colonialist hegemony of foreign governments and societies and the concomitant poverty and social inequality?

I write this from a café in the west Village where before me lies Saturday's *New York Times* with the special coupon insert and I focus my attention to three ads: one for Fisher Fusions, a snack that comes in the following flavors—"ice cream sundae," "cinnamon roll," and "energy blend"; another for liquid "nutrition drinks"—Ensure, Myoplex and Glucerna; and a spray cleaner "Extend-a-Clean" by the Johnson company. These advertisements/coupons subtly underscore the very problem of how North American society perceives various external political realities.

Similar to our social approach to eating and housecleaning, we fail to see the obvious connections between what we put into the environment and our bodies and what our bodies and the rest of the world produce in return. In the United States of America, we are an overweight society whose reality is centered upon the consumption of myriad products and foods, while conterminously we are obsessed with losing weight. Reflective of such antithetical thinking, there are now food products which *disguise consumption as non-consumption*, which turn the act of eating into the act of losing weight. Paradoxically, one of the most publicized ways to losing weight in North America is to eat *everything but the real food* to which much processed food alludes: snacks *which taste of* cinnamon rolls and ice cream sundaes, but they are not these actual substances and diet foods specifically made to give "nutrition" without any real or whole food substance. In short, we attempt to achieve "health" through the most unhealthy methods and we attempt to average longer lives through acts which are proven to bring about untimely death and disease.

Likewise, we buy sprays that make bathrooms "stay cleaner longer," when in fact it is common knowledge that substances cannot actually keep anything cleaner "longer" since cleanliness is an ontology. Cleanliness cannot be maintained by a product for purchase simply because cleanliness is a state of being *maintained only through action*—it is the act of not introducing dirt to an area and of its actual removal. No substance can do either of these actions. While I adore the absolute irony of Canadian and United States material fetishisms, there is an underlying sadness and lack of self-reflection when such products are the paradigmatic basis for thinking about all things be they social, political, economic or somatic.

Here in New York's west Village, people send me good wishes for my work in Haiti and I am inspired by the many who would like to take time from their jobs to join me. Others are finding ways of collaborating from afar—before coming to Haiti while packing up my house in Montreal, I had telephone, Internet and physical meetings with fundraisers, artists, and programmers, all of whom are collaborating in their own ways. A few hours ago a woman told me she was about to go to a meditation group to send good feelings towards Chile so as to heal the people there in the aftermath of the earthquake which occurred this morning. Most people mean well and many humans make efforts to do good yet there is a disconnect between what the political machinery avows and what the people who vote these machines into power actually desire. Likewise there is a synapse between the messages of urgency and danger that are propounded by our media and the reality on the ground as to what is truly a danger or an imminent human crisis.

In North America we overeat and we throw millions of kilos of food away each year while people in other countries starve, we silently support our governments and international agencies which impoverish countries like Haiti, and then we act out the other side of catharsis: our hearts bleed when people die of starvation and thirst and when they are crushed to death during an earthquake as a result of poorly constructed buildings. Some go even further as they jump to adopt the children of the very people we have indirectly starved instead of taking political action, instead of sending funds to help our brothers and sisters raise their own children in Peru, Guatemala, and Haiti. We kill with one hand and adopt with the other, all in the guise of benevolence and good will.

It is time to recognize that eating what looks like dog food and is called "cinnamon roll" couldn't be further from a cinnamon roll. Perhaps we ought to question why we would eat such substances. Is it that there is an alleviation of guilt for not eating a multi-caloric cinnamon roll and instead we have created a panoply of substitute eating? What does this say about ourselves and our quite unhealthy relationship to food? Clearly we ought to acknowledge that if we want to give our bodies nutrition and to lose weight perhaps we ought to re-discover eating and dispense with consuming. Let's return to grains, fresh fruits and vegetables rather than giving the good people of Abbott our money for Ensure, a liquid that was not designed for losing weight and certainly not intended as a food replacement for anyone who does not have their jaw wired shut. There is a striking irony that in North America we are starving ourselves through malnutrition of a different sort. Just as we engage in endless "wars on terror" which attempt to realize peace through creating violence, we similarly struggle to regain health through ingesting imitation food that is slowly killing us.

The problems are as evident as the solutions on the inter-related political and somatic fronts. More to the point, the solutions to these quagmires involve changing personal, social and political patterns and we need to take the necessary steps to open our individual and collective consciousness so as to bring about the necessary dialogues within our communities. We should perceive poverty as a preventable condition in all its interconnected dimensions from the countless situations of civil and political unrest worldwide, to myriad dimensions of domestic poverty, to poverty as a direct reflection of the media and political framing thereof. Likewise we need to study how our governments' policies inflect and create poverty internationally while realizing how our lifestyles necessarily inform our political structures and world economies as our over-consumption depletes natural resources from people who are no less deserving of food and water than we are.

Waiting or Claude Speaks

A lovely worker on his lunch break offered to drive me to the Haitian embassy after I asked him for directions. Edwin had a huge truck and he explained to me that we had to go in a round about way to the embassy way due to construction on one of the nearby roads. Santo Domingo is lush with color and bustling with energy as we pass a coconut stand and several fruit trucks before arriving at the embassy. I thank Edwin for the ride and he tells me to call should I need anything. I really was far from the coldness of Montreal in every sense.

I walked several steps towards the embassy and an explosion went off in front of me. My face felt the movement of air and I saw a bright burst of fire just ten meters in front of me that lasted only a moment. I turned around and asked a woman who was leaving the embassy what had happened since I saw no damage from this explosion aside from a dead bird which I saw die in mid air and then quickly drop to the ground. She explained that there was a pigeon who touched two different power lines which caused it to be electrocuted. I was incredulous that such a small bird could cause such an explosion—his body lay limp in the intersection. I forgot momentarily about my task at the embassy and then I went over to the corner where I had heard that daily buses depart for Port-au-Prince. Next to the embassy was a group of Haitians whom I asked about transport to Haiti and one man stood out to me.

Claude is 37, an accountant trained in the Dominican Republic who returned to Santo Domingo after January's earthquake with his wife and children. Faced with starvation Claude returned to the city where he studied at the university, Santo Domingo, and where his wife was gainfully employed. Here he drives a taxi in an attempt to support his family. Claude is angry, frustrated with the situation back home, and it would seem that he has every reason to be so.

"Anyone who says that Haiti is gong to recover is lying," he tells me. "Just look at the situation there: you have Canada and the United States who say they will go to help and so they send engineers and doctors. And they fund these services to employ their own people," Claude relates, "They spend thousands—one doctor from Quebec told me that he was paid $3,000 to come from Quebec; yet we HAVE many doctors and engineers here. We don't need your professionals for we have this—we don't need any more. We need to have education and for people to stay and develop our country. But we cannot stay because there is too much debt and no salaried jobs. How can Haiti ever recover when every Haitian's dream is to go to the United States and Canada?" I ask Claude what he sees as the solution and he responds immediately, "Erase the debt and financial reparations. We need hospitals and schools. We need literacy and we need to join forces to fight the hegemony of Canada, the USA and France—to stop them from imposing their politics on us. They "give" us money and the they tell us how to spend it. Do you realize that one reason Aristide was deposed is because he wanted France to pay reparations to Haiti?" Claude spoke.

Claude was standing under the trees that lined the street along with another ten Haitians. Some were Haitian-Dominicans others were Haitian immigrants who, since ten or eleven years, were all working in the Dominican Republic. Just as the immigrants to Montreal from where I had just left, foreigners held jobs here in the Dominican Republic for which they were highly over-qualified. How can there be a revolution—and let us be frank here, the kind of change that is needed in Haiti is not the rhetorical change of Obama but a real change driven by the people—when the very people who wish to make revolution are starved into emigration, driving our taxis in Montreal and Santo Domingo, and removed from their families and communities?

Claude sees his life as physically better in the Dominican Republic but he is despondent for the future of his people.

Dios Me Protege

One notices a familiar site in Santo Domingo that is common throughout Latin America: that the from roofs of already-constructed one-story homes sprout various metal rods, cinder blocks and plumbing which announce the arrival of the soon-to-be second floor. These pipes and rods sticking up from the roof are are a sign of hope, a symbol of the anticipation for a tomorrow with more money to continue that dream house. Rare is the house that is built in one gesture and the house with protruding metal pieces in much of the world has become the sign of a prosperity to come.

As I travel to the embassy to take the bus to Port-au-Prince, I am reminded of this city's richness, colors and wonderful smells, not to mention the people who are quite welcoming, generous and loving. The talk radio in the taxi, however, is quite critical of the racism in the Dominican Republic against the Haitians whose number is approximately two million in the capital alone. There is an acknowledgement of a problem whose depths are properly being discussed for which solutions seem far off. I notice that on the taxi driver's glove compartment there is a Jehovah's Witnesses sticker. I ask the driver, Monny, if he is a Jehovah's Witness. Monny says he is not, stating that he is Catholic. He told me that he bought the sticker because people were selling it at the side of the road one day and he found it beautiful. He asked me if I was a Christian and I said I was not and went on to explain a bit about my syncretic childhood, my religious education, and my family in India, all practicing Hindus. He told me that there is only one God. Of course I could not resist this affirmation and asked Monny, "How do you know which one is it?" Monny responded, "Well, in my religion we are taught that there is only one." And I repeated my question, recounting him the story of Hanuman and Ganesh. Monny said, "But God cannot be an animal... he cannot be a chicken." "Do you really think God looks like the blonde haired, fair skinned image you see in this sticker?" I replied adding, "What if these images are all metaphors for the plurality of God that is us?" At that very moment I saw Monny was wearing a beautiful bracelet made of wooden squares upon which were painted on each block a different image of Jesus and Maria to include several images of what seem to be clerics and nuns. No sooner had I exclaimed how beautiful was his bracelet than he pulled it off his wrist and gave it to me.

I went to the side of the Haitian Embassy and the tiny bus, which would hold no more than eighteen people, was getting ready for the trip. Men were strapping pieces of cardboard around a huge mattress and box spring.

Behind the bus was a small trailer in which went various pieces of luggage and boxes, upon which would eventually rest this cardboard-wrapped mattress and box spring.   I saw Claude around the side of the Haitian Embassy sporadically throughout the day and before leaving to pick up his daughter from school.   While awaiting clients, he recounted more of his story about Haiti to me.

First he warned me to be prepared for the destruction and the horror, telling me to "double up" the masks when I walk around the city due to the stench of dead bodies.   He had left Port-au-Prince eight days after January's earthquake to return to Santiago. Claude saw the situation in Haiti corrode by the hour and decided to move back to Santo Domingo where he and his wife had previously lived and studied in order to protect their ten year-old daughter.   Claude's younger brother, a twenty year-old student who was studying in Santiago, went home to visit their ailing father, a blind and elderly widower.   Claude's brother was studying civil engineering in the Dominican Republic; thus he could not stay long to care for their father.   Claude wished me well and had to run off to take a client in his taxi.

I went to the vendor on the corner and asked for a sandwich for the trip and Jean-Jean, a young eighteen year-old approached me, asking me what I was doing.   He told me how he was going to the Haitian Embassy to renew his passport since he wanted to go back home to see his family.   Jean-Jean had been living in Santo Domingo already ten years and was full of curiosity as to why I would go to Haiti, asking what I would do there. I answered his questions and attempted to get in a few questions of my own. Jean-Jean showed me his birth certificate which was on a carbon copy paper handwritten in a script that seemed to be crafted after years of training by nuns, a script that was perceptibly as perfect as any computer font. He wanted to go back to help his grandmother, aunts and uncles who remained homeless and to be of support to his family as his cousin had died in the earthquake. The bus was about to leave so I bid Jean-Jean a good day and I took my seat in the front row just behind the driver. Directly before me was the driver's mirror from which was dangling a plastic head of Scooby Doo. On the mirror was a red sticker that read "Dios me protege."

We commenced what was to be a long, hot and beautiful journey across the Dominican Republic with the music blasting, people laughing with only a brief pause the moment talk radio went to the latest political sex scandal when people listened silently for only a moment, their patience worn thin. Upon hearing a minute of discussion on this subject, the entire bus moaned and one woman popped in a CD of more salsa to the jubilant cheers of my fellow passengers. We stopped at the border several times for exit stamps on the Dominican side and entry stamps once in Haiti. The town was known as Jimaní and the scene was one of a typical market day, except this was a scene of such a day in dire poverty. People were not just selling fruits and vegetables, housewares and pieces for water pumps—people were selling their own clothes, used shoes, kitchen items.

Nonetheless people on the bus seemed exuberant to be back home and it was clear that we were no longer in a land with houses half-built. Instead, we were definitely in a space of no fixed living quarters, tents, metallic and boxed homes, collapsed buildings and a very fragmented sense of hope. Despite what seemed to be a shocking arrival for many, since arriving to such poverty is shocking even to returning Haitians, there was an air of levity and happiness. One women returning to the bus after a passport check was greeted by one of my fellow passengers who made a comment to her which I could not understand. He smiled at her and his eyes were fixed on her breasts. She returned his comment, made in Creole, with a glare that burned through his smile; however he laughed even more. The gentleman beside me also laughed when he heard her comment and I turned to my fellow passenger and said, "Did he just flirt with that woman?" He laughed and said, "No, he congratulated her on her beauty."

We pulled away from the border and in front of our bus was a truck upon whose side was written: "Les RICHES et les PAUVRES SONT Beaux DEVANT La Mort" (*"The RICH and the POOR ARE beautiful BEFORE Death"*). Indeed, we had arrived in Haiti.

The Jesus Complex

What I have always loved about living in Central America and the Caribbean is how certain tasks are simply easier. Traveling by land, for instance, is generally not all that difficult. The passenger is to show up at a certain place and time, she buys passage (no pre-booking necessary), and while traveling, food just appears before your eyes—from vendors entering the bus with treats of fried plantains, to women pushing through the passenger window a basket of freshly prepared tamales, to young kids shouting out repeatedly the drinks they are selling. You don't even have to leave your seat and you are fed. And sometimes you can complete home shopping from your seat with many products being circulated around the bus on each and every stop—brooms, washing detergents, colanders, hairpins, children's socks, deodorant, perfumes, kitchen utensils and the like. In Port-au-Prince such services are everywhere as you travel in buses or walk down the streets. Even in the markets as people remain in fixed places selling their goods, there are just as many men and women circulating with differently competitive products. Competition is stiff and everyone is trying to make a living in circumstances that are far from ideal, far from normal.

In Port-au-Prince, most everyone is either living in a tent, metal and wood hut, or, if lucky enough to not have lost their homes, they are hosting neighbors, friends and family inside and in front of their homes. This is the reality all over the city. I am staying at the home of three Haitian women who grew up together and in this house are currently living neighbors, a local boy whose parents work in another town, and about fifteen international medical doctors, nurses and a driver. Thus, every corridor, terrace and square foot of floor is occupied by medications, condoms, various ER kits, scrubs, and mattresses. There is a sense of solidarity and goodwill here and the collective sharing of space and tasks reflects such intentions. Elsewhere I have met families whose homes are in perfect condition, but due to the news that is given about the possibility of another earthquake, the residents refuse to sleep inside their homes and instead are camping out meters away from their house, only entering it in the morning to prepare meals and shower. The house has become a space of communal cooperation and refuge and conterminously a place of fear and distrust. This would likewise describe the relationship between people where, on the one hand, solidarity is visible everywhere from people helping their neighbors remove stones and rubble from in front of their homes to friends coming over to help the injured with household tasks.

As in any community, there are those people who are not at all participatory and who even cause damage: from those who robbed homes split into two in the first hours after the earthquake on 12 January before the occupants were able to arrive home from work that evening; to the adolescents who pretend to be orphans in order to garner services and food from the thousands of NGOs (non-governmental organizations) in this country; to the various administrators in institutions who are both overwhelmed by the quantity of work and incapable of managing the massive numbers of volunteers. There is a sense that many people in positions of power do not know what they want to achieve and a result of such indecision is chaos that dominates despite the semi-transparent façade of organization. As one might understand the frustration of the volunteers who are often badly managed, it is far more frustrating for Haitians to be told to go to the hospital for medical support only to be turned away, to be told they will be given tents only to be forced to sleep under bedsheets stretched upon thin long tree branches. The scene is confusing: there are massive problems in communication from hospitals and relief organizations towards the public: doctors who cannot reach hospital administrators, people who are promised food and tents only to be told there are no tents, and many local institutions seem to be more interested in making contacts with more international NGOs and to extend their funding possibilities rather than help those in need. The good will of these institutions who are present in the post-tragedy support is not always clear as the lack of organization often obfuscates what good will there might be.

Hospital directors complain of having too many volunteers and in the same breath all their complaints indicate that their resources are sorely managed. Many Haitians complain that the disaster relief money is going to subsidize foreign doctors which is only partly true as many foreign doctors are in fact volunteering their time and services to the NGOs which bring them in. Yet disaster relief monies are used to fly in these medical professionals and more money to feed and house them despite the fact that all the doctors I have met from Haiti and abroad are strongly committed to helping those in need. Likewise I have heard many stories of Haitians who are abandoned in the public hospitals—one man's mother was left for the past four days in a hospital without a doctor to treat her for malaria. Stories such as this only demonstrate the lack—and not the excess—of Haitian doctors.

Doctors, both Haitian and foreign, work incredibly long hours to help those suffering and they make do with a severe shortage of supplies and the lack of infrastructure in continuing their mission to help those in need. Another common situation is when doctors and nursing teams are invited to hospitals from afar and then no sooner do they arrive they are told to leave.   Doctors were asked by one children's hospital to come from Germany and no sooner were they in the country than were they asked to leave. Likewise, organizations and individuals are invited to help organize the continued education of nursing staff and then are likewise told that the hospital has "changed its mind."   What was twenty-four hours ago a pressing, extremely urgent need is suddenly not at all a concern. Administrators vacillate upon decisions and refuse aid while Haitians wish for more help.   Even late last week Préval announced that he wanted there to be less aid. It is difficult for both volunteers in the country and the many

Haitians in need to trust words. Actions are visible in the shifting camps of various medical groups who have been instructed by the government not to remain in the same place from one day to he next so as to discourage people from camping out and establishing permanent domiciles at these sites. Movement is crucial to these health clinics' survivability and stasis and continuity are not only discouraged, but they are considered signs of danger as they pose a threat to the already existent Haitian health services. With such logistics, it is hardly surprising that organization in the capital is so seemingly unrealizable. Everyone speaks about the poor, the sick and the children but everything remains discursive, floating on the surface of "goodwill" that remains performative in nature.

Monday morning's sermon at St. Damien's Children's Hospital was given by Father Rick Ferchette, a Catholic priest and medical doctor who has been living in Haiti for over twenty years. Father Ferchette spoke of the major problem affecting the realization of relief projects in Haiti: that there were intense bidding wars for contracts which delayed most relief efforts. Ferchette, clearly a Liberation theologian, discussed the unjust nature of poverty and sickness, of the crimes of humanity that would leave children abandoned on the streets. Ferchette spoke with passion, citing the Bible from Isaiah 65 and this passage from John:

> After the two days he left for Galilee. Now Jesus himself had pointed out that a prophet has no honor in his own country. When he arrived in Galilee, the Galileans welcomed him. They had seen all that he had done in Jerusalem at the Passover Feast, for they also had been there. Once more he visited Cana in Galilee, where he had turned the water into wine. And there was a certain royal official whose son lay sick at Capernaum. When this man heard that Jesus had arrived in Galilee from Judea, he went to him and begged him to come and heal his son, who was close to death. "Unless you people see miraculous signs and wonders," Jesus told him, "you will never believe." The royal official said, "Sir, come down before my child dies." Jesus replied, "You may go. Your son will live." The man took Jesus at his word and departed. While he was still on the way, his servants met him with the news that his boy was living. When he inquired as to the time when his son got better, they said to him, "The fever left him yesterday at the seventh hour." Then the father realized that this was the exact time at which Jesus had said to him, "Your son will live." So he and all his household believed. This was the second miraculous sign that Jesus performed, having come from Judea to Galilee. (John 4:43-54)

The efforts of altruism are visible from the Haitians who stand in the hundreds lining up in a cue outside the rubble of a fallen school, all passing buckets of mortar from person to person to clear the premises from the tons of debris in order to make way for the eventual site of the new school to the thousands of volunteers working to take care of urgent medical needs, to the nurses assistants at St Damien's who are stretched to the limit as children need to be fed throughout the day (with individual feedings often necessitating enormous amounts of time due to the manner of feeding via syringe), medications administered, bottoms cleaned, bodies washed, and clothing changed. There is barely the time for these nurses to dedicate themselves to the necessary coddling and loving of these children, especially those children who are abandoned. This passage above speaks about altruism as Christ-like, implying for the congregation that they must behave as Christ would have in order to help others. This is the more patent, obvious reading of this passage. However, there is another interpretation that is more sinister and perhaps more pertinent to the situation here in Port-au-Prince: that of how the volunteering self sees herself—as Christ.

Certainly the danger in behaving as Christ is believing that one is actually a "god-like" figure. Sadly, this behavior is not so uncommon in Port-au-Prince among volunteers and many NGOs as I have seen much of this volunteer machismo, what I call the "Christ complex." Individuals who have been on site for longer than new arrivals "pull rank" on them, underscoring the time they have been in Haiti, their title and their links to x or y organization worrying more about their framing in the scenes of rescue

than their work with and dedication to the actual people in need of help. This is not to say that this Christ complex is imperatively innate to Christian organizations—it is not—or that non-Christians do not take on this pretense—they do. Just as problematic are the scenes of those who are more concerned about photo opportunities with children in the hospital where I was working. The notion for parental permission is not considered, I am told, as orphans' rights are co-opted by the institutions that ostensibly help them. The exchange is this: the price of hospitality is paid by their sickly, smiling faces posted on websites and brochures as hospitals such as St. Damien's raise money through the use of these children's bodies. The director of the St Damien's sister orphanage from Mexico, an American woman, passes through one of the children's wards posing with the abandoned children for the camera. She is playing the role of Princess Diana as she would move from child to child, sit down, take a child from its bed and cuddle for a moment and then pop that child back into its bed to move on to the next child photo op. When she entered into the children's ward where I was working this woman actually took the food I was feeding an infant from my hands to pose for that photo. When I asked her kindly to ask me before intervening in my work she told me curtly, "I have been here for two months." This woman had a sense of entitlement and clearly demonstrated that everything she touched she controlled, from the children to my own participation in this child's meal. Onward Christian soldiers.

The situation grew markedly worse when this woman returned to the ward where I was working and continued her photography of the sick children who could not authorize such photos. That morning I had spoken with the other nurses and learned that it was not acceptable that a person comes into the ward to take photos of the children. Yet none of the Haitian nurses dared speak out for fear of repercussions from this white woman. They were, as they told me, too afraid to speak out. So when Princess Diana entered the ward, I did speak up and I told her that she needed to look at the UN guidelines for photography of minors and as well many other media organizations which likewise detail the ethics of this form of photography. She stared at me as if she had never been broached with such ethical questions and I had to spell it out for her, "These children cannot possibly give informed consent. When I am doing fieldwork or when anyone works with children in any professional setting, you must have informed consent at the very least from these children's parents." She cynically turned to me and said, "But they are orphans" to which I responded, "And as such you have an even greater obligation to protect their likeness and persons."

Princess Diana went on to protest that the photos she was taking was for adoptions of these children through the Mexican orphanage which she ran. Shocked by this news, for the laws in Haiti do not permit children to be transferred as if cargo between countries for adoption elsewhere, I stated that any sort of transfer of children in that manner would be considered trafficking. She stormed out of the room and within an hour I was summoned to the office of the assistant director of the hospital, Phadoul Amisal. I was quickly told Phadoul that these children "have no rights," that this American could photograph them at will and that I should no longer volunteer at this hospital. I said that was fine for me to leave but I still demanded answers regarding this "inter-country adoption scheme" which this American orphanage director inadvertently admitted. Phadoul became flustered. I asked to see the hospital's official statement on adoption and he said, "We don't allow adoptions." Something was clearly amiss as I had repeatedly heard that week from the American woman from Cuernavaca, Mexico that adoptions did take place. Later I was told that in fact this hospital was one of many organizations which shifted the geographical location of children without any regard to legal procedure. As in many western countries where children are regarded as paychecks to foster parents within the social welfare state and where salaries are associated with taking custody of children, Haiti was not any different. Children were often a means to an end within myriad economic, religious, and social welfare/developmental models such that of course this American woman felt that she owned these children in this hospital. For all practical purposes *she did*.

The stories I have heard form Haitians who have felt overrun by foreign volunteers and by volunteers who feel usurped by the disorganization are multiple and it seems that many volunteers are feeling their efforts wasted by sheer one-upmanship. Some have left frustrated while others continue looking for a project in which to integrate their skills. Certainly there is a balance for these volunteers to establish between lending their efforts to an organization which knows how to manage their talents while likewise being able to be present for those in need and not for the larger political or career advantages that many seek in establishing themselves as the saviors of children. Acting like Christ and mistaking oneself for Christ are two very different actions in theory. Yet, I begin to wonder how the politics of volunteerism have become such a scene of personal self-affirmation and professional demonstrability such that people mistake the acting like Christ for being Christ. And in the volunteer's rush to run for the laurels, those in need rarely see any benefits. More problematic is how the Christ complex feeds into the structural problems central to the various institutions which demonstrate the inability to collaborate, listen and cultivate dialogue. Hence the colonial invasion of "good will" professionals where Haiti serves as the backdrop to the perceived need of people who were never extended an invitation.

Father Ferchette also recalled Thomas Aquinas in his sermon: "He who is not angry when there is just cause for anger is immoral. Why? Because anger looks to the good of justice. And if you can live amid injustice without anger, you are immoral as well as unjust." Indeed, remarking the injustices of poverty and the lack of infrastructure here is not enough. Behaving as Christ would behave is likewise not enough and I would dare say that the infusion of religious doxa in the language and the mimetic formations of Christ render toxic the planning of relief efforts here. Each NGO acts alone and rarely in concert, government agencies and military of every sort are on constant parade, and as I await a tap tap (local transport made from brightly painted pick-up trucks with make-shift seating) to return home outside the hospital situated next to one of the UN bases, I am witness to a display of wealth and power which speaks to where much of the money has gone.

There are twice as many shiny, new, white SVUs and jeeps with the UN letters emblazoned on the doors in black as there are tap tap. UN blue helmets and weapons of all sort are held in a ready position by the UN police who patrol the city. Meanwhile, people must wait hours to return home, each tap tap stuffed with workers and students, while the UN vehicles are often empty aside from the driver. Interspersed between the UN vehicles are any number of the vehicles originating from any of the various 10,000 NGOs in the country. Logically, travel is rendered impossible for the average Haitian. And standing there in t-shirt and blue jeans held up with a piece of blue clothesline, I attempt to find any transport that is not full or which is not official UN or NGO transport. The traffic is so congested that a four mile trip is often two to three hours since most of the congestion on the streets of Port-au-Prince is caused by the plethora of the NGO and UN vehicles. The irony is that these organizations hold the major presence on the roads and yet their efforts, six weeks after the earthquake, have yet to be seen or felt.

Discourses of Color

I have spent my first week in Port-au-Prince working at Saint Damien's Children's Hospital in a ward which I was initially told treats malnourished, abandoned children and orphans. By the end of my first days working in this ward, I learned that most of these children were neither orphaned nor abandoned. In Haiti, a child is considered an orphan having lost *one or both* parents. These children were, however, as many of the patients in the hospital, malnourished. I have been doing whatever was asked of me—changing diapers and clothes, bathing and feeding the children, and a taking care of coddling, holding and playing with babies. In the short time I have worked at this hospital I have witnessed parents who suffer greatly watching their children writhe in pain from meningitis and others who come to the hospital to relate their problems to me, coming to me specifically as if I could offer assistance in their need to accept the loss of a partner or a child. Many saw me as a source for possible NGO funding and I often had to inform all too many Haitians that I came to volunteer my services and that I had zero affiliation with outside funding. My presence often served as a means for me to understand not what I could do with various communities but rather what I represented to certain people and communities.

It is a common event in Haiti for non-Haitians to be stopped to answer questions such as: Where are you from? Is this your first time in Haiti? Are you a doctor? What is your name? It can quickly become an inconvenience to have to constantly answer such questions, but such is life in a country where communication is central to all activities, especially when a one is a foreigner. Learning how many gourde (the local currency) the tap tap should cost for each trip is a challenge as you are constantly cited different prices until you enter into discussion with the driver about the relief problems. Those five minutes of dialogue have magically turned the foreign version of the tap tap fare (15 gourdes) into the local price of seven gourdes. It is at this moment when the questions and answers stop resembling the *mis-en-scène* of tourism and approach the daily discourses of real life. With the omnipresence of NGOs from around the world it is a fact of life that so many Haitians make assumptions about those with lighter skin, for better or for worse.

Color, however, is a discourse ubiquitous throughout Haiti not because of what it represents in terms of some outdated colonial *pensée autre* of beauty, but because color represents a way out of poverty, of misery and for many, out of Haiti. As I move about the city in local transport, I have seen first-hand the role that lighter skin plays with complete strangers: I have had a twenty-five year old ask me to adopt her, Haitians follow me to the hospital to come looking for me to ask how to get food aid or a job, others who ask how I might help them go to the United States or Canada to study. One woman actually called up the hospital and attempted to use my name as a reference to get a job. The desperation is clear and color is often the only factor which distinguishes between privilege and poverty, between occupier and occupied.

So as I regularly hear the use of the words "blanc" and "noir," I wonder if these terms might inflect something unique to the post-earthquake invasion of aid workers or the pre-earthquake occupation of the 10,000 NGOs dispersed throughout the country. What is most troubling is that there seems to be little distinction between outside forces—both monetary and military—and Haiti's own bodies of power. Aside from the national flag and the police there is no sense of government as the occupation of Haiti has been long-established. The colors of uniforms are insignificant as it never really matters who asks you to pull your car over on the street since it only matters that you slow down and hope that it will not take too long as the UN soldier, Haitian police officer or the French soldier glance into the car. Uniforms tend to be drab browns, greens and grays and Haitians just know to stop when they see these colors flag them down.

Of all the children in the ward where I worked I found one paradoxical child, Gertrouille. She was a young girl of two and a half years of age whose body was emaciated, her leg broken and her eyes stared outward all day long. My first days in this ward I found that she would never engage me, she would simply stare outwards and not move when I would change her, refusing all affection. Then suddenly one day Gertrouille just started crying in the middle of eating her lunch. I went to her crib and removed her bowl and spoon and took her in my arms. The nurses immediately started laughing hysterically. When I asked why this girl cried, one nurse replied, "She doesn't like this color," pointing to her own arm, her skin. I thought she was joking and the nurse, noticing my shock, repeated, "It is true. There is another woman who comes here for the child each week, a white woman. Gertrouille calms down whenever she sees light skin." I was horrified and in disbelief for this little girl was living at home before

the earthquake. This meant that if she developed this type of behavior it was in these few weeks following 12 January. Still in a state of disbelief to what these nurses told me, one of the nurses turned to me and said, "Watch this." She then walked up to the small child and sure enough Gertrouille wouldn't let this Haitian nurse hold her. However when I would go over to her she would immediately stop crying. The nurses said, "She won't even let her mother go near her." This was a shocking story for me to digest. And after asking the nurses about this child I learned that the theatre of the child who performs for people with lighter skin is not so uncommon here in Haiti in both the pre and post earthquake era.

The facts of life are brutal in Haiti but many children are abandoned by their parents, not for a lack of love or desire, but for an immense love for their child, the will to see their child survive the poverty into which she was born. I would eventually learn from the nurses that every single child in this ward was abandoned at this private hospital where parents can be certain that the staff will not only re-nourish their babies, but also be guaranteed that these children will go on to be transferred to the orphanage this hospital has created near Kenscoff. Each and every one of these children was registered by a parent, yet after checking their child into the hospital, these parents would never return. Similarly, some children with parents are likewise instructed to tell foreign workers that they are orphans so that they will be taken away from Haiti (or, as they believe this will happen). As such the theatre of poverty performs for those who chose to be its spectators and skin color is all that separates the poor from the rich, those who are able to afford tickets into and out of the country from those who cannot. It is a theatre of cruelty which has no age limit and the actors like Gertrouille are never too young.

The reality behind such representations made for the foreigner are, in large part, a conditioned response to the longterm historical presence of the approximately 10,000 NGOs. The creation of aid organizations in the west have created a marketplace based on development where the stock market for this enterprise is desperation and poverty. Sadly the fact of poverty has served a culture of development that has detrimentally created a schism between those with money in Haiti who are involved in business, enterprises, and even the arts and those without money who could benefit from the local wealth and knowledge. The forty-year-old NGO base in Haiti has effectively eliminated the possibility of community efforts in creating new spaces of dialogue whereby local resources can be used differently in ways that radically break with the NGO model which uses only certain agents as the intermediaries who generally control projects from the top down.

The reality today is that many Haitians have created their own national NGOs and have made a healthy living from them; yet, the money often doesn't trickle very just as in the case of their model, the international NGOs. Monies are raised and accountability for the funds rarely required. The richer nations taught Haitians how to make money from the poor and NGOs have become the business model for not only international development projects but for many businesses run by Haitians. Almost everyone who works in Port-au-Prince is employed by an NGO or government agency and dependency theory models retain a certain relevance in analyzing the relationships of money and power here. The lesson Haitians have learned is this: start an NGO and you have already assumed yourself a role outside poverty due to the symbolic and real access to funding that is attached to most every NGO in the world. In essence, starting an NGO allows access to funding in this country far more easily than starting a business. It is not surprising that so many seek to solve their own poverty problems by setting up organizations that propose to solve others' problems relative to poverty. Poverty is as paradoxical to Haiti as the shade of skin is to Gertrouille: both function in relationship to perceived outside forces' ability to contain and/or influence the flow of wealth.

Yesterday I was invited to a school at Carrefour Feuilles which was reduced to rubble in the quake. One of my new roommates who also runs an NGO and one of the teachers from this school asked me to teach and help assess what was needed in terms of pedagogical tools.[1] I started to work at the school immediately after leaving the children's hospital. When I arrived in Carrefour Feuilles what made my heart jump was not the ruins of the former school site but rather the resilience of the people. In a line spanning over 200 meters were about 250 neighborhood residents of all

---

[1] I would learn later that this roommate along with the other two women in the house ran an elaborate child trafficking ring, the school as NGO being the cover. I would also learn that this was not an uncommon practice in Haiti for people to start an "orphanage" or "school."

ages and sizes, queued up from the pile of rubble down the incline of the mountain to the street where a truck would receive the pieces of the former school, handed bucket by bucket across each person in the line. This has gone on for days as the community wishes to have the school re-built. For the past week the school has been re-opened in a nearby home but the space is extremely limited. Children are now divided into different school days—levels one through six attend on Monday, Wednesday and Friday and levels seven through twelve on Tuesday, Thursday and Saturday.

I sat with the entire group of students in the morning as they sang songs. Then at one point they were split up into two groups and I was left with the second and third graders. We did a great deal of staring at each other and after a few moments I asked the students to tell me the story about Toussaint Louverture. Although the students recognized his name, only one could say that he was a former slave with no other points of this story. So I commenced to tell the story about this man who was liberated from slavery at the age of 33 and who would go on to organize the world's first modern-day slave revolt. And then I went onto explain how this act de-clenched a series of slave resistance movements throughout the Americas.

One constant I kept hearing throughout my first days teaching was the language of the students, specifically their use of the words "white" and "black." And after we discussed the story of Toussaint Louverture, the terms of color came up. So, I asked the students who was black? They told me they were. I turned to one of them and pointed to his bag, "What color is your bag?" He answered, "It is black." "Is your skin that color?" I asked pointing to his bag. "No," he answered. I asked the students still pointing to the bag, "Have you ever seen someone with that skin color" and they all shook their heads. "Indeed, your skin is not black. But what color is it?" One of the shy students looked at me and said softly, "Brown." I smiled at him and said, "Exactly. Brown is the color of your skin." I then pointed to one of the student's shirts and asked, "What color is her shirt?" The students exclaimed in unison, "White!" "Have any of you seen someone this color before in your life?" They all shook their heads. I then pointed my arm and said, "This is also brown, light brown." The students then smiled at me and we all put our forearms in the center of the group to observe the various shades of brown we embodied. "Black and white are fictional ways to divide people. As you just saw the use of these words "black" and "white" are not even scientifically accurate terms when applied to skin color. All humans are one color: brown," I told them. Many of the students whispered the words, "I am brown" as they would smile at one another and at me.

Isn't it interesting how we use language to separate people?

The Pornography of Poverty

This is an ingredient list for a product distributed and sold all over Haiti. Read the ingredients and guess what this is:

Water, sugar, orange, tangerine & lemon juice from concentrate, citric acid, food starch-modified, anthan gum, corn oil, potassium citrate, natural flavors, ascorbic acid (vitamin C), sodium benzoate & potassium sorbate, as preservatives, yellow #5 & #6, beta carotene

If you guessed "citrus punch" produced by the good people at Tampico then you are correct. You know the type of citrus punch with corn oil, don't you? This product represents one of the many forms of aid "given" to Haitians. Shortly after the earthquake, Tampico's CEO announced a donation of $25,000 in direct monetary donations to the American Red Cross and he also pledged an additional $100,000 for disaster relief in Haiti. What does this money really mean and where exactly did it go?

After further investigations I learned that most of the money from this "donation" went right back into the purchase of the company's own product. This money is used to buy the very same oil-infused drink and this beverage is—according to many Haitians here in Port-au-Prince with whom I have spoken—the only "aid" they have received. While some of this money was said to go to the Red Cross, most of it went back to the company which made the original donation. This is the phantom donor effect integral to many NGOs: money is postured as going to "aid" and that aid could be anything—medicines, vegetables, a corn oil drink, SUVs, and even extremely generous salaries of foreign relief workers.

This scenario has been played before in other countries facing crisis from Sierra Leone to, more recently, Iraq. Disaster money pours in an contracts are almost immediately bid out to multi-nationals—*rarely Haitian firms*—where the money goes not to Haiti, but rather through Haiti. It is a well-accepted fact that much of the money raised has ended up in the hands of highly-paid consultants, corrupt government officials and UN bureaucrats, not to mention UN programs that have nothing to do with development. To see Port-au-Prince one would think that there is a war going on rather than a thoughtful reaction to poverty and disaster. Moreover, there is quite clearly a theatre of relief efforts taking place here, ad with a few exceptions, very little of the aid money has reached the needy. Essentially, this business of poverty is thriving and it is the same situation of old in hyper-drive: NGOs and the international community increase their efforts to bring humanitarian aid to this devastated country and the Haitian government is increasingly losing its control—what little control it has—over where the money is to be spent. It is clear that Paris, Ottawa and Washington are making these decisions, often channeling their influence through NGOs and programs such as USAID.

Let me be clear here: the poverty in Haiti is real but it is a poverty in large part constructed by foreign aid and this fact is self-evident after spending just a few weeks working with NGOs and being intimately involved in the life of Haitians. The history of aid to countries in times of crisis (ie. the tsunami in southeastern Asia) has only demonstrated how aid exacerbates the problems by allowing yet another entry point for foreign capital, further destroying the ability for grassroots movements to retain their autonomy and communities. Wealthy countries need to rethink how to be of aid to countries like Haiti and to evaluate the ethical implications in the planning and execution of humanitarian relief while also developing private and extra-national interests. Ultimately, we need a new model.

NGOs are a business and this is evidenced by the throat-cut politics I have already witnessed. For instance, it is not uncommon that wealthier NGOs will outbid smaller NGOs or that these organizations will bribe officials for space to house refugees. Such practices secure more funding, making future funding easier—all guaranteed by the mediatized photograph of hungry children in safe shelter, credit given for "saving the day" goes to the NGO, often acting in concert with a grander political agenda, whose logo is emblazoned on the side of a new tent. I have heard of cases as recent as this morning of organizations which are being bought out by richer NGOs, all to get a cut of the "poverty pie." I have witnessed first-hand NGOs refuse to give food to Haitians who are not practicing Christians or who do not say a mealtime prayer. In a similar mealtime genuflection to the power that feeds the self, Government agencies are likewise promised aid based upon their having accomplished the privatization of certain sectors. This is the age-old story of the economic ploys of the last forty years in Haiti. The stories of money flowing outward towards private companies, Haiti's NGOs or of aid not reaching its due end would indicate, to the non-critical subject, pure corruption. But we need to look beyond such facile notions that render aid as somehow always good or which frames problems with aid as uniquely linked to corruption. What if the biggest source of corruption are these very humanitarian agencies which ostensibly help the poor while in reality they have created a market of donorship based on liberal guilt, neocolonial pretense and the exploitation of economic vulnerability? The back-door business deals are rarely—if ever—mentioned in the mass media and those who watch CNN's coverage of a recent site of disaster relief are shown the UN camps, tents given out by World Vision, even images of hungry children. In response to the mediatization of misery, many will pick up their telephones to donate money believing this is the *only* solution because this is the relationship forged between the media and relief agencies.

So, let us examine momentarily how business arrangements function whereby the image of the starving child has become itself a type of political currency for maintaining neoliberal policies of "aid." Currently in the west there is an unhealthy relationship between media and fundraising which creates what I call a "pornography of poverty." It is a theatre of cruelty which has no age limit and the actors range from the young to the old with, often, small children's faces being used to pull at the heart strings of the liberal westerner who has no idea where the money she sends actually goes or that perhaps sending money might worsen the situation. For instance, the images of poverty and disaster were pumped through the media for the first five days after Haiti's earthquake without any discussion about such reifications, nor about the ethical implications in using children's faces. Haiti soon filled up with people who came from around the world to make their careers as photographers. One photographer I met here in Port-au-Prince proudly told me that she is "making a photography book on Haiti"—she runs around the capital with paid escorts as she speaks absolutely no Creole, using disaster as the backdrop to her career and images become about "crisis" and "disaster," rarely about the subject. In a delicate moment when photography should be carefully measured, there is no push from any organization or individual to re-evaluate the visual modalities of exploiting disaster. Instead photographers plunge ahead with the same methods and logically reap the same disastrous effects. These photos serve the larger system of pity which aliments the liberal's need for exoneration through charity (rather than through political reforms) while keeping the viewer focussed on the children's faces such that we do not bother to think that this type of aid is merely a neocolonial fiction of "solidarity." For this is how Haitians view this entire process.

Likewise, former military contractors have descended upon Haiti in the name of investment through an NGO called the International Peace Operations Association (IPOA). If it were not so tragic, it would be comic—an organization that linguistically sells peace while in reality it sells death. Here is their mission statement from their website:

> *IPOA's mission is to:*
>
> *-promote high operational and ethical standards of firms active in the peace and stability operations industry;*
> *-to engage in a constructive dialogue and advocacy with policy-makers about the growing and positive contribution of -these firms to the enhancement of international peace, development and human security;*
> *-to provide unique networking and business development opportunities for its member companies; and*
> *-to inform the concerned public about the activities and role of the industry.*

The IPOA is an umbrella organization for private military and logistic corporations. It is the Halliburton of Haiti and we should all be worried. The aim of this summit held on 9-10 March, 2010 in Miami, was to bring together "leading officials" for "private consultations with attending contractors and investors.."[2] After discussing the objectives of the company with IPOA's president, Doug Brooks, he referred me to the summit's website which professes development in these terms:

> *Utilizing a unique format that combines informed content with the opportunity for private consultation with senior decision makers, the company has forged close ties with international governments, leading public bodies, multilateral institutions, non-governmental organizations and the global business community to provide a wide range of business opportunities for those companies keen to do business at the highest level within some of the world's most lucrative markets.*

---

[2] Fenton, Anthony.   http://www.globalpolicy.org/home/172-general/48778-haiti-private-contractors-like-vultures-coming-to-grab-the-loot.html

One thing is painfully and disturbingly evident from this mission statement: Haiti is up for sale and it is being done in the name of benevolence through NGOs, foreign governments and now the IPOA which couches the language of benevolence as a "business opportunity."

The reality behind the representations of the "orphan" and of the starving and malnourished masses is that these images are made specifically for the foreign donor while lending legitimacy to the 10,000 NGO marketplace. The even harsher reality is that most of Haitian "orphans" are not at all orphans—these children are victims of poverty. At this moment in the St Damien's Children's Hospital are nine abandoned children, all checked into the hospital by their parents, all abandoned there. Haitians have come to regard NGOs as surrogates to their own state and sometimes to their own families as the cases of child abandonment at the footsteps of hospitals and orphanages persist. So is it all that surprising that there is also an expanding NGO presence of orphanages in this country?

Agriculture provides a telling example of this loss of control over public funding as Haitian journalist Nazaire St. Fort reports: "[M]ore than 800 NGOs work parallel with the agriculture ministry, but most define their own priorities." The Association National des Agro-professionnels Haïtiens (ANDAH) contends that of "3.4 billion gourdes (91 million dollars) budgeted for public investment in 2006-2007, 3.2 billion (85 million dollars) are managed by NGOs." In brief, Haitian resources and farming are contracted out and the government is barely present in any of the steps central to planning, implementation, and development of farming. It is no wonder that local experts predict that the worse is yet to come in the rainy season (ie. high rate of infant mortality and stalled food production).

Poverty was never the normal state of Haiti and its "underdevelopment" was not a result of an accident or natural disaster—it was made to happen. Prior to 1950, Haiti produced more than 80 percent of its own food and exported products that kept it's economy strong: coffee, cocoa, meat and sugar. Since this time Haiti has been crippled by foreign encroachment in the form of political and economic instability from the late 1950s with the election of François Duvalier who increased taxes, destroyed the infrastructure, shut down unions and worked in solidarity with the US government as a force against Communism in the region. Since the 1970s and 1980s there has been a move to push Haiti to reduce its tariffs and open its markets to foreign investment.[3] This process destroyed economies in the rural parts of the country since farmers lost work due to the US imports forced upon Haiti as part of World Bank and IMF policies. As a

---

[3] Nazaire St. Fort and Jeb Sprague. "Haiti: Once-Vibrant Farming Sector in Dire Straits" http://ipsnews.net/print.asp?idnews=41454

result, people flocked to the cities to dwell in slums.   What one notices today about Haiti is the absence of shops with most everything being bought and sold on the streets.   There is the occasional auto parts store or the posh stores of Petionville, but there are few stores comparative to other parts of Latin America or the neighboring Dominican Republic.   Haiti was made to grow dependent upon other nations as its "debt" was crafted carefully by those offering Haiti "relief."   With relief came more debt and poverty.   And the lucky few who are employed in this country generally work either for the government or an NGO.

It is not surprising that NGOs have brought Haiti to this level of despair. Even Haiti's former Prime Minister, Michele Pierre-Louis (2009-2009), used NGOs to create her political career.   Before becoming Prime Minister, Pierre-Louis ran FOKAL, the Fondasyon Konesans Ak Libète (Fondation Connaissance & Liberté in French), a foundation created by George Soros' Open Society Institute (OSI) in 1995.   Given an annual budget of over $4 million (US), FOKAL was known as one of the most powerful NGOs in Haiti. Such NGOs actively weaken the political system by corroding grassroots organizations that would keep revenue in the country, detering reasonable prices for Haitian produce, and ensuring that products like Tampico reamain on the shelves.   Specifically FOKAL was used to delegitimate Aristide's government as Kim Ives details how Pierre-Louis used her power within the NGO to do this:

> Politically, Pierre-Louis became alienated from Aristide and his Lavalas Family party in recent years.   In league with the bourgeoisie's "civil" opposition front Group of 184, FOKAL played a small but visible role in late 2003 and early 2004 in characterizing the Constitutional government as repressive and intimidating.[4]

Pierre-Louis' position within FOKAL eventually granted her political access to the seat of Prime Minister. The NGOs continue to dominate and atrophy the state while the production of local fruits and vegetables remains unsure; yet Tampico, La Vache Qui Rit and other international products flow into the country. On the export end of Haiti, poverty porn continues to flow outward into the media from the news to NGO publicity websites where Haitians are used as the photographic shopping mall for this stock market on poverty. Most non-Haitians are clueless as to why all this relief money has not reaped any fruit. Except, of course, for the fruit and oil of Tampico's own investments.

---

[4] Yves Pierre-Louis and Kim Ives "Préval Nominates Michele Pierre-Louis for Prime Minister" http://www.haitianalysis.com/politics/preval-nominates-michele-pierre-louis-for-prime-minister

Naked in Port-au-Prince

Yesterday I went to a meeting on Rue de Miracles in downtown Port-au-Prince, the center of the worse destruction of January's earthquake. I was to attend an ecological encounter led by Hunter and Rodrigo, two specialists in permaculture who came to Haiti to teach Haitians about ecological methods for recuperating their homes and sanitation. The workshop they organized this day dealt with all aspects of the human compost toilet and Rodrigo and Hunter gave detailed instructions to all who attended. This free seminar aimed at helping communities use found and recycled material to build a human compost toilet and the participants in the workshop consisted of people from all over Port-au-Prince, especially the city's poorest sectors of Carrefour and Soleil.

I was most impressed with the presentation of these two young men who were eager to take part in Port-au-Prince's reconstruction in a way that offered Haitians the possibility of self-empowerment without the use or reliance upon NGOs which typically end up in a cycle of dependence or the lack of government interest in continuing such projects. Both men have been working in their own countries—Hunter in the United States and Rodrigo in Portugal—to educate people about ecological tools of home construction that are both readily available and economically feasible. The audience ranged in ages from teenagers to grandparents, each individual ready to hear about how to rebuild their homes and communities. Instructions were given regarding various methods for funneling urine and composting feces; for building sustainable outhouses made of found objects such as used tires, recycled wood and mortar; and for creating awareness about sanitary methods of waste removal, pathogens, and insect cross-contamination.

All the participants were extremely engaged with the presentation and I was surprised by the enthusiasm of everyone present. Notes were taken, questions seriously asked, and through an interpreter information was shared. Even more embarrassing subjects were cut through with frank talk: the words "shit" and "piss" were used so as not to exclude those who might not engage more technical terms and the topic of men needing to urinate sitting down rather than standing up was treated seriously.   These city dwellers wanted to recuperate their homes and learn how to construct anew their domiciles such that they might have more active control over their lives, rather than remain tethered to the need to purchase modern toilets that would remain outside the reach of most Haitians' pocketbooks. This seminar was one in a series of seminars aimed at directing Port-au-Prince residents towards self-empowerment through recycling materials in their immediate physical space and through communicating in cooperation with neighbors such that these facilities might serve the immediate needs of several homes.

Walking to this meeting, I passed dozens of collapsed buildings, each one unrecognizable with the occasional pancake stacked arrangement of floors. Most, however, were just rubble. All down Rue de Miracles were rubber stamp makers, shoe shiners and cobblers, a small store selling everything from men's suits to the 2 gourdes 200 mL. was in upheaval. I have met a police officer who has no choice but to live on the streets as his house was crushed in the quake and the city has done nothing to alleviate the stress on its own police force. He usually sleeps in his car. The displacement of well over a million people in this country is most visible in a city where approximately 10% of the buildings are destroyed (estimated at approximately 300,000) and hundreds of thousands of people are displaced living in any one of the hundreds of tent cities throughout the capital where these individuals simply live on the street.

The city is in ruins with most every destroyed building still unmoved. Thousands of televisions and refrigerators remain in the rubble and it is daunting to think of the human cost of this disaster when the rainy season starts later this month. Lead, cadmium, PCBs, mercury, and compressor oil will sink into the ground causing even more damage to the city's drinking water which is already tainted by the massive garbage rivers through the cityscape. To look at Port-au-Prince is to see a seemingly insurmountable series of political, economic and ecological obstacles. It is difficult to fathom that this city could eventually be one day beautiful, or even acceptable, with garbage lining the streets and flooding every dry river bed. More daunting is the news that Typhoid, Malaria and infant mortality are steadily rising and this will be protracted with the rains.

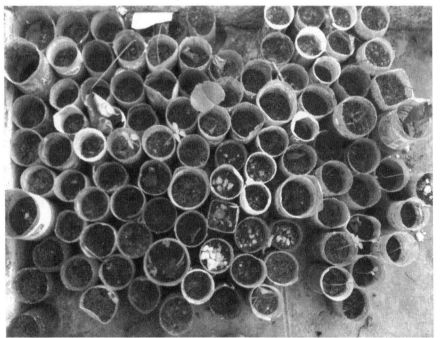

After we finished the first part of the morning workshop we head over to Carrefour to examine a spring in the middle of a public garden. The students of this afternoon's workshop came from a program where they are studying *prayanama*, *asana* and human values. They ranged in age from the late teens through the late fifties. The garden was beautiful and we were greeted by many individuals who looked after the flora and spring.

As we moved deeper into this space we could hear the rushing of water and finally we saw the spring which meandered as if a river. I could not keep my mind from thinking about swimming in this water as the temperature was about 38°C that day. The long ride over to Carrefour was full of discussions about the NGOs and the political absence of a central government; we spoke of the need for reforms, for civil protest, and ultimately for change. And yet it was clear that this river in front of us presented us a far less great obstacle—how to get into it without getting our clothes wet. The options were limited: we either got naked to get in or we would have to forego swimming.

I told the eight women with whom I walked to this spot of the garden that I needed to swim. I added that I would jump in naked if they would. They all laughed, embarrassed. This was the center of a poor Haitian quarter, men were everywhere, men who later would try to "help us" climb up ledges or steep inclines that day despite the clear independence of these women. After many minutes deliberating, one women crossed the spring on a branch extended over the expanse and she said she would go in with her pants. I suggested we get rid of the men—so we asked the two boys and the one man to please move further along in the garden. They left, looking back over their shoulders to see what we would do. Once out of sight, I ripped my clothes off, behind a tree so the men in our group, busily planting seeds, would not see. I then jumped into the spring and all the women laughed. Then one by one, Martine, Carline, Nicole followed and soon we were all in the river naked and laughing. The women spoke of us starting a revolution and I could see the parallels of courage. After all, if seven Haitian women of all ages can get naked in the middle of a public park in Port-au-Prince, what is to stop the Haitian people from reacting to the dire situations of ecological and political urgency with an equally radical public performance of resistance?

Croix-Desprez

Today I went to a recuperated school in Croix-Desprez.   I say "recuperated" because like most schools in Haiti, the school in this neighborhood was destroyed in the earthquake. Like most schoolchildren throughout Haiti, many are unaccounted for while their teachers are likewise missing.   So, what Croix-Desprez represents are the concerted efforts of a group of a few teachers and high school students who have decided to recuperate the elementary school by teaching the students from 2 through 16 years of age on the premises of a building that was cleared of its rubble.   This semi-permanent arrangement is called Gespam, an open-air school housed under a large canopy and divided into four, sometimes five, different learning spaces separated by various vertical separators.

Although this neighborhood seems almost middle-class at first glance, there are many pockets of incredible poverty now gravely demarcated by the catastrophe here.   The displacement of both the poor and extremely poor has pocketed this neighborhood with tents on its streets, in front of and behind houses, and even inside the confines of private gates. What is unique about the students of this makeshift school is that almost all the student body is living in tents within the stretches of this neighborhood in one of the highest parts of Port-au-Prince, many without parents or family. As one teacher, Gerda, told me, "In about six months this city is going to get a brutal awakening to thousands of pregnant thirteen and fourteen year olds." She is currently working with several of these pregnant adolescents and conducting theatre workshops directed at the massive number of adolescents in this community to provide sex education, underscoring the importance of pregnancy and AIDS awareness.

Gerda invited me to the school to help with the children, to lend my advice regarding the organizational matters, and to render a pedagogical assessment so as to assist the teachers and older students organize courses as closely as possible to the regularly programmed agenda. Most schools have been closed since the earthquake and many are now slowly beginning to open in this type of community-formed alliance. This is a grass-roots efforts to bring students together—often at the site of rubble or in private homes—in the hopes of continuing the younger children's' education in this moment of crisis.   The results are often hopeful, but also disheartening since it is painfully clear that Haitians have to depend on their own volunteerism and frugal resources which is why NGOs present a seemingly magical solution to the weakened state structures.   So at one point in the day a teacher uttered, "At least the NGOs offer us some relief from this," quickly adding, "But the price we pay for such relief is too high." NGOs are contemplated as temporary forms of relief here since these organizations tend to be the places Haitians go in times of need for momentary relief with a mini-grant, for example. Bandages are patched over festering infections and the larger troubles are never truly resolved.

So I asked Gerda, "What does the Minister of Education do to help you out in these times?" She laughed, "We don't even know where he is, if he talks." I suggested going to meet with the minister and asking why the students here do not, at the very least, have access to water and toilets, the minimum anyone could hope for. We shall undertake this project on Monday, should we be able to find where the Ministry of Education, also destroyed in the quake, has been relocated. All this must be parenthetically stated perhaps, because none of us expect any real answers. Blah blah and more blah is the order of the day in Haiti as newspapers and radio confirm and confusion only alleviates any responsibility for this government. What is more troubling is that the government is clearly deferring to NGOs in the aftermath of 12 January and there is great complicity in the government's handing power to these organizations.

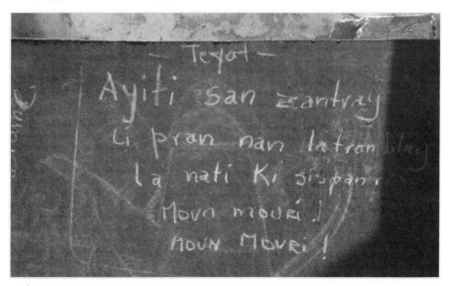

This is a poem entitled "Theatre" which I found on one of the chalkboards in this makeshift school site.

> Haiti without its entrails
> It took on the earthquake
> Nature no longer lives
> We died! We died!

This poem addresses the world "stage" of those people watching the tragedy from afar and it makes known this fact as if to say, "We know you are watching us."

From all that the eye can see, the earthquake has destroyed the lives of at least a third of this city's inhabitants and those who are willing and able are helping their neighbors and communities. What is most evident, sadly, is that this government abandoned its people long before 12 January, 2010. The signs of desperation are grave, paralleled by the hope and tenacity of the few who fight for their communities. The false hopes which NGOs plant publicize growth, change and betterment are nothing other than fictions made to ease the neoliberal conscience which would rather reach for the checkbook rather than her Senator's or Minister's phone number or email. Money will not change this problem alone and our compulsion in the west is to throw money at problems—and it cannot be overemphasized, for it is difficult for westerners to grasp—that throwing money at this problem under these conditions will simply not help.

No schools, no books, no teachers, no water. Yet, every NGO in sight is sporting new, expensive vehicles and highly paid international staff imported from around the world, all compensated by recent donations. Haiti is clearly dying and many whom the earthquake did not kill, will be taken through false hope of this their postmodern grim reaper, the NGO.

Living *la vida loca*

Great news for Ricky Martin! If only all closets could be opened. What is refreshing about "coming out" a closet is the affirmation that some new consciousness might be revealed. Of course, there are always those who will say, "I knew since the day you were born," and others who simply shrug their shoulders, finding this no news at all. Yet, opening up closets may very well produce friction, denial and anger.

My dear friends, let me tell you a very nasty story about denial—a story that begins and ends with capital, desire, and colonialism. The paradigm is here, Port-au-Prince, but the examples are numerous as "third world"[5] children serve as the proxies of first-world "salvation." Far away are the crusades or the missionaries of the twentieth century to save your souls. Indeed, there are now atheists and Democrats, liberals of all shades and sizes, coming to save you—or rather, your children. "Jesus loves you" might be the theme of the day on most every tap tap, but the colonial drive of adoptions in this country is the meta-narrative of salvation, and it is the western Dollar and Euro that will do the saving. Adoption is a business in the west and its ugly anus is here in Port-au-Prince. Allow me to share with you the bowels of neoliberalism that has most every adopting parent—who has or has not cried on Sally Jessie Raphael about their desire to have a child as if this were a Maslovian first-tier necessity—couching their desire to adopt as an act of "charity."

To begin, there are many moral issues with any approach to adoption that portends charity, aside from being utterly condescending and orientalizing. There is also a central psychological problematic that must be posited here: Is it at all healthy that people adopt to "save" children? This assumption that has long been part of the personal politics of adoption in the sociological and psychological fields needs to be critiqued. After all, since when should having a child be anything other than a selfish desire on the

---

[5] I use the term "third world" as what I find to be the most suitable and non-derogatory nomination of poorer nations. The term western does not really work because there are many countries in the East (ie. Japan, Taiwan, Australia) which are economically rich. Likewise "developing countries" is problematic since all countries are developing and much of what we call development say in the United States is merely an over-valuation of material over the social, not a very developed way of thinking of doing. So in the indirect reference of Chilean writer, Diamela Eltit, I have adopted the use of the word, "el cuarto mundo" (the fourth world), to label many wealthier "first world" nations whose way of thinking about social structures and social welfare is far more corrupt and malevolent than any "third world" country run by the stereotypical despot. I am merely re-arranging cardinal orders such that they mean something, yet they mean nothing. I will keep "third world" in quotation marks to keep this ironic and subtle difference at hand.

part of the parent(s) to have a child? Ethical issues surrounding the emotions of charity by those who wish to adopt need to be seriously critiqued. But this is not yet my point. I am dancing around the shit of what I have found myself in the middle.

One week ago, I discovered that the home where I rented a room was actually an elaborate operation of child trafficking. The alleged NGO run by these three young Haitian women, all in the their mid twenties, was a front for an elaborate child trafficking ring from Haiti to the Dominican Republic. Of course, when I found out, my brain exploded. I was quite aware—as everyone reminded me constantly—that my life was in danger. Here in Haiti, knowing things one should not know ends badly for many. Speaking out about things ends even worse. Yet in just two weeks I had found two very different forms of child trafficking in this city—one under the auspices of a an international charity/orphanage/children's hospital, the other a local NGO comprised of women who themselves were products of this "fake adoption" industry as they had been symbolically in Germany.

So, there I was listening to this director of a school here in Port-au-Prince admit one evening that the school's director had smuggled several children over the border from her "orphanage" to Santo Domingo without passports. The next day, I was given confirmation by several teachers at the school, all hesitant to speak out for fear of losing their jobs, that there were thirty children taken over the border that day. I was not entirely shocked by this revelation because I had discovered in my brief time in Haiti that this kind of practice was not uncommon—that many orphanages are "cover operations" for child trafficking wherein the "orphanage" would claim not to conduct any adoptions, but occasionally would allow adoptions for a fee. When I found out about this trafficking operation, it was a head-spinning moment for me as I had just ten days before discovered that a children's hospital was more interested in taking in perfectly healthy abandoned children to stock their orphanage than in accepting sick children. I had been coming to learn about the epidemic increase of "orphanages" each year in this country all whilst living under the roof of three child traffickers. Interestingly, what I witnessed at the children's hospital was upsetting mostly because it allowed me to see how a child who is considered parentless is co-opted in an incredibly perverse way: as both an object of adoptive fetishism made to "complete" the western infertile couple and as the symbol of this couple's stated claim to save a child from poverty and misery while conterminously the servicing hospital/orphanage basks in the media glory of "saving children." There are serious moral questions to be raised when an institution's participation in reducing child abandonment actually increases and promotes this phenomena and when an institution fails to encourage political and judicial action concerning child abandonment. That is, if we are really to believe the narrative they spin.

But there is an equally grave problem in the cultural construction of how adoption is spun in the west with the potential parents sweeping into disaster sites to "save" children from misery, posturing themselves as heroes and the child's life preordained as part of a larger neocolonial structure of "betterment" a the hands of people who hide their personal greed behind the veil of "charity." Most of us have all heard the stories and the bleeding-heart reasons from prospective parents about the reasons to adopt which frequently spin on the notion of "benevolence". However I have yet to read cogent discussions in the fields of psychology or human rights which demand an investigation of such social practices where the desire of the individual to create a family hinges upon this extremely perverse, colonial narrative which conflates personal desire with political machinations that claim to be "helping" a child. I have rarely seen governmental agencies discuss if such attitudes might be unhealthy: children need love, not pity. And it seems that this fetishization of the adopted child precludes love in favor of the posturing of charity, pity and a very colonial—if not mentally unhealthy—attitude towards these children.

Since the earthquake two months ago, there has been a flurry of North Americans showing up at Haitian orphanages and hospitals looking for a child to take home. There has also been growing critique of this practice by agencies such as UNICEF in New Zealand[6] which posit that adoption is likely not the best solution when these children who have simply not been identified, nor their families located. After all, It is common knowledge that when any object, say a crumpled piece of paper, is given a value and people desire to have this object, the value of this product will constantly shift. We have seen people throughout history go to all lengths in order to possess objects and even to reproduce the means to attaining said objects (ie. counterfeiting). Indeed, having that object of one's desire is a most important "task" for the western subject who today seems to think she can do anything (or that she ought to be able to do so). In the west we no longer die from consumption and polio, our houses do not fall down so easily in earthquakes, and when a tragedy hits our beloved New York, it does not even come close to the daily loss of human life to famine worldwide. When we suffer it is special because we are special. Or so we assume ourselves to be.

And so the story goes that when the western subject wants a baby, it is no holds barred: fertility clinics are on the rise throughout North America as infertility is becoming a major money-making, treatable health concern.

---

[6] "Haiti Ripe for Child Trafficking." *The New Zealand Herald.* 25 January, 2010. http://www.nzherald.co.nz/world/news/article.cfm?c_id=2&objectid=10622184

Big bucks are being made and even people in their twenties are having to get help in order to acquire their dream family. But many fertility stories do not have picture-perfect endings and this is where transnational adoption fits neatly into the neoliberal subconscious where materiality of the "third world subject" is excluded, where freedom is yet another unlimited consumer choice. When this foray into the "family that must be" becomes a colonial conquest wherein we turn our sights to "developing" countries which our governments have historically helped to impoverish, there is another series of questions that we must ask—both as citizens of rich nations which no longer have access to children to adopt within their own borders and as individuals. We must ask ourselves if it is moral to adopt a child whose mother and father are simply too poor to feed it. We need to hold both the state and the individual to a higher standard and we need to ask these questions and debate these dilemmas in open forums.

I long for the days when I will never have to hear as I did last summer at a picnic in Woodstock: "That is my adopted daughter over there...We got her in China." Gee, thanks, but I sort of figured some of this out give that you are blonde and she is Asian. But does this "fact" even need to be stated? We need to question if this form of parenting is at all acceptable given that adoption is a private issue which, once granted, is a narrative for the child to share (or not). Lofty interpretations of parents who see themselves as "saviors" of needy children or as good samaritans need to be critiqued and scrutinized by those specialists who confer the right to adopt upon hopeful parents to be. Announcements of "origin" need to fall into the history books along with notions of miscegenation, race and colonial occupations.

Back to the commodity fetishism of small, dark-skinned Haitians. Indeed the facts are cruel as both Canadian and United States adoption agencies charge on the average $30,000 per private adoption. Today I asked the director of the Institut du Bien Etre Social et de Recherches (IBESR, the Institute of Social Welfare and Research), Madame Jeanne Bernard Pierre, what her office planned to do regarding private adoptions which in Montreal look wonderful, but from here smell of child slavery, prostitution, organ harvesting and child selling. It is easy to idealize your family and prepare that family-photo, annual Christmas card when you don't have to think about the woman who couldn't afford to feed her child or who was in fact robbed of her child. These are not uncommon occurrences in Haiti as any Haitian will tell you. All except for Madame Jeanne Bernard Pierre, who at first yelled at me in the huge makeshift office sprawling across the courtyard of the earthquake-damaged building behind her claiming, "I have never heard of any child selling!" I turned to

Madame Pierre and without thinking I exclaimed sarcastically, "Wow! That is amazing, you must be the most naïve person in this government...or the most corrupt." As soon as the words were out of my mouth, every single person in the makeshift office in the courtyard was silent and they looked at me as if to say, "No she didn't." After many minutes of discussion, Madame Pierre calmed down and changed her tune, suddenly claiming she understood quite well the dangers posited by private adoptions. Indeed, people might have been upset about Ricky Martin not telling Barbara Walters that he was gay, but in the big scheme of things, that was Ricky's business. Child trafficking and paying $30,000 for a child through private adoption is ours. Well, ours and Madame Pierre's of IBESR.

Certain closets need to be opened and as the police from the DCPJ, Direction Centrale de la Police Judiciaire (Central Directorate of the Haitian Police) told me yesterday, child trafficking is all but uncommon in Haiti. The other day a teacher at a school where I have been working in Croix-Desprez, from the balcony upon which I was standing told me to look left, "You see over that orange rooftop to the metal one...There used to be an orphanage there. That woman just disappeared with the children." Then I was told to look over towards another area of Port-au-Prince on the right, "That building is another orphanage and everyone knows that children are sold there." Why is this the open secret and yet our governments continue to allow—even encourage via tax breaks and monetary incentives—private adoptions with Haiti?

UNICEF, an organization with which I do not always agree has come to see the inherent dangers posed by inter-country adoption:

> Over the past 30 years, the number of families from wealthy countries wanting to adopt children from other countries has grown substantially. At the same time, lack of regulation and oversight, particularly in the countries of origin, coupled with the potential for financial gain, has spurred the growth of an industry around adoption, where profit, rather than the best interests of children, takes centre stage. Abuses include the sale and abduction of children, coercion of parents, and bribery.[7]

The dangers have been demonstrated as this and numerous other reports indicate and as Inspector Myrthil, second in command to Haiti's Direction Centrale de la Police Judiciaire Brigade de Protection des Mineurs (also known at the BPM, the Brigade for the Protection of Minors) related to me earlier this week recounting the countless cases of child abductions and trafficking. In effect, Inspector Myrthil tells me, his hands are tied and his office can only investigate certain cases but that the head of operations is

---

[7] UNICEF's position on Inter-country adoption http://www.unicef.org/media/media_41918.html

untouchable and quite protected. He said that I ought to be careful to whom I pose questions and suggested I go to UNICEF to make a report there. Two women police officers also told me to be careful of going to any other police prefecture due to police corruption and police officers' involvement in child trafficking. So from the offices of the DCPJ and UNICEF on Monday, I went to the ministries who make and administer Haiti's laws on adoption. Clearly this problem has many dimensions and both sides of the adoption process share the blame.

When I reached UNICEF I found Caroline Bakker in an air-conditioned room hunched over a computer. I began to tell her about the cases of child trafficking I had discovered, but she just shrugged her shoulders, told me to go to the police and spun around in her chair to return to the computer screen. When I told her I had already gone to the police, she stated, "I am not responsible for child trafficking." Dazed by this interaction, in time I found the name of a child protection officer from UNICEF, Myriam, who was interested in working on this problem. A few days later Myriam contacted me and thus began my journey into the bowels of UNICEF.

But this sort of apathy and deflection of ethics can be found anywhere uncomfortable questions are asked. In 2007 while looking to adopt a child, a Montreal adoption agency told me that they charge $30,000 for an adoption. When I asked why the prices were so exorbitant, I was told, "Those are our costs." After reading more about international adoption it became quite clear that the "costs" of such agencies are about keeping people employed and nothing to do with the welfare of children. How have we come to this era when children's lives are still bought and sold?

So today I sat in a special parliamentary session wherein an "avant projet" is being constituted to reform adoption laws in Haiti. Deputy Gerandal Télusma from Artibonite, the president of this committee, is attempting to update the 1974 law and I am hoping to convince her and other politicians to deny all adoptions which are not public and free in the country of the adopting parent/s. She recognizes the problems of both the unsecured nature of the thousands of orphanages in this country (of which nobody seems to hold a precise number) and the fact that these orphanages contain few—if any—orphans. The deeper ethical issues in any sort of adoption pre or post-earthquake must be addressed from both our political representatives and those who work in sociology and psychology.

Haitian children are being abandoned, left at the doorsteps of NGOs and embassies, and confided to the good doctors at the children's hospital. From all that I have learned there is no investigation undertaken to attempt to find any parents or relatives. Children "found" or abandoned are like stock shares that bring in extra revenue for the many orphanages in this country. The fewer questions asked only means—just as in the case of the wallet you find on the street—that what you find is yours.

This is a newer, crueler colonialism that engages the subject, driven to the throes of desperation, starvation and the unholy alliances of bandits that will do anything to have a piece of $30,000. Even $100 goes very far in Port-au-Prince. I have spent the entire day traveling between the Ministry of the Interior, the Ministry of Education, the Ministry of Justice, the Institut du Bien Etre Social et de Recherches, and the Parliament. I didn't spend more than a dollar for all my tap tap travels.

We are spared the grotesque reality of child selling and slavery that dominates much of the developing world as the adoption agency serves as the pimp between the child we claim to love and the family that has been, in one way or another, robbed of their child. This is not a family photo Christmas I ever hope to receive.

Jesus Speaks Kreyòl

As I was walking towards the tap tap yesterday morning, I passed the local barber near the bridge by the house where I live. We stop and chat daily, but today I received the wave in—several clients, other barbers, and few neighbors were watching the story of Jesus as can only be seen in the orange colors of Vistavision cinema with cheesy fake beards and pearly white skin that of course Jesus not only had in "reality," but which is maintained throughout every representation I have seen thus far in Haiti. In these films, Jesus is not only white, but he also speaks Kreyòl (Creole).

In Haiti there is a lot of mention of "white." As I walk down streets here I am often called "blanc" (irrespective of gender) or more indirectly there is often the mention as incidental. After I jumped into the truck cab, an elderly lady wanting to ride up front guilt tripped the other passenger in the cab seated nearest the window who had told her to go to the rear of the lorry. The woman protested, "But you let the white person in." A gentleman sitting between the woman and myself gave his seat to the grey-haired elderly woman and he went back to sit in the carriage of the truck with the other passengers. The woman sat next to me and I turned to her and said in Kreyòl, "What makes you think I am white?"

Many Haitians of this woman's generation are quite religious, many of the younger generations are not at all. This current Christian holiday, Easter, celebrates the suffering of a human who was also God is markedly ironic in the setting of Port-au-Prince, a city where people are themselves suffering—more than a million in camps, no sign of major debris removal, no water for the schools despite their impending opening on Monday, the rise of malaria, cholera and typhoid, infant mortality is already soaring, and buckle your seatbelts: massive deaths are yet to come as the rainy season is expected drown people in these tent cities. I am approached by Haitians each day for tents and currently with permaculture specialist from Portugal, Rodrigo, we are organizing the construction à la Hasan Fathy and his architecture for the people, to erect recycling sites and buildings from ready-made material—earth, rubble, pieces of wood. The rains are non-stop for five days here and flooding is a reality. These tents are soon going to be the instruments which will drown people in six weeks' time.

Rodrigo and I discuss the project on which we worked yesterday—we went undercover posing as a couple looking to adopt a baby. This all started when the day before while leaving the UN's WASH (Water, Sanitation, and Hygiene) meeting, just outside the gates next to the UN guards from Nigeria, Rodrigo and I were approached by three men, holding photos of infants and adolescents, showing us documents of their orphanage, asking for money, looking for help for these "orphans." Light brown skin here indicates money, NGO status, and upward mobility for those with none. I asked if they did adoptions and the older gentleman, a preacher by the name of Louis Estivenne Etienne, said that they did. I asked if they gave discounts for more than one child and they said we would have to discuss it further but that of course anything was possible. They showed me documents from the Office of Social Services certifying their orphanage from 2001. I asked if that was their latest certificate and he said it was not but that he did not have a more recent certificate to show me. I pulled out my iPhone, pretending to speak on the phone, and recorded our transaction of the children taking pictures of this incident to present this to the parliament on Tuesday with whom I was working on drafting up better child protection and adoption laws. I likewise made plans to visit the orphanage, Orphelinat de Sion, in Arcahaie with my "husband," Rodrigo. So a few days later, off we went.

I realized immediately that Pastor Estivenne, his son and son's friend were not a high-end child-smuggling operation. I suspected that they were economically strapped running an "orphanage" beyond their means and sadly had no idea of the ethical problems of shopping children's photos on the streets. While Estivenne had told us Thursday that he had 70 children, in reality we saw Friday that they had only 32 present. Where were the other children? At that the children we saw were miserable and were clearly posing for us, all in clothes that were tattered, mismatched shoes, and amongst the already thin bodies, a few girls were extremely malnourished. They were, as is typical in Haitian schools, in audience for the "visitors." And after the director presented us, they broke out in song from English, French and Kreyòl about Jesus and his love bestowed upon us. One girl, about eight years of age was so emaciated that her arms were no more than five inches in circumference, her knees bowed. Most of these children had families who could not afford them, but clearly neither could this orphanage. The Ministry of Social Services and the Office of Social Welfare offer no relief, so is it any surprise that I found these men looking for their light-brown skinned savior of children in the bodies of the UN, UNICEF and other NGOs in this part of the capital? Of course Jesus is light-skinned when the only people holding salvation, sic money, are those who come from afar with questionable forms of help.

I heard stories about Sean Penn's having travelled down with a suitcase full of cash handing it out directly to people to get the job done given that little had been done before his arrival by any other NGO or government agency. As I write this article are hundreds of thousands of Haitians without tents who sleep in their cars, under linens stretched over tree branches and some in excavated tombs of the Petionville cemetery. Penn rightfully distrusted NGOs who to this day have generally done very little for the million plus Haitians living in utter misery and so his handing out money directly to the people demonstrated how quickly things could be achieved. Despite the fact that the camp which Penn's organization has created is not the final solution, it beat out all other organizations here who discuss action and yet are slow to engage it. This camp established in a matter of days relatively safe living conditions for approximately 50,000 people. This was not the situation of his orphanage in Arcahaie.

The director of the "orphanage" and his son were extremely well-dressed on the one hand, while the 32 children slept in two rooms of approximately eight by fourteen feet—in the boys' room two beds on frames for adults and three mattresses on the floor to be divided by 16 boys. And for the girls no mattresses whatsoever and two proper beds for the women guardians. There were no changes of clothes for any of the children. At whom to be angry I asked myself? The non-existent state which had been long marginalized and made surrogate to the IMF and World Bank deals? The greedy preacher who just wanted to construct himself a church and hence, having little of a congregation, fills the church/schoolhouse with these children whose appearance and origins he can barely explain? Children are just delivered to him, yet somehow there are families that must sign off on the adoptions I discuss with him. Likewise, it is clear that these children are not receiving education as they cannot read, are listless and sad. This preacher was willing to sell me children in exchange for funding of his orphanage and this was a small fee. This gentleman had lost his funding after Aristide's ousting when the Christian Revival Center out of Atlanta, Georgia had been sponsoring them to the tune of ten children. This is the price of sponsorship and it is rarely long-lasting and comes at the cost of children working the land as the preacher later told us.

The brutal fact is that these kids are *restavèk* (indentured servants, from the French, *rester avec*, "to stay with"), as our preacher tells us how it was his dream to have an orphanage while the children remain seated staring at a wall in the courtyard, waiting for us in order to sing to us our "welcome song." In this courtyard there are extremely complex English sentences on the blackboard behind us; yet none of these students speak any English aside from the memorized song with which we were greeted. In the church/schoolhouse chalkboard are countless Bible verses in English that are beyond these children's grasp. How is it that such an "orphanage" can legally exist as the conditions are inhuman and the fraud so evident.

Indeed, reading historical texts it is interesting to see how slavery has been morphed throughout the years by those who control it. Long gone are the slave ships—for that is too expensive. Let's starve countries, charge individuals for visas and air transport and then underpay migrant workers. And when our population is unable to reproduce let us buy the children from these regions. It is *restavèk* all around the world from Haiti to France and few seem to think there is anything wrong with the current situation. In the more traditional form of *restavèk*, the family typically leaves their child to be raised by the plantation farmer in order to ensure he is fed while he must work as a slave cutting cane for his life "indebted"—much in the same way Napoleon indebted the Haitians to pay indemnities for their liberation in 1829—to this master. Children are often "given" to others due to poverty and misery in Haiti and international adoption has ironically followed this very same model. But you cannot simply give a child to slavery as you cannot give her to another person. *Restavèk* is commonly practiced in the country and even here in the capital as you will find that stuttering child or an adolescent who is "too slow" for school serving as the house boy or girl. Though Haitians are aware of this practice, many are not aware of the abuse inherent to this practice. So whenever a foreigner tells me, "But her mother told me to take her," there is clearly no difference between this ignorant woman from British Columbia who sees herself as helping a child by co-opting her and that ignorant preacher from Arcahie who thinks he is saving children and doing the "Lord's work" by taking in the abandoned and utilizing this life as labor for his coconut and banana plantation.

The *restavèk* of the orphanage and the private adoption companies are cultural practices which need to end. We ought to have learned from our ancestors in western nations that buying humans is immoral no matter what you call it in whatever language you choose to employ: be it slavery, *restavèk* or adoption.

Shit: The Sequel

Last night while dancing with British permaculture expert in Kenscoff, Richard Higgins, someone yelled over to Higgins and asks him if he is having fun. Higgins looks up at me and exclaims, "I'm having loads of fun...after all, I've been stuck in a convent for over two months!" Higgins, like many other independent volunteers, came to Haiti to share his knowledge about permaculture and human composting with Haitians and has been living with a nun in a convent in Port-au-Prince's Canapé Vert neighborhood alongside a community of tents to number approximately 5,000 inhabitants between three camps.

Using the methods of farming elaborated by Sir Albert Howard and Yeshwant D. Wad in their book, *Waste Products of Agriculture: Their Utilization as Humus* (1931), Higgins advocates thermophilic composting of wastes which in turns humanure into an extremely rich fertilizer. Thermophilic composting as known as the Indore Process, a method of composting developed in Indore, India, between the years of 1924 and 1931 reduces the destructive tilling of the earth and results in low or zero impact agriculture which does not leave the land stripped of minerals and full of fertilizers, fungicides, herbicides and pesticides. In this process all aerobic bacteria are killed and the kräusening process (such as that used in the processing of beer as Higgin's colleague, Andrew Loxham, introduced) allows for the composting procedure to utilize the fungi and bacteria already proliferating in previous batch material.

Richard Higgins has created in Canapé Vert's center a series of palettes upon which this IDP (Internally Displaced Persons) camp's composting is created from nearby human composting toilettes where urine is separated from feces. This entire operation takes up approximately sixteen by fourteen meters of space between four central palates and one final resting pile. As I walk around the latrines and the composting area, I would never know that feces were the source material. It smells of earth and the sanitary conditions are better than most public toilets in North America.

At the meeting Saturday afternoon are various members of CRS (Catholic Relief Services) and IOM (International Organization for Migration) as well members from other NGOs who are interested in sharing ideas on this subject. But this is not a new technique in Haiti according to Higgins. These very same methods were used 80 years ago in this area when Haiti was a rich agricultural country before the late 1950s. People like Jane Wynne, whose father began an organic farm in Kenscoff, have been doing organic farming for decades and know very well the agricultural and health benefits to permaculture as her farm has become a teaching model for other Haitian agricultural specialists.

Higgins is being sought ought by CCCM (Camp Coordination Camp Management, part of the UN cluster system) to solve their problems of sludge tanks built on the north side of Port-au-Prince which have been the repository for waste from all the camps within the capital. The toilets in the camps were typically chemical portable toilets the results of which are the accumulation of numerous acres of sludge on the outskirts of Port-au-Prince. Predictably disastrous, the waste from these sludge piles reeks and harbors dangerous pathogens in a crucial moment when a local clinic has already reported seven cases of typhoid in the past ten days. The rainy season has yet to come and tens of thousands of deaths are predicted by doctors here. Eliminating waste in a sanitary manner is an urgent matter and Higgin's pilot project should serve as an incentive for the Ministry of

Environment. But will anyone truly listen to Higgins, much less follow through?

The center of Haiti's health and economic woes can be traced to the massive ecological disaster here which includes every corner of Port-au-Prince—rivers, sidewalks, backyards, gutters, city streets, to the areas where garbage is tossed out of bus windows. It is impossible to see any part of the city which is not covered in plastic bags, bottles or cans. To boot, the air quality is equally lamentable as toxins are released into the air from the all too frequent burning of metal and plastic. One of the biggest ecological problems is not even this—it is that trees are disappearing in the tens of thousands as people go to farms and hack away at them for firewood. To be perfectly blunt, the city of Port-au-Prince is a dump and there are realizable ways to resolve these problems.

On each of the four palettes the compost is turned three times and rotated as it is introduced to three different kinds of fungi. After ninety days the compost mixture is turned out onto a maturing space where it lies ready to be used after another period of lying dormant. Higgins is trying to get the UN and NGOs like the CRS to adopt his system and it is actually quite a struggle, as I notice at last Thursday's WASH meeting at the UNICEF offices. Many of the NGOs present are there to find fast solutions—UNICEF is looking to get rid of the sludge not concerned at all about the reasons for such ecological disasters. Meanwhile, Higgins offers a way out of creating sludge for the people in these tent cities which, instead of resulting in ecological disaster and a contamination of the water table, offers a clean, renewable system of waste disposal and a conterminous source of fertilizer for agriculture. The answers are clear and it would seem that both the Ministry of Environment and the major ecological NGOs would hook into Higgin's project as it safely eliminates waste and creates revenue for communities since these communities could save money on the purchase of fertilizer, sell the excess fertilizer and create an ecologically rich environment for the eventual growth of food crops.

The choices are in the hands of many—the MINUSTAH (Mission des Nations Unies pour la stabilisation en Haïti), the thousands of NGOs which desperately need to collaborate with each other, the government which needs to form a central agenda for dealing with this ecological catastrophe, and the people of Haiti who are still throwing trash in the streets and rivers and burning plastics and metals each day. There is a communication problem in Haiti—clearly many people are uninformed about the dangers they pose to themselves and the only signs of public education in sanitation are pre-earthquake items such as the indications to hand wash and cover one's face while sneezing to avoid The H1N1 virus. Yet NGOs are unable to function as a government and if they are to be of any use to Haiti, they should be organizing their movements with each NGO taking up a separate task, focussing upon one community while another NGO is working in the next community. The NGOs do not always involve the government as the government representatives were conspicuously absent at UNICEF's WASH meeting last week. So the ack of coordination and a clear mandate is also part of the problem. Some here say there are "too many cooks in the kitchen" while others completely give up on the government and the NGOs altogether. Certainly it is likely that the government did not represent itself at these meetings because the NGOs overshadow—dare I say overpower—the government. So ecologists such as Higgins and organic farmers like Jane Wynne, whose Wynne Farm has maintained organic and self-reliant farming for over thirty years, remain concerned for the future of this country. There we were dancing to *soca* in the Wynne Farm kitchen discussing how to effect environmental and political change in Haiti. Everything seems both so possible and yet so hopeless.

Ms Deeds Goes to Town

Let me state up front that I didn't hold out great hope for my trip to the parliament on Tuesday. I didn't imagine anything out of *Mr. Smith Goes to Washington* or any of these Capra-esque films where the "little man" beats City Hall. But nothing could have prepared me for the circus which awaited me at the Haitian parliament.

Yesterday at 9h30 I showed up early for a special session of parliament which was to start at 10h00, a session dedicated to reform Haiti's 1974 adoption law. 10h00 came and went and only one deputy was present as well as St Pierre Beauboin, who represented the National Association of Haitian Magistrates. In the following ninety minutes the others trailed into the large portable room: Rigaud Duplan, president of the Haitian Bar Federation; Yva Samedy from the National Association of Nurseries; and Collette Lesponasse, Chief Coordinator for the Support Group for Repatriated Persons and Refugees. An hour and a half late, the circus began.

The president of the Commission for Social Affairs was Gerandal Télusma, a Haitian deputy from Gros-Morne in the Artibonite whose charisma kept this parliamentary session animated and who wielded her power to divert or dismiss discussions throughout the sessions that week. She began by letting people know that the "debate" over the proposed changes to the current adoption law would take place; however, everything but debate occurred. The president gave the speaking order to those who were punctual with great doses of protest from Madames Samedy and Lespinasse. Rigaudon Duplan went through the 2007 proposed legislation, page by page, which for no clear reason became the "rough draft" for this year's legislation (ie. Did the 2007 law take this long to discuss? Did it fail in votes?). Duplan was quite distressed by Section II, Article 11 which gives the child the right to have an opinion about his own adoption, "Who ever heard of a child having rights at eight years of age?" he exclaimed. In Haiti this is certainly a sentiment felt widely and demonstrated by empiral reality of children's lives, as demonstrable through jurisprudence which has yet to fully address the rights of children and through the social treatment of children wherein UNICEF estimates at least 300,000 children are *restavèk*. Indeed for Mr. Duplan the child ought to have no rights, to be exchanged in silence because he claims that a child has no valid opinion, much less judgement. Of course he went carefully over the prohibitions of incest and marrying one's own child, as if such iterations were necessary.

The rest of the session was entirely homophobic—not to mention sexist—and the phobia was everywhere to be found at the small table discussing this document.   Such issues taken for granted were that the adoptee lose her name, that she *must* take on the name of her father and not her mother, that only adoptions from heterosexual married couples, heterosexual cohabiting couples, or divorced men or women are permitted. Now to anyone reading this list with a healthy sense of humor, these requisites for alleged heterosexuality are quite funny—after all the law is aimed at avoiding homosexuals raising these precious children (to whom the government turns a blind eye regularly when these children are trafficked).   Yet, as is common knowledge, one of the possible myriad reasons for divorce in a "heterosexual couple" is in fact one partner's latent homosexuality, so the "safeguard" against homosexuality could be easily dismissed.   In the end, the charade of the "moral parent" took precedence over any discussion of child trafficking.

At one point in this week of hearings, I addressed Deputy Télusma and I told her that I had been approached by an "orphanage" to "adopt" children and "help sponsor" their orphanage and that I had encountered three separate cases of child trafficking in my first month in Haiti. Télusma was dismissive and wholly disinterested in discussing the deeper issues within Haitian culture of child abandonment, of poverty, of the sale of children, of the practice of *restavèk*, of the government's lack of surveillance over the still unknown number of "orphanages" around Haiti, and of the non-existent public sponsorship of these "orphans."   She was more focussed upon the restructuring of the 1974 adoption law and the creation of a new paternity law which would make Haitian men who father children financially responsible for them.

You will notice, dear reader, that I employ an awful lot of words in quotes, a necessity in the spirit of academic honesty and likewise a conveyance of irony from which I take as much disgust as humor. Disgust for the obvious reasons surrounding the cultural and media obfuscations of the reality behind Haiti's orphanages.   The humorous part is simply because since I have stepped foot in Haiti I have had these moments where I find myself giggling thinking of Kathy Griffin's references to her having "dental work" (her code name for plastic surgery) or her allusions to Whitney Houston's "singing" (a euphemism for Houston's crack habit). Indeed, one can hardly use the name "orphanage" in Haiti without coinstantaneously thinking child trafficking, kidnapping and/or slavery. Sadly, these euphemisms reveal the tragic underbelly to this practice that is called "international adoption": the result of our societies' refusal to interrogate this practice is that most people in the west have as little concern for the true identity and conditions of their adopted child as those who, a hundred and fifty years before, believed buying Africans off a selling block was acceptable and serving a social good. There is a moral obligation central to adoption and our media and legal processes in the west have crafted the adopting parent as a tragic figure for whom the "third world" surrogate is everything but present. Welcome to neo-orientalism, brothers and sisters: no longer the tableaux of Delacroix's musings of a world he created in his head and then in his studio with women's bodies serving as the colonial backdrop to his fantasy of Algerian women. Instead, we remove the foreign elements of poverty and disease and we "save" the offspring, allowing the family to rot "off camera."

There I was in Parliament asking delegates and ministers to change the law and to make all orphanages fall under state control, to maintain strict vigilance over the quality of these spaces, to ensure the well-being of the children, and to outlaw private (for fee) adoptions internationally. Last week Gerandal Télusma had told me to continue to come to parliamentary session, but the reality of this "invitation" was met with a wall of silence. Deputy Télusma came to me during the debate and said, "It is actually against the law that a foreigner speak to the parliament.   I will have to invite you."   So, I waited through the discussions from Mr Duplan's reading verbatim of the document for an hour, to a thoughtful, if brief, intervention from Mr Beauboin about the rights of children, followed by Gerandal Télusma's adjournment of this debate.   I was not invited to present the data and information pertinent to the abuses of "orphanages" in Haiti, nor the photos I had collected from Saturday's "undercover mission" in the orphanage in Arcahie.   It was clear that Gerandal Télusma did not want to acknowledge the very serious and interconnected problems of child trafficking, adoption and *restavèk*.   Hence trivialities and not substantial issues were discussed because it is so urgent that the child has the father's name, compared to other more frivolous issues such as child slavery and trafficking.   It was as if these officials believed their own lies; yet none has to this moment been able to supply me with a precise number of "orphanages" in Haiti much less engage in any cogent discussion regarding the funding and control of such institutions.

When I approached Gerandal Télusma afterwards, I informed her once again that I have more information related to child trafficking to include the photos I took of the documents and "catalogue of children" I was supplied when approached by an orphanage last week.   I was troubled by her refusal to directly address this issue in session and even more distressed to have been lied to since I later learned there is no such law that a foreigner cannot address parliament.   Gerandal Télusma's query to me after the session: "Do you always travel from so far to advocate for political rights for others?."   She then told me to wait for five minutes and never returned.   The moral depth of this parliament could be measured by the fact that there were no recordings made of the special session, no attempt to hold a public forum audible to all present through the use of the microphones (which worked for the press conference immediately after), no presence of child psychologists or social workers, and no media presence, despite a group of journalists far away from earshot of this "debate" (yet they were joking and speaking rather loudly such that the "debate" could hardly be heard for those of us present).   Hence, every twenty minutes Télusma had to ring a bell and/or yell at the reporters asking them to be quiet.   At one point she took a fellow parliamentarian's head under her left arm and squeezed his head tightly, rubbing the top of his head with her right hand as if a routine from the Three Stooges. Conveniently, the noise from this cluster of reporters meant that the politicians did not have to answer, much less pose, legitimate questions and it was painfully apparent that this parliament was about the theatre of government, not about substance and certainly not about working through real problems related directly and indirectly to "adoption."

So, there I stood under the tress at Académie, at the Haitian Parliament's new headquarters, awaiting the return of Gerandal Télusma and I was befriended by a young law student and radio journalist who knew the score. "I hate Haiti and I am not afraid to say it," he told me. "The politicians are corrupt and they are idiots—but of course they are stupid given that everyone here is so uneducated that they vote for these charlatans...I just want to immigrate to the Dominican Republic or Martinique!" I felt this person's anger and frustration and I wanted to join him in leaving.

"That's Hot"

For those of you who are wondering if Paris Hilton is here in Port-au-Prince: no such luck. I have yet to see her form amongst the tap tap riders. However, I have been inspired by a lovely former student of mine, who ironizes what is really hot by saying or more recently writing to me in reference to political or philosophical discussions reiterating Paris Hilton's: "That's hot." Since leaving Montreal, I have missed Hugo's lovely mannerisms, his curly hair, his beautiful fashion and his philosophical sensibility. Our discussions range from the more academic to the musical underground of French punk music of the 1980s and to the current, sad politics within our university in Montreal. And what I miss most—though I was reminded recently via his email—was how Hugo's invocation of Hilton's "that's hot" renders intellectual the banal and borrows a most trivial phrase, flattening it and punctuating the here and now with a reminder that life is always much more than the depth of current discourse. Life is multiplicity and somehow Hugo's invocation of Paris reflects the impossibility to take everything too seriously.

And with this spirit, I took to the market on Monday, eager finally to eat. I tend to eat every other day in Port-au-Prince because of the necessity to capitalize on daylight as women are constantly reminded not to travel alone at night and my workload is beyond any habitual conception of intense. I am my own NGO and my chauffeur is the nearest tap tap, hence I must boogie until 18h00 every day. Monday, however, I didn't see any food that inspired me, everything had been sold or was dried up. I had half an hour before my next meeting and bumped right into a retired French teacher who was sitting in next to a sign for replacement windshields and sitting directly behind a makeshift desk upon which was set an old typewriter. This reminded me of the typists that are found at the entry to Rabat's old city on Avenue Mohammed V, where there is a line of typists under the walled entrance, middle-aged men ready to write letters of employment, obituaries, and love letters. Inspired by this letter writer my dear retired French teacher and I shared the next forty minutes together. I decided to write a letter to the men of Haiti, or more precisely to those men who follow me around the streets calling me "blanc," asking my name, telling me constantly to watch out for the passing cars as if I hadn't the knowledge to watch out for traffic. This gentleman, in his late sixties, with great patience and calm wrote the letter in longhand with no ruled guide, each letter perfectly formed, each line in polished linearity. The French system of education was present in every fibre of this man's redaction and he was ever so graceful as he turned to me and asked, "*D'ailleurs* is with an apostrophe, *n'est pas*?"

And there we were, sitting on an elevated step of the market street in Petionville as I dictated my letter aloud and he patiently listened and wrote. People selling meals and edible goods nearby turned and watched, others passed by busy looking for their tap tap, others stopped to listen. We discussed syntax at moments, gender at other moments and then polished off each sentence. It was a collaborative and imperfect effort. I would stall mid sentence and then change a thought, a verb, and retrace the thought process. The French teacher would suggest another manner of finishing the phrase. We were creating a text which began as story and oral narrative but which was transformed into a cursive-written proposition and ended in a formalized, 1970s typewritten text. We dialogued and laughed an awful lot. With each line he would write, I remained utterly amazed because I could never write in such a straight line—not even with ruled paper! The precision of each letter, the artistic grace of his handwriting left me wondering if I ought not to leave the project in the written form.

After all, if anything the surrealists have taught humankind is that art is a process, not ever really a product. And here in Port-au-Prince the ready-made the "found object," and the retooled recycled "trash" is everywhere. In Haiti not very much goes to waste and I made an attempt at recycling words from oral to written forms, utilizing a forum which still has its place in a town with few computers, and creating a discourse between various spaces, social elements and consciousness.   I was certain this project should be a failure simply because there was no measure of success given this letter would remain forever unread in its original form.   It was meant to communicate only to the few for whom it was never really intended: the girls selling dry beans, the boy passing with cans of milk, the men who may or may not have themselves been *dragueurs* (men who catcall women) and the older women who kept smiling and laughing.

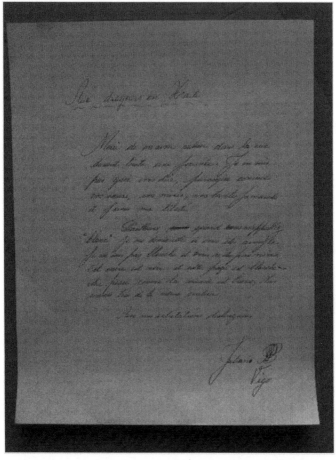

As we created each draft we would read the words out loud and meanwhile the small crowd grew bigger as we approached the typewritten performance.   The retired professor was initially curious with my idea and by the time he finished the handwritten version, he was wholly devoted to the project.   I thought that I must collaborate with him again because what we choreographed was much more than merely two pieces of paper and a live performance.   He understood the discursivity of a discussion that I would never have with these dragueurs since the moment you engage a *dragueur*, you do not "get away" so easily and you are tasked to reason with him as to why you must hurry to work or why you simply do not wish to have his phone number. This letter was a discourse/non-discourse. The French teacher had decided he liked me and requested my name and number and we both laughed as he signed the letter for me. I rather fancied his signature over my own and here below is our product:

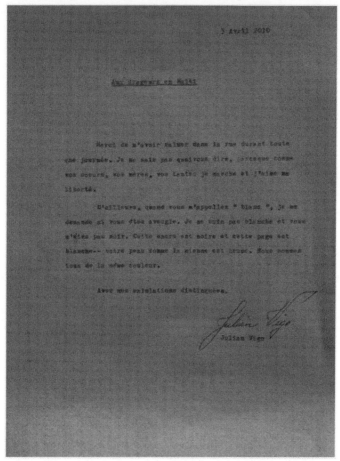

I took the letters, thanked the gentleman for his collaboration and immediately thought of Hugo's invocation of Paris Hilton: "That's hot."

Pa Gen Jistis

I went to Delmas 33 on Wednesday to visit the Hôpital de la Paix which until 12 April is being run by the "Proyecto Integral de Salud," the Cuban-sponsored brigade of healthcare workers.   Before 12 January, Cuba maintained a strong presence of medical staff in the country with a 400 member staff, half of whom were doctors.   Now Cuba along with Brazil, Ecuador and Bolivia maintains a team of 1,500 medical personnel 200 of which are members of other Latin American nations who studied in Cuba. This brigade has occupied pre-existing hospitals around the country and has created four additional mobile hospitals in Carrefour, Léogane, Arcahaie and Croix-des-Bouquets with plans for 101 permanent health centers for primary care which will attend to 2,800,000 patients, 300,000 emergencies, 160,000 births and three million vaccinations annually.

Hôpital de la Paix was quite modest but bustling with patients, doctors attending to all with extreme calm and care.   I was waiting for the chauffeur who had invited me to the hospital last week and I sat in front of the green medical curtain, admiring this calm space. There was none of the "third world" atrophy of bureaucracy and crowded spaces that I was accustomed to find in Montreal.   This emergency room treated patients with the respect and care I have rarely seen in my own country as I recall having a miscarriage in a Montreal hospital last year, and no staff was present at the front desk, the guard had no idea what to do and the intake nurse disappeared for half an hour to take a smoke break only to return to scowl at me, "Step on it!" as I could barely walk, the nurse refusing me a wheelchair or any help whatsoever. Hôpital de la Paix made me appreciate gentle, professional medical care and gave me a sense of some form of social justice being executed in this country.

Luis Alberto Medina Garcia, a twenty-five year old Colombian doctor, has been in Haiti for two months and is practicing general medicine at this hospital which specializes in surgery, pediatrics, obstetrics and emergencies. Dr Medina Garcia discusses how this eleven-year-old Cuban medical brigade has worked on Haiti to create 85 hospitals throughout the country in an effort to compensate for the lack of public healthcare. He would like to stay here to continue his mission and will soon be transferred in a few days to another hospital. He is committed to his work here and like all medical staff I am meeting in Haiti, he has off time and work has become what he knows best about Port-au-Prince.

This hospital brought to me a sense of hope and I brought this hope to my second radio interview of the day at Radio Digital, wherein I spoke of the problems of Haitian "orphanages" and child slavery. It is hard to have hope in Haiti where nothing really functions—from the electricity to the police, sometimes it works, most often it does not. Fortuitously, the pharmaceutical director of the hospital, Vireland, after my asking her which tap tap to take to get to the radio station, accompanied me to the radio station to ensure I would not return home alone when traveling at night after the interview. She turned to me on the first of a very long three tap tap commute and announced, "I am doing this out of solidarity." I wondered if this was a personal sentiment that Vireland had always honored, if this might have been incited from her work with the Cuban brigade or if this too was a sentiment entrenched within Haitian culture. It seemed almost too perfect since Haitians' relationship to non-Haitians tends to fetishize the foreigner—children on the streets regularly stop NGO vehicles begging, consciously skipping Haitian-driven vehicles and I am learning not to give my number out too often as this often leads to dozens of phone calls asking for tents, jobs, money, etc. which sadly I cannot supply. What people are too embarrassed to do in front of other Haitians they do over the telephone and by SMS. While it is totally understandable that desperation drives this behavior, it renders living in Haiti difficult for someone who is not Haitian and not working at an NGO because the perception here is that every non-Haitian has a posh job or works for the UN and has tents stuffed somewhere in their bag. But who can blame

Haitians for thinking this given that in the bottleneck traffic each morning a good 40% are UN and NGO vehicles? Virelande escorted me to my interview, sat with me under the tarpaulin of the makeshift studio replacing the one damaged in the earthquake, and later that night accompanied me to Petionville. We exchanged phone numbers and Virelande went to Delmas.

I returned home to find everyone in my house sad about the death of a family friend, Daniel. I was one of the last people to see Daniel alive. A 28 year old out of work programmer, Daniel was at home one night when I arrived needing to find an Internet Café, desperate as I was to write an article on a computer rather than my iPhone. Daniel took me to an Internet place a good distance down the street from my house and he insisted on waiting for me as I wrote despite my telling him that I would be ninety minutes. So I wrote, posted to my blog and I dug into my pocket for the fifty gourdes only to find ten. I was quite embarrassed and asked Daniel if he had forty gourdes to lend me until we arrived back home and of course he did not. He smiled stating, "Everyone here knows me and loves me and they will just want to make me happy." He whispered something to the young guy at the head computer as I dug for change in my Kinder egg. I found four more gourdes and Daniel said, "Don't worry" and on second thought, he gave the computer guy the four additional gourdes. "Everybody loves me" he repeated in a way that was neither over-confident nor arrogant. He just stated this as a simple fact.

We spent hours speaking that night in the courtyard at my home and he told me about his life in such an honest way that I didn't feel as if I was being performed for. There was none of the typical sale pitches that I hear constantly with men here: "Do you want a Haitian boyfriend?" or my favorite when I demonstrate no interest in my interlocutor and he utters, trying to manipulate me with: "You are not racist are you?" There was none of this nonsense with Daniel and he seemed to be a straight-shooter. He said he was miserable not working and informed me that he had not had sex in two years. We spoke of the many injustices in Haiti—"*pa gen jistis*" ("There is no justice"), I said in an attempt to exercise my expanding Creole vocabulary. Daniel was extremely drunk and I kindly reminded him that drinking and sadness were terrible companions; however, he stated that he was only drinking that night. I suspected differently. Daniel asked me about my life and I answered his questions with my usual candor which happily did not shock him. Once Daniel heard that I sleep with men and women, all bets were off. Daniel said, "Cool, so you will understand this," and he commenced telling me about his six-month career in pornographic films in Cuba several years before. He gave me the most vivid descriptions of sex I have heard in my life and proceeded to describe his— *ahem*—"qualities." I was as elated to have a completely frank conversation with someone here as Daniel was to share his story. I imagined that I was the only woman to whom Daniel told this story given his religious surroundings and his proximity to the men in the family from whom I rent. Daniel was also proud to tell me about his films since I also make film and video and as he saw it, so did he. We shared a medium and that brought us into the details of the only properly paying job Daniel said he ever had in his life. Like many Haitians, Daniel studied throughout secondary school, was a self-taught programmer, and remained unemployed after his studies. His only real job, he claimed, was his short-lived porn film career.

The next day while drunk, Daniel climbed up a three meter high wall and fell on his head. He died shortly after reaching the hospital. Daniel is one of the millions of Haitians who see no future in their own country and alcohol is one common way for numbing the current reality of high unemployment, no central government, no hope. On the way home tonight with Johny, broken up over the death of his dear friend, I learned that in fact Daniel had never been a programmer, had never left the country, and that not only had he never had a porn career, he had never had sex. "He just drank a lot…and he was a good liar," Johny declared, "That is what he did best. But I miss him. He was like a brother to me." In the absence of possibility, fiction became Daniel's way out of Haiti. *Pa gen jistis.*

Crazy in Port-au-Prince

There are days when the tap tap comes and goes regularly; other days when you are left waiting for hours as people shove by, pushing one another, jumping onto the empty tap tap. Men can be the most brutal and in order to jump onto the end of this converted pickup truck, they shove women, children and smaller men out of their way. I have done what I call the "run for the Gold" when trying to board a tap tap, joking later with people that this should be in and of itself a unique Olympic sport. I tell Haitians they would definitely win the gold medal in the "Race for the Tap Tap Competition." In Haiti size is often a factor in political domination: if you are too large to make the run for the tap tap, too fat to fit into the seat with other people, or tall and thin such that you become a desirable commodity as your legs are turned into a sofa for those who prefer to sit on you rather than stand hunched over. Size maintains your ability to throw, quite literally, your weight or jettison towards a tap tap which never slows down to ensure that only the fittest will be able to board, thus eliminating fights to enter a parked tap tap. There could even be a separate competition for those with children, since the skill in being able to push your child onto the tap tap and then jump in yourself is an art form.

And then there are the politics of sex and the tap tap. If it weren't bad enough walking down the street here as a woman having men constantly remind you to look out for cars, pushing you perpetually as if you hadn't the eyes, ears and brain to figure that one out for yourself, the tap tap brings up an entirely different set of sexual politics. Often when sitting with the driver there will be a third person who wishes to crunch into the very same seat. I gladly move over if the person boarding is a woman, but if a man is boarding, I step out and allow him to sit in the middle seat, next to the driver. On many occasions I have had men tell me, "You know that is not your place...your place is between two men." I inform these men that they are misinformed, that not only do I not have "a place," it is certainly for me to decide if I feel comfortable being surrounded by two men whom I do not know. One man yesterday told me that I "need a man to protect [me]" to which I responded that it was in fact the women in Haiti who protect the men,[8] and not the other way around, citing him what is a commonly accepted fact amongst most Haitians men and women alike: that women do most of the work inside and outside the home (and this

---

[8] Well let's face it, this is an international fact: women do two-thirds of the world's work and receive ten percent of the world's income.

paradigm does not change around the planet incidentally). He grew furious and started yelling at me insisting that I didn't know "my place." I reminded this gentleman that not so many years ago, this same rhetoric was uttered by Europeans towards people of African origin, who likewise told them to get in *their place*. Of course, he denied the parallel structure, repeating that I needed his protection. I let him know that his anger made me think I needed protection from him, not by him. The driver laughed quite a bit as I spoke of the history of Haiti while this man screamed at me, claiming to "know everything" (as well as his reminding me that men are stronger than women, etc). Asking him to recount certain facts about Haiti's release from slavery, I find out that the screaming man's words were not backed up by facts and that he had little knowledge of Haitian history whatsoever. So I recounted him the liberation of the slaves, the late 18th through the early 19th century with Louverture's work around Saint-Domingue and I reminded him that only the individual decides where she wants to be, for whom she works, and where she chooses to sit. He was still screaming when I left the vehicle to change tap taps.

There are other days when the tap tap exists at a premium: the driver holds up his fingers to show three fingers. What was once a ten gourde ride (two Haitian dollars) has suddenly become fifteen (three Haitian dollars). One woman in the back of the tap tap last Tuesday protested and I joined her asking the driver, "What are you offering us that the other tap tap for ten gourdes are not?" He grunted, "That's just the price." Everyone paid the three dollars begrudgingly in this exceptional act of having to pay up front—the driver knew that people would not pay fifteen gourde if he had to collect when they descended the tap tap as is the normal practice here. Nonetheless, resistance was expressed on the tap tap ride as a gentleman seated in front of me announced, "Ok, he charges us more, but we are not letting anyone else onto the tap tap." As is the usual score with tap tap, they comfortably seat five and if no large people are on board, often six. But there are many rides which simply are pushing the limit in forcing six adults to line each side of the tap tap. So this gentleman told each and every person who attempted to jump on and do the hip crunch that there was no room. We were ten in the tap tap and everybody joined in this act of resistance, refusing the driver more passengers thereby avoiding the sardine effect. We all laughed as we continued our journey towards Académie refusing passengers, with everyone finally giving in and letting a gentleman holding a rooster in his left arm stand on the back of the tap tap for the last kilometer, hanging on only with his right hand.

This morning, there were no tap tap at all. Well, there were a few, stuffed with men and boys, brimming out of all open orifices, reminiscent of the packed Delhi trains during morning rush hour, and dozens of people lining the streets hoping for more transportation. The older Haitians, women and their children, stayed at the side of the road and there was a particularly high number of school children unable to go to school waiting in the Petionville market. I waited a good twenty minutes and realized that there was no getting a tap tap given the plethora of students gathering, so I went to the nearest motorcycle stand hoping the students would get to school. I tend not to take motorcycles here as they are more expensive for foreigners (as a volunteer, I am on a tight budget) and more importantly they are bloody dangerous. I have done a great many crazy things in my life and the motorcycle sans helmet is not a new adventure—even riding without a helmet, an obstacle course of bad roads, plus driving chaos I have also done. But Port-au-Prince is by far the most dangerous place I could fathom riding a motorcycle: the roads of this city are full of ripples and holes. Also, the use of the horn creates more confusion than clarity and the main roadway is not a concept that is respected here, such that cars will literally pull onto a major roadway with speeding traffic being forced to grind to a halt simply because the offending vehicle is larger. Coming down Delmas, a main road in Port-au-Prince, the motorcycle driver took a cautious yet expedient pace and each and every time a car or truck approached the main road, the motorcycle driver would not just slow down, he would stop. This is the land of bigger is better—bigger takes precedence. This is evident everywhere where those who are smaller and poorer have no place on the road or the cityscape, while the bigger and posher are given carte blanche to all spaces.

So, we continued down Delmas, turned right at Delmas 33 and whenever anyone would cross the street or when we would enter a tight pedestrian marker, the horn dominated the road as the driver would honk repeatedly to rush people out of his way. This is the dictionary entry for the vehicle horn in Port-au-Prince:

1. Get the fuck out of my way. 2. Move your ass you mere pedestrian walking with grocery bags! 3. I have a big, new car—look at me! 4. Don't even think of going there. 5. Hey, friend, it's me. 6. This is a horn and it indeed works. 7. I am running you over—goodbye. 8. Cogito ergo honk.

Now for anyone who has been in a rickshaw in Delhi or has crossed Tahrir Square on foot, you are aware what crazy driving is. For those of you who think that crossing Broadway near the Flatiron Building is dangerous, suffice it to say that we are simply not in the same solar system of "danger." The reality on the streets is both daunting and light-hearted: amidst the most surreal situations from traffic disasters, to the infamous *blocus* (congestion) that occupy most every morning and afternoon traffic pattern, to the market scenes that reveal the only true signs of livelihood within a chaotic tableau of conterminous desperation and prosperity.

Sunday morning, while shopping in the Petionville market, I was looking for avocados to bring up to Kenscoff and none were to be found. I bought greens, onions, tomatoes, garlic and mangos, but I was persistent to find the avocados for my friends in the mountains. Forty minutes later I gave up my search as everyone in the market informed me that the avocados were not yet ripened—it would be a few more weeks before I would be able to have my much dreamt of avocado, tomato, salt, olive oil and lime salad. Walking towards the tap tap, I looked up and before me walked a fifty-year old woman who was entirely naked from head to toe. Nobody in the market seemed to notice and I was having a definite crisis of conscience—my heart raced as I wondered if anybody noticed this woman aside from myself. People were talking with one another, parents were walking with their children to church and through the market were those who like me had the task of shopping, the phone card sales boys were strolling around with their red vests with phones in their hands front and center, women were selling eggs, and men selling friend plantain chips, all conducting their transactions as normal. Nobody looked up shocked, nobody pointed, gawked or pointed—it seemed as if this woman was invisible. It was after a full two minutes of thinking where I might find someone with a large piece of cloth, looking to the woman to see if she was injured or even to see if she was simply mentally ill (as if looking at her would discern this). My eyes would dart back to the masses to see if they reacted. Finally I went to the youths selling the phone refills and asked them wondering if I might have imagined this woman, "Do you see her?" They laughed at me and I thought to myself, "Maybe I am mad?" I went to the women selling the eggs and fried pastries and asked if they saw her, to which they said, "Li fou" ("She is crazy"). I persisted, "Are you sure she is crazy?" They smiled and assured me this woman wanted to be naked, barefoot walking down the streets of Petionville. I turned and pondered this scenario a moment and then continued walking in search of a tap tap.

Arriving in Kenscoff I found out that a nurse who had, with an American doctor, rescued a child from an "orphanage" and admitted the child into a hospital for treatment, was being threatened with legal action from the "orphanage" who was demanding the immediate return of the child. The orphanage in question is well known in Kenscoff for utilizing the children as sexual slaves, sending girls out daily to prostitute themselves, and this fact has been chronicled by the local police and recently by the US Army Military Police. A Child Protection Officer from UNICEF asked me to investigate the orphanage after reports came from the Haitian Police and the US Army that this orphanage was selling young girls into prostitution. Still the IBESR has done nothing to shut this "orphanage" down and there is no sign this "orphanage" will be put out of operation any time soon.

After hearing the story of this good samaritan being threatened with legal action from Sister Dona's lawyer who attempted to distort the medical care given to the child as kidnapping, I became so cynical about the situation. I even told the nurse not to worry simply because the government would rather keep a corrupt orphanage running rather than shut it down and admit their own wrongdoing—namely, that they did not take action months ago when agencies and local police were warned.

My task that morning was to go to the orphanage and chronicle the conditions of the children as well as to attain information regarding adoption for my research on the use of orphanages in illegal adoptions. So I showed up at the orphanage, my iPhone in pocket. I was met at the door by a young woman dressed as a nun who told me that Sister Dona was not in. I told her that I came from the United States, that I was with a "church group," and that I was interested in adopting a child. She invited me in. She showed me the children in the back of the orphanage, broken down into two groups, those under seven and those above seven, having what seemed to be like lessons without a teacher present. All were seated underneath a blue plastic tarpaulin. Strangely mulling about were two young men of approximately 18 years of age who had no place in any orphanage.

I was shown around the premises as I had asked where the girls and boys sleep. I was shown two separate rooms where light filtered in through concrete blocks up high as triple bunk beds served as the sleeping spaces for these children. From the numbers it was clear some had to double up. This young "nun" avoided showing me one room on the left front building's second story which she claimed were uninhabited. This is the room where these young girls were said to be raped. At one moment while she took me around, my "husband" called. My "husband" in these sorts of investigations was a method I employed in such situations when I would take out my iPhone and have a fake conversation with nobody while I would use my thumb to snap photos as I fake-discussed how beautiful the children at the orphanage were. I walked around the premises clicking away and by the end of my conversation, I came back to the "nun" and asked her what it would take to adopt—how much money, essentially. She told me that "many foreigners make a donation of $6,000 US." So this was the price of a Haitian child's life.

She then offered to show me the registry of names of people who had come to this orphanage. I looked through the list of signatures and addresses and people from around the globe who had visited this orphanage to include some officials within various embassies in Port-au-Prince. Next to almost every name were the names of children, the "wish list," of each signatory as if reserving that specific child. I was able to sneak in a photo, albeit a shaky one, when the nun left the room for a moment.

As I write this article, the "orphanage" of Sister Dona called Sœurs Rédemptrices De Nazareth is still operating, its doors wide open.

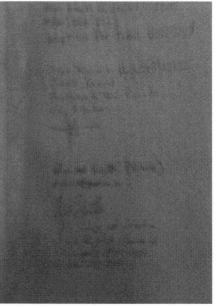

The naked lady walking in the market in Petionville suddenly didn't seem so crazy after all.

Biopower and Adoption

UNICEF estimates that approximately 300,000 Haitian children are *restavèk* (child slaves) and that 3,000 children are trafficked out of Haiti each year. However, these figures are widely considered conservative both because there are no serious studies to date on this subject and because the very definitional basis of trafficking needs to be rigorously redefined in order to more precisely represent the reality of children whose lives are bartered, traded and sold under the guise of various legal and illegal institutions.

Before the earthquake of 2010, UNICEF estimates that 400,000 children (approximately one in ten children) were living in an orphanage. While most of these children were not orphans (ie. the word "orphan" in Haiti is mostly a misnomer as most children in these places are abandoned), many were abandoned by their families in the desire to have their child raised outside of extreme poverty, often with the hopes of their child being adopted and raised in a rich western nation. This attitude is not uncommon in Haiti and there is an increase, not a decrease, in the number of children being dropped off at orphanages, children's hospitals, and churches as this comportment has become a social trend amongst this country's most disenfranchised. Tangentially, there is a grey space surrounding inter-country adoption which avoids addressing the necessary moral dilemma of creating economic enterprises wholly based upon an ethos of "adopting out of poverty" and likewise which does not confront the problematic relationship between the comparatively wealthy, first-world adopting parent and the poor Haitian family unable to afford their child. Currently, such discussions are not being addressed by either international legal bodies or specialists in the area of international adoption.

Haiti approves approximately 1,500 adoptions per year and many of these adoptions take place through American and Canadian adoption agencies which charge fees beginning at $30,000 USD. Likewise, there are local Haitian adoption agencies which require adoptive parents to support their child while awaiting the completion of the adoption process (often $200 USD per month in a country where most people live on less than $1 per day) with the total fees often amounting to $25,000 USD. Such fees are estimated to bring in $20 million each year calling into question both the ethics of buying human life as well as the parallel polemics of "conflict of interest" as most every agency works with specific lawyers, notaries, social workers and other facilitators whom are all paid through the adoption agency. As such, there is no external control of these adoptions and the organization which ostensibly oversees all orphanages and adoptions within Haiti, the IBESR (Institut du Bien Etre Social et de Recherches), has reported to have absolutely no idea as to how many "orphanages" there are in the country. With such a lack of knowledge of and control over these orphanages, it is understandable how corruption and private financing leads to a blurring of the lines between economic assistance and purchase.

Correlatively, there is a slippage of the term "orphan" which lends a certain authenticity to the situation of the human life represented: "orphan" connotes a credibility of need due to the absence of parents. By employing the term "abandoned child" or "center for abandoned children" the myth of the Haitian orphan would not only be dispelled, but the employment of a language that more accurately describes the current social reality for many Haitian children would function to inform the international community of the social conditions behind all these Haitian children that are today largely believed to be orphans. Hence, it is essential to understand both Americans' and Haitians' notions of the "orphan", the "orphanage" and the "abandoned child."

Over the past three decades there has been a deepening social crisis in Haiti regarding the co-optation of children for various exchanges, specifically that of adoption and *restavèk*. Though adoption and child slavery might seem like diametrically opposed cultural practices, they often operate in tandem with one legitimating the practice of the other (ie. adoptions are legitimated because some perceive them as saving a child from slavery) or one covering up the other (ie. adoptions are often exchanges of children for the sole purpose of child sexual exploitation and/ or child labor). What is also important to understand the relational dynamics between these two practices is how the seemingly innocuous practice of international adoption has fed a larger system of economic exchange between richer western subjects and poor Haitians whereby the material exchanged is a human life, regardless of the underlying emotional and moral issues buttressing contemporary practices of adoption. More directly, there is a clear analogous correspondence between the surrender of one's child to another (albeit richer) Haitian in the more traditional system of child slavery, *restavèk*, and the contemporary measures of international adoption which actually do replicate this same social and economic ethos: that of saving the child from an uncertain future, resuscitating the child's life through a now foreign other. While it might be uncomfortable to examine these stark similarities, it cannot be overstated that any study of child trafficking in Haiti would be remiss for not examining the social parallels present between a parent seeking the economic "salvation" of a child through *restavèk* and through international adoption.

Similarly, the relationship between various traditions (sic institutions) which "take over" parenthood due to economic poverty and the creation of "surplus value" based on the economic exchange of human life must be examined in relationship to child trafficking. This surplus value, while it is often measured in monetary terms (ie. high adoption fees which are legitimated by claiming to include psychological evaluations, home studies, legal and transport fees), cannot only be exacted economically as there is also the symbolic value that is attached to adopting a child and giving up a child for adoption in Haiti and in the United States. For instance, many Haitians who voluntarily give up their children believe that their children will necessarily return to them at the age of eighteen. These parents simply do not regard their giving up their child for adoption as a permanent status, but instead, many regard this practice as a "prêt", a loan. In the minds of a great number of Haitians who give up their children to for adoption, there is a firm belief that their child will become economically enriched and one day return to help out the originating family that made their ultimate sacrifice. Conversely, there is often the attitude among westerners adopting children out of poverty that theirs is an act of selflessness and there is a conscious elision of this posture within the bodies of jurisprudence and social psychology which directly effect adoptions in wealthy western nations. There is a comprehensible need to address directly the larger moral quagmire created by a cultural practice which makes acceptable an ethos of adopting children out of "pity" or "benevolence," rather than out of love.

Contiguous to this question is how the larger developmental politics of international aid by foreign governments and NGOs, together with the widespread and growing practice of international adoption and sponsorship, lends to an unhealthy relationship of economic and psychological dependence on a macro-political and social level and likewise on the micro-political scale of the parent who often believes that it is the role of these outside bodies to help them raise their children. By creating a market of adoption in such a milieu of international aid and charity, it is not difficult to comprehend how this structure aliments the widespread attitudes held by Haitians that foreigners are better equipped (sic economically) to raise their child. There is a tautological relationship thus created between these two structures: on the one hand, the "need" or desire for children by western families feeds the "voluntary" abandonment and illegal co-optations of children in Haiti in the well understood relationship of supply and demand; on the other, western subjects are fed images of starving, neglected and "orphaned" children and consequently the western subject creates economic ties of symbolic parenthood through "sponsorship" (thus receiving their annual hand-drawn sketches to hang on their refrigerator) and often undertakes the expensive process of international adoption under full approval of the Hague Convention and national adoption laws. This entire scene of the able westerner who can sponsor and/or adopt a Haitian child takes place within the theatre of commonly accepted social and institutional "norms" that simply does not question the ethics intrinsic to these acts of "charity" and exchange and which likewise turn a blind eye to the reciprocal relationship that such attitudes and practices might impose upon the society which "willingly" gives up its children. Hence the relationship of charity to international adoption functions very much as a social and economic surrogate of the parent in the absence of a national state mandate and social assistance. Poverty thus becomes doubly exploited through the exchange of the child through both legal and illegal structures: first, at its origins within the social reality of the poor family and secondly, on the symbolic and transnational level of adoption where the richer family is paradoxically "awarded" a child by the mere relational value of wealth and circumstance. Tangentially, parenthood is perilously becoming an institution that no longer is related to the somatic, the social structure of family, or emotions of love; now, parenthood is becoming a transnational fabrication being decided by default where economic wealth determines rights to parenthood and the paradoxical basis for such constructions are perverted as much by the western constructions of entitlement as the Haitian attitudes towards wealth.

Biopolitics is a central facet of international adoption which is implicitly present within the search of western subjects who adopt children outside of their own national territory. Since the 1980s, sex education, birth control and access to abortion have reduced the rate of unwanted births in the west resulting in fewer babies to adopt domestically. There are even countries such as Italy and Canada for whom immigration is vital to these countries' economic stability due to the otherwise dwindling population; thus adoption is not only needed, it is often facilitated by the state. Likewise the notion of family has also changed such that today same-sex couples and single adults are turning to adoption, not to mention the problems of fertility facing richer nations. The response to the problems of reproduction, the decrease of available children to adopt domestically and the concomitant measures taken by governments to encourage transnational adoption has resulted in a bio-political project in the west which creates and institutionalizes orphanages in developing countries and directs the global flows of children from the developing world to western shores. I am extending the theoretical concept of biopolitics to the actions and policies of orphanages in Haiti and international adoption institutions within the west. According to Giorgio Agamben (1998) and Michel Foucault (1997) control over life is the core of biopolitics. While Foucault focuses on the state's concern with the biological surveillance and control over populations (ie. disease control, sanitation, education), Agamben modifies this notion of biopower, slightly expanding Foucault's definition to include the control of populations through what Agamben calls "bare life." Borrowing from Aristotle, Agamben characterizes biopower as law which maintains the power to define the simple fact of living, "bare life" (zoē), of its citizens. Agamben demonstrates how this simple fact of living is actually excluded from law since the end of political discourse is not "bare life." Opposing "bare life" to "politically qualified life" (bios) Agamben maintains that "qualified life" is the focus of the modern state in its drive to create competing articulations of "life according to the good." In this way, Agamben proposes that "bare life" is a simple, unqualified fact of living included within the discourse of politics through its very exclusion. Demonstrating that the power of law is to actively separate political beings (citizens) from "bare life" (bodies), Agamben maintains that there is an inclusive exclusion at the level of life itself which is often called into action during a "state of exception". Thus the subject of "bare life" remains conterminously absorbed by the law and yet rests outside it since the ultimate goal of the state is, in the end, to transform "bare life" into "good life". In this way, law creates a field of inclusive exclusion which allows for certain humans to be treated differently–even as non-humans–in their exclusion, while their inclusion is implicated through their transformation from "bare life" to "political subject".

Taking this concept of biopower from Agamben and applying it to the paradigm of legalized adoptions, we could read the political being (the citizen) as the adopting western subject for whom jurisprudence demands that the subject obey certain laws regarding domestic adoption. But, shift the scene of adoption away from the domestic space of legality and social scrutiny and another order is revealed: the third world child who is rendered "bare life". International adoption is the state of exception and the law creates an exceptional case for this form of adoption: the adopted body is separated from the domestic social order, certain laws are suspended and other rewritten on an exceptional international order, and the "bare life" of this child is co-opted through legal discourse set upon an international theatre of bringing this "bare life" into the "good life". Though the "bare life" of the abandoned child falls outside the official political discourse of transnational adoption, its "bare life" is nonetheless implicit through its exclusion in law. The very exclusion in legal discourses of the child adopted from the developing world hinges upon the delegitimization this "bare life" in its geo-political space, the confused and disordered third-world. It is then that the law recuperates and fully legitimizes this life through her eventual adoption into the first world. The "bare life" is rendered legitimate as "good life" only at the point of its inclusion as a political being–its body and the body of her family excised from the scene of legal discourse. These "bare life" subjects simply do not exist as subjects within the law and as such the "bare life" of the child hinges upon the transformative power that the combined forces of professed wealth, democracy and social order abroad offer her as she is ushered into the "good life" of the western family. The biopolitics of international adoption can therefore be seen as managing crisis and combating poverty while conterminously promoting humanitarianism through which the "bare life" of the child is pushed into the past (along with that of her poor family) in order to embrace the "good life" she is afforded in the future.

The very nature of international adoption implicitly engages the ethos of biopolitics—namely the appropriation of human life from one nation to another through the formalized implementation of legal discourse which simply converts the practice of somatic appropriation and importation into law. The legal discourse which renders legitimate the attainment of the "good life" is buttressed by the various cultural practices which couch international adoption as "good will", such as those private and public foundations that claim to "save" children through adoption and monetary, long-distance sponsorship and as well the media which pushes images of the third-world other as a subject entirely incapable of caring for herself.
The neo-colonial implications of biopolitics are unavoidable and the attitudes both in Haiti and in the west are reflective of these constructed relationships which portend to save or to be saved. The biopolitics of family creation through adoption are rarely discussed amongst legal and psychological experts in the fields of adoption and social welfare and the dangerous underbelly of adoption biopolitics is implicit throughout Haiti's growing number of orphanages.

One can simply not examine the practices of child trafficking without conterminously studying the very cultural and legal institutions which serve as the paradigmatic basis behind the illegal act of trafficking (ie. that the child will have a better life, that he will be fed and clothed, that she will receive an education). Likewise, one cannot study child trafficking without examining the residual effects of legalized practices such as international adoption whose fees reify these children in creating jobs and institutions based on the appropriation of human life. When discussing child trafficking, it is imperative that the legal aspects are scrutinized as much as the overtly illegal activities in order to fully understand what might actually be a similarity in spirit amongst all these licit and illicit operations of child exchange.

One cultural aspect that must be directly addressed is how there is often present—even within the overtly illegal activities of child trafficking—a moral imperative of helping children to attain the "good life." The mother who abandons her child at the church, the father who sells his son to the orphanage, the parents who send their daughter to the country as *restavèk*, the adoption agency which organizes adoptions in Haiti, and those who traffic *restavèk* to the countryside all believe on some level–just like the lawyer in Toronto who adopted her child from Haiti–that they are helping these children escape a life of poverty. In short, the biopolitics of legal adoption should necessarily be as central to any discussion of child trafficking as the more overtly illegal practices of human trafficking and *restavèk* simply because what drives, in part, the illegal trafficking of children and the continued practice of *restavèk* is the combined and complementary forces of two types of exchange value of human life: monetary value which deems the child exchangeable at a specific price and ethical value which posits subjectivity through the transformative power of the subject from "bare life" to "good life." In the end, it must be asked if there is a cultural belief being created from all sides of these exchanges of humans, as indicated from current reports, that the ends justify the means in this collective aspiration for granting children a "good life."

Minimum Wage

Once a week I come to a commercial center, Complexe Louverture, to plug in and write. My iPhone is my computer and the guards here are kind enough to let me charge my phone as the electricity where I rent is rarely on. The wealthier businesses which have their own commercial spaces (for the few who can afford the rents of Petionville) hire guards—the gas station, walk-in pharmacies, bookstores, clothing shops and restaurants are all furnished with guards who carry shotguns or pistols. The guard sitting on the barstool next to me is a young man of twenty-three and is carrying a .38 calibre pistol. He works twelve hours a day and he works Fridays, Saturdays and Sundays. He is paid 3,000 gourde per month which is equivalent to $75 USD per month. This young man was given one month of training and he hopes to find a better paying job eventually.

Friday, while working on a project at MINUSTAH, I drank a coffee at the canteen and met a Haitian programmer who works as a technical consultant for the United Nations here in Haiti. He told me he was not getting paid very much but when I asked him his precise salary, I could hardly agree with his estimation of his salary. This twenty-six year old programmer makes 30,000 gourdes which is approximately 750 USD. Plus for each day he comes to work he gets a 550 gourde supplement bringing his total earnings to $1,025 USD. What he was saying when he said that he was not getting paid "very much," he meant that he was underpaid compared to the foreign workers here which is a common occurrence by the UN and NGOs who hire locals.

Yet, I understood immediately why so many Haitians want to work for MINUSTAH and why these Haitians were slow to protest the presence of such an organization which, while helping in certain ways to "stabilize" Haiti, also destabilizes this country. To date in Haiti, there is no real job creation coming from any NGOs which many efforts to create a theatre of job creation such as the launching of pilot projects to help collect rubbish from the litter-polluted environment or to clear post-earthquake rubble where Haitians are paid an equivalent of 2.50 USD for six hours of work, Haiti's minimum wage. The UN has created 5,600 jobs with UNDP (United Nations Development Program) having already created 50,000 by the end of February with plans to create 400,000 jobs by the end of the year. These jobs, however, are generally not longterm contracts.

An incredibly large portion of Haitians are unemployed (85% unemployment) but these figures do not take into account the majority of the workforce: the women of Haiti. It is striking how little men—

unemployed or not—do to help women in the home.   While their are
exceptions to this rule, they are few and extremely far between. So Haitian
women take on the non-stop charge of work while they raise their children,
feed their households, care for the sick and elderly, wash clothes, maintain
the home, as the men are commonly sitting around watching television or
hanging out with their friends. (It should be underscored that women still
work more than men inside the house in every country around the planet.)
In Haiti, women often work outside of the home as well and usually occupy

the traditional jobs of waiter, cook and cleaner. This morning while looking
for lentils in a nearby grocery store, the guard holding the shotgun was a
thirty-year old woman. Women run Haiti and it is immediately clear that
the men who often insist on women's "place" in tap taps and on the road
(men are constantly telling me to be careful about a hole in the footpath, a
passing car or motorcycle as if I need for them to tell me what my eyes see,
what my ears hear) are compensating for a role they no longer have. Yet,

many men are slow to recreate their roles and compensate for wages not earned, or simply to lend a hand in the quotidian tasks of the hearth by stepping into a new role as husband, brother or father and to do their fair share of work in the home. But change is, after all, an individual choice and act. In the family with whom I live, everyone participates—from the boys who sweep the yard at six o'clock every morning to the elderly aunt who helps look after the children.

Meanwhile in the some of the IDP camps, food distribution programs for adults have been halted as a means of encouraging people to provide for themselves. Some relief organizations are aware of the dependencies that the many decades of NGO presence creates in Haiti and thus today "work for cash schemes" are increasing as NGOs with various international government-sponsored efforts are attempting to create a means for men and women to earn their meals rather than to be given charity. There are reports from IOM (International Organization for Migration) of people having left their homes from Cité Soleil to move into the camps so they could receive food aid. Yet even though there are of some people abusing the aid, there are more cases of aid not reaching the smaller camps. The World Food Program has expanded to schools as children are now the major focus of food distribution efforts.

I learned just recently that all the free post-quake clinics in the IDP Camps have all but destroyed Haiti's private healthcare system. So while goodwill has helped many, it has likewise helped to destroy a thriving private sector economy. Meanwhile there are Haitians, long accustomed to aid who want to see it continue as their president warns against this and rightly foresaw this dependency hurting their economy and agriculture (which is already a reality). So while many Haitians want jobs, others want the security of a sure meal and lodging. The decisions that need to be made are inevitably painful because of the decades of charity. Dependency is a difficult bond to break as many people claim they will never leave the camps and others are simply worried how they will afford groceries with few jobs on the horizon in the private sector.

The housing crisis is yet to be resolved by the IOM which is trying to figure out how to accommodate all 1.6 million Haitians from the camps to more permanent structures. The government has recently allotted land for 50,000 people, but the structures are far from a reality. Sean Penn's organization, J/P HRO, is in the middle of a massive relocation of 6,500 people whose tents are in extremely dangerous positions to handle the rains. There are critiques from various NGOs about the ethics of translocating these people to outside Port-au-Prince, far from their extended families, from public transport and extremely far from any form of employment.

As I finish writing this piece, the skies are now ominously grey, the wind is cooler and the guard, now changed from his uniform to civilian clothes, is awaiting his replacement for the next shift. When I ask what he will do tonight, he says "Anyen mem" ("Nothing special"). He will return to work here at 6h00 tomorrow morning.

Walking to the town center this morning, as I turned towards Saint Pierre, a bunch of teenagers saw me and yelled out "Obama..Obama." It was as if saying his name gave these young men a sense of hope. And while I did not vote for nor do I support Obama, nothing logical came to mind with which to respond to these young men except to yell back, "Obama."

On Corruption

I was crossing the street at a pedestrian crosswalk and was hit by a car. When the police finally arrived, they refused to make a report explaining to me "Madame, you are not hurt enough." This accident did not happen in Haiti—it happened 26 November, 2006 in Montreal, Canada. I was not only refused a police report, I was harassed at the police station (PDQ 38 Est) when I tried to follow up on the case and was told that I "must have imagined being hit due to [the pregnancy] hormones." I was just over six months pregnant when I was hit by that car which many activists involved in my case now believe to have been driven by an off-duty police officer. I filed reports with the Police Ethics Commission of Quebec for being hit by a car and for the harassment I faced at the police station. the result of my filing this report was that I was harassed for many months after this. I persisted for years for an investigation of the original incident and then each count in turn of harassment. Such incidents of harassment went like this: a police officer I had never before seen in my life showed up at my house one morning at 7:30 and he glibly told me to make a complaint about him stating, "Please make a complaint to the Police Ethics Commission about my coming here and let's so who they believe." He proudly showed me his name tag as if to demonstrate to me that nothing would happen to him in the event that I actually file a report against him for this early morning harassment visit. And indeed, this bully, replete with his monosyllabic grunts, was correct: I filed a new report with the Police Ethics Commission for this new incident of harassment and nothing came of it. Just as their results for their "non-investigation" when I was hit by the car in 2006 or for the incident when the police told me that I had imagined being hit by a car, verbally harassing me, the Police Ethics Commission of Quebec concluded no ethics were violated. This is how ethics operate within institutions where there is no control of conflict of interest and absolutely no transparence in the procedures. When I asked for an outside investigation after I received only stonewalling for several years, Louise Letarte, counsel for the Police Ethics Commission, told me last year, "I have closed the file on this case and it will not be reopened." My only proof of an "investigation" I received is a form letter which predictably did not put into language my accusations. Instead this letter silences what happened to me in the bureaucratic metalanguage of "allegedly" with no mention of the real actions that were committed to my person. Only the words "incidents" and "events" are employed to refer to what happened to me and all violence was censured out of history. The report reads "the alleged incidents of 26 November, 2006", mirroring the exact language of the reports I received later about the more recent complaints I filed related to my attempts to have an investigation conducted of the original crime as well as the harassment I suffered by different officers. Each "report" was written in exactly the same language and phrasing with the same repetition of, "the incidents of [x date]," being the only link to the violences I had suffered. The specificity of language, just like the police report denied me after being hit by a drunk driver in 2006, is refused the subject. The only power the individual has before the state is taken from her and twisted into bureaucratic mumbo jumbo that reveals no information, no details, and zero accountability. The message is clear: you are not hit by a car unless we damn well say you were!

In my years living in Montreal, I learned an awful lot about ethics, or rather the total lack thereof. In the Université de Montréal where I taught for eight years, two other colleagues and I were harassed since we arrived in 2002. I received the brunt of the harassment since I was a junior colleague and my other two cohorts arrived already with tenure agreements. The harassment was sexual from one colleague, from the other also a former department chair, it was intellectual and over time these two women worked in concert to harass me over the years. The harassment came began with tiny lies. For instance, the former chair would tell me that I was not allowed to conduct research outside the country during the summer months, she would invent complaints to the Ombudsman from students (which I later learned were fictitious) in order to force certain votes in departmental meetings, she would demand several weeks into the semester that I redo a syllabus to reflect her criteria of grading despite students voting against her wishes time and time again. The harassment was brutal and it was constant. In 2005 while on an ethnographic field project in Morocco hearing from a doctoral student who was told by this colleague that he must change advisors since he was falsely informed that I would not be returning to the department. These were just a few of the slews of lies these women would tell. Everything these two women said in the context of their profession proved to be a series of fabrications and were motivated, I suspect, by the arrival of three new colleagues all of whom were innovative in their specific fields of expertise and all of whom were inter-disciplinary in their approaches to the field of Comparative Literature. Such petty politics are not uncommon in academia, but the lengths of harassment which I endured certainly were.

My colleagues and I made numerous complaints to the university where I taught but typically, nothing was done. In fact, instead of investigating the harassment, the Université de Montréal would eventually jump on board with the harassment as I was to later learn in the true spirit of Sweeney

Todd's lyrics, "The history of the world, my sweet, is who gets eaten and who gets to eat." I was to find a thirty-three page document of defamation circulated in the very week of my tenure review by the one person in that department who had sexually harassed me. When I filed a new complaint of harassment after discovering the creation of this defamatory document being circulated against which almost every one of my colleagues spoke out, I was then put on "academic sabbatical." Meanwhile I was to learn that aside from these two women, there was another colleague or two who traded their votes against my tenure for votes for their future promotion to full professor. Two colleagues told me of this fact and from this attempt to denigrate my character, the department was split.

These colleagues who organized and executed this defamatory campaign against me (along with those who tagged along for future rewards) are still holding their posts and functioning within the complete permissiveness of the Viagra-pumped institutions of the aging, impotent province of Quebec. The Université de Montréal speaks of justice through its toothless mouth, all the while there are well-known problems of conflict of interest as this is one of the few universities in North America which employs an enormous number of professors who did most—if not all—of their studies at the same university, from BA through PhD. Of course its website boasts being "one of the best institutions in the world." Such rhetoric is unbelievable as any decent institution of higher learning would take action to protect professors from being harassed. More directly great institutions do not need to engage in self-promotion since such appellations require critical distance and intellectual integrity, none of which this university maintains.

Meanwhile my "academic sabbatical" which was to last a couple weeks, lasted for approximately eight months. An investigation was launched and was headed, of course, by a very close friend of the vice-dean dating back from their studies together in 1965 (when they studied in the same department and have since taught in this very same university). This fact alone openly demonstrates the Université de Montréal's complete lack of ethics and utter conflict of interest for which, paradoxically, every professor at the Université de Montréal is not only accountable, but to which we must attest in writing annually. This smacked to me of the visit from the police officer who let me know that the rules do not matter for those in power. In the end I won the case as nothing of substance was found by this investigation and I received what I call "la subvention de l'Université de Montréal," a payout from the university which allowed me to conduct my research, human rights work, and make films without any financial worries. In hindsight, I am quite happy to have left that corrupt institution and province. My life has grown professionally and emotionally

from this experience and I was forced to see the vast moral and ethical gaps
that such institutions create when power goes unchecked.

Moreover, these events have led me to understand that corruption in
Québec is not only rampant, but is quite accepted—that is if your last name
is Pelletier, Normandeau, or something of the sort. Or if you have the good
fortune to be so deeply engrained and obedient to these very corrupt
systems that you are part of the "club." Thankfully, younger Quebecers see
this corruption and react against it, but their voices are also stifled as they
find the petty behavior towards Anglophones and English as counter-
productive. One Quebec college student told me how she received
"tickets" from her high school teachers for speaking to her friend, outside
of the classroom, in English. Another shop owner had his bookstore shut
down because he exposed English language books in the window. Quebec
is a province which espouses the discourse of identity and nationalism—
albeit through a discourse which is ghettoized—seeking to chisel out
identity as if a faint remembrance of a glorious, colonial past from the
shards of that which hockey and *poutine* cannot enunciate. Such toils of
the state when veneered onto the human functionary leaves the hollowness
of a Catechism (as well as a void of the morals of the Church which the
"Revolution Tranquille" eviscerated) whose only genuflect is to the
absurdity of empty rhetoric. Maple syrup, the Montreal Canadians and the

oh so KKK-esque Fête de la Saint-Jean-Baptiste. Need we marvel at how someone like Celine Dion took the province by a storm?

An extremely xenophobic province, Quebec's distrust of foreigners demonstrates its reluctance to transparency and dialogue: its corruption functions in honor of its xenophobia and tautologically in the reinforcement thereof. I remember a taxi driver shocked at the coverage of a hockey game over the radio in January as the announcer would refer to the Montreal Canadian hockey players of French origin as "pure laine" (literally "pure wool," to imply pure race) and the players of other origins were referred to as "les autres" ("the others"). I would even say that the inability of most Quebecers to criticize their culture and their own political structures is a self-manifesting fear by a people who are so timorous of losing their culture, that they fail to realize that there is absolutely no singular culture in Quebec to protect or to lose.

Sadly, the results of the 2007 Bouchard-Taylor Report which investigated "reasonable accommodations" of ethnic and religious minorities only further polemicize not just the nature of the problems of xenophobia in Quebec, but moreso this report demonstrates the absolute myopia omnipresent within the social and political fabric of that province and its concomitant inability to discuss these or any problems. Police brutality is as much a problem as are discriminatory hiring practices as is anti-semitism: however, any mention of problems or corruption simply results in the real or metaphoric harassment "visit" to put the subject in his place. As the Bouchard-Taylor report tellingly reveals through the language of "reasonable accommodation" that immigrants are merely to be "tolerated." This social reality demonstrates these politics of tolerance with Quebec showing appalling statistics for immigrant unemployment with a ratio of 17.8%, almost three times the 6.3% ratio of native-born Quebecers. Yet, if you speak to most Quebecers, they will proudly tell you how there are no problems—there is certainly no racism as the interlocutor begins a sentence deflecting all discourse of racism to the United States. Indeed, the United States has been a convenient scapegoat for all of Canada, but there is no comparison between the debates and movements actively taking place in the United States in the fields of immigration and civil liberties and the absolute contrition and elision by many Canadians on this subject.

These are the lessons of life that I have taken with me to Haiti where, despite the seemingly insurmountable problems on all fronts, Haitians know exactly where their problems lie and how to name them. There seems so little hope here, but then I am reminded of the fact that in my work in Port-au-Prince, I have had four ministers sit down and discuss the problems of child trafficking and the environment with me in person and that I was, after all, able to make a police report about child trafficking. I was not accused of being a "hysterical woman" or other such nonsensical deflections. No matter how much Haitians critique their government I am reminded of how relative corruption is and how institutions in Canada purport a certain degree of oversight while they simply pay lip service to the language of ethics.

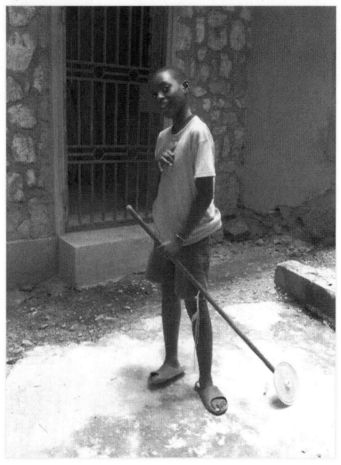

When I pushed for an external examination of the police force as my file had never been properly examined, I was told that this could never happen. I was not even given the consideration of a dialogue, an explanation as to how a woman, six months pregnant, hit by a car is refused a police report and harassed by the very same police force for years because of her attempts to effect justice. I was never granted a meeting with the person who allegedly conducted the Police Ethics Commission investigation and doors were constantly slammed in my face. The scene became comic-tragic on 26 October 2007, when the Police Ethics Commission, after eleven months of my pushing for an investigation finally granted an investigation. That morning I received a phone call from the investigating sergeant who told me that she could not investigate my case because she thought I had waited a year to press charges. I did not know if to laugh or cry for it was clear that the Montreal Police Department was operating in an orbit of utter ignorance, if not also intentional miscommunication, in order to undermine investigations before they even occurred. Until today, no government official has agreed to ensure that justice would be, if not served, then at least attempted.

With such ethical practices in the center of the government, it is not surprising that Moroccans, Algerians, Iranians, and Haitians holding undergraduate and advanced degrees are barred, by and large, from public service positions and are regularly discriminated against in the private sector in Quebec. As a result, many are driving taxis and performing jobs far below their competence and education. Conversely, I have been in Haiti only five weeks and have already had doors opened for me professionally. Most recently I have been asked by the Ministry of the Environment to create sensitivity training for teachers and students regarding all things ecological and health related. The differences could not be more stark: the reception I have received in this country should serve as an embarrassment for those Quebecers and for those who laud the "Bouchard-Taylor Report," a document which minimizes the trenchant and violent abuses of racism in a province that fears the very immigrants who can likely save this limp province from its own auto-asphyxia.[9]

I arrived home on Saturday from the market and found a boy from next door playing with a toy he invented from a piece of wood, a nail and a plastic lid. He was about nine years of age and found immeasurable happiness playing with this toy—literally, a re-invented wheel—all throughout the networks of the courtyards, in and between houses, and on the main street. From garbage he created an object of play and life fled from this child's actions as he happily posed for a picture for me. The sheer innocence of his actions and ingenuity of his invention spoke volumes about the potential for growth in this country. Despite the tremendous amount of work required to build up Haiti, there is so much hope here simply because Haitians are able to take what they have— garbage and all—and examine their social and political realities in the desire to create, reinvent, and embrace that which does not fit the age-old schemes of cultural control and fascist notions of "pure" identity.

---

[9] I must inject that my experiences with younger Quebecers, most of whom are aware of these problems, inspires some hope.

Do Not Read This

There is a new Olympic event involving the tap tap. It goes something like this: a full tap tap is going up a hill and the vehicle in front of it brakes unexpectedly forcing the tap tap to follow in suit. The tap tap's motor dies and it must be empty to make it up the hill, so all the team members get out of the vehicle as the tap tap starts its motor up and heads to the top of the hill with the entire "équipe" (team) running to meet the tap tap lest their seat be taken.

I love this place! I think the most eventful moment on Montreal's mass transit was a bus being diverted from Laurier to Saint Joseph and people sat in absolute silence staring ahead as if a Stepford wife. Sure, New York's subway offers professional artists and acrobats and the Paris metro sports its occasional anarchists who board the car just to make a lightening-fast discourse to the onlookers who actually seem interested. But here, nothing is "normal" and despite the lack of time schedules and apparent order, life takes on another type of order which is more organic and sane.

Last night when leaving MINUSTAH, the paperwork had not yet been finished for my transportation but the men in the transport division had no problem taking me home. For all our love of requisition forms, waivers and other bureaucratic procedures in many countries of the world, life in Haiti just happens without all this procedural stamp, sign and photocopy. Though some might say that we are better off with "our order," I would argue that the generosity of the people here replaces the systems of authorizations, protocols and checkboxes. For the many times I waited for a tap tap and it seemed hopeless I would ever find one, there was always someone who picked me up. Yet, some Haitians are horrified when I tell them I hitchhike—those who warn me against it are the very Haitians who have never hitchhiked, of course. The informal modes of transport found through hitchhiking can be exquisitely more pleasurable should they have air conditioning on a particularly hot afternoon—after all, most of the modes of transport in which I have taken as a hitchhiker are far posher than the tap tap. And as wonderful as the tap tap are for all reasons of language, learning and life, there are just so many occasions when the tap taps are full because you are mid-route and inconveniently situated to get a ride on a vehicle. Thus the only way to get to one's destination is to call it out as private vehicles pass by, hoping one stops to let you on board. Things are never as they seem in Port-au-Prince and there is something both exhilarating and, at certain times, precarious about life here.

One out of ten Haitian children are in orphanages[10], and this means that they are almost all abandoned children. Since the earthquake, there has been an increase in child trafficking and there is not enough that can be done to curb the many associated abuses. This morning at a meeting with the Royal Canadian Mounted Police who are working in Haiti to uncover pedophile rings, I heard many things I wish I had not: of men who make pornographic films of themselves and children—as young as two years of age—and they trade them with other men online. Apparently, there is a fetish of collectionism and these men set out to obtain all of the pieces of the "collection," often using other men's films as models, visual challenges for them to reproduce their own. And when you are talking about "collections" of rape films, this means that the "collection" is never closed and always remains open and perpetual. Some of these people, these officers told me, create "instruction manuals" as to how to rape a child and avoid leaving traces which usually involves locking the child up for several days as evidence will be more difficult to prove. Foreign men are the predators and tens of thousands of children are enslaved for part, if not most, of their childhoods.

I do not remember at which point I reached the apex of horror or when I just became numb with the information I was given. Human slavery is much more a reality than anyone, myself included, cares to admit. The International Labour Organization estimates that there are approximately

---

[10] Maohadjerin, Mashid. "Haiti's Orphan Industry." *The Wall Street Journal.* 26 February, 2010.

27 million humans living as slaves. This is more than double the number of slaves taken from Africa and taken to the Americas during the trans-Atlantic slave trade. Indeed, it is easy to turn the channel or to avoid thinking about it. Most people prefer not to think about such things as it ruins their "sugarplums and fairy dust" view of the world. In my own observations, I have found that most people living in privileged cultures are unable to accept the horror within their families, their societies and their political structures, but the reality is that child prostitution and sexual slavery exists within our own borders. Women and children are trafficked at rates that are only unbelievable because many of us prefer not to think about this, not to frame this as *believable* by marginalizing these facts as "unpleasant" or simply not central to our lives or where we pretend that such events happen "over there." It is preferable for many to live in a world where nothing "bad" happens. However, that is usually because one's eyes are closed.

One of my pet peeves in humans are those who say, "I don't like to think about unpleasant things" and those others who say, "I'm not political." Life is not a shopping list of items we wish to have happen to us, or not. If you breath, then you are a political subject. We have few choices with life's events that come before us, namely sickness, death, natural disasters and even those malevolent forces who do harass you at your job, who rape, who steal and so forth. Despite this, we also have an enormous amount of choices about the decisions we make, the actions we take and those transgressions that we either take on or leave as unfulfilled fantasy. Denouncing injustice, treating others humanely, loving our fellow humans—this is the stuff of life that must be encouraged and celebrated.

Inevitably, we have an obligation to be judicious and thoughtful and often we realize we are not at all. Many humans negotiate their imperfections with as much grace and self-critique as they permit themselves and hope that they grow from these experiences. In short, I simply cannot imagine a world where adults enslave and sexually exploit children. This makes no sense and simply breaks the limits of the mind to fathom such acts of violence and sadism. But of course there is no sense to most things in life, and certainly no logic to cruelty. A friend of mine who has been struggling with cancer, horrified by those who suggest that her illness is related to her lifestyle or the infamous "negative thinking," told me recently, "Nobody asks why you win the lottery."

Last week I went to a restaurant in Petionville for a plate of rice, beans and that ever so delicious sauce, full of sliced raw onions. A surprisingly elated, Farah, the twenty-year old waitress, was excited to see me. I did not except this reception as the last time I was there we had a long discussion about religion wherein she expressed shock at my non-belief in a god, to which she repeated, "But where did you and I come from?" And she pointed to the restaurant, the roof, and held her arms out to show me that all this her god had created. After I delicately explained the Big Bang and the rudiments of evolution, she said, "But God exists! He made you, he made me." Needless to say, I was a bit surprised when I walked in the door this last time and the waitress, Farah, greeted me as if I were a long lost friend. I had mistakenly presumed that I had been relegated to the "hedonistic other" category. When Farah saw I had a camera function on my mobile phone, she insisted I take a photo of her. She stood and posed in a *Life* magazine kind of affectation from the 1950s, her huge smile and a slight twist to her torso, gazing into the camera showing sheer confidence and joy.

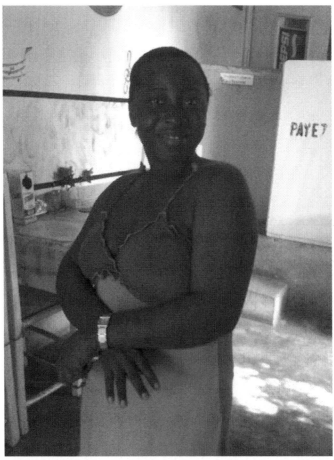

I expressed my inability to take such photos as I am rarely comfortable before the camera. So Farah took one of me with her camera and of course, I came off looking lime Patti Hearst in the infamous "wanted"

photo. Farah then offered to make me cherry juice. I did not believe it was real cherry juice because quite often "fresh" can mean a freshly opened bottle full of sugar, artifical colors and very little juice.   So before accepting I queried, "It is freshly made?" She replied matter-of-factly, yes. I repeated, "It has no sugar and it is really fresh?" She assured me it was fresh, all natural, and thus I agreed. It was my first cherry juice in my life, a beautiful salmon colored drink which tasted better than cherries. It was impossible for me to imagine such a drink, yet that moment of sipping the cherry juice punctuated for me this innocence which much of my recent work with child trafficking had blunted. That juice was liquid heaven in a world where innocent souls are swallowed by utter depravity and madness.

The Uncertainty Principle

Someone at IOM (International Organization for Migration) recently told me this: "What Haitians want more than anything else is not a house, not even food. They want a job." I almost fainted having found myself in the presence of someone working with an NGO who actually understands Haiti. He pondered if what might be best for Haitians—as has been suggested—would be to give them the recent UN funding, directly, in their hands Sean Penn and Alison Thompson style. After all, what Sean and Alison discovered by bringing hard cash into the country, is that Haitians want jobs and when they have one, they get the job done quite well. Their camp is the best oiled machinery of humankind in this city and I am beginning to understand that IOM might be a close second given their deft handling of a child trafficking law which goes to vote at this very moment. Apparently IOM is using underground methods of communication with those in power within the government. This is not your typical pomp and circumstance of NGO theater for the spectating donors—IOM embodies the world of savvy young actors who have found a way to the government that is not through the front door of ministries or the parliament. The relationship between getting a job and getting the job done presents often disparate realities in Haiti and it would seem between these two organizations, a radical rethinking of the politics of relief and development is in the brewing.

Most of the people I have met who work for NGOs and the MINUSTAH are highly educated and intelligent people. Most, in fact, are as critical of their roles in this country as they are of the institutions for which they work. I have heard many speak of the inefficiency of these organizations which bring people into the country for anywhere from two weeks to three months and then there is a rotation over to a new team. It is difficult for there to be any continuity or dialogue between teams as each communication is abruptly broken, records are often not kept (depending upon the organization) and projects are frequently begun and not finished or proposed and never realized. Most everything tends to rest discursively and not within a practical framework. Instead, communications tend to take place within the organization acting as proxies for the actual efforts of carrying out action or protocol. Rarely, if ever, are these organizations invested rethinking their approaches to development work.

Other criticisms are those typical of any enterprise—from too many meetings, to overwhelming amounts of paperwork, to all talk and no action. But in the world of NGOs these are crucial critiques made from the bowels of organizations who ought to have their maneuvers streamlined and who should know how to get away with as few meetings and as little paperwork as possible in order to spend more time effecting change, educating cohorts, and resizing and rethinking actions. And then there are many who are entirely conscious of the problems that they they are actually creating instead of remedying. Or, as one UN worker told me, "At this point we are inducing more damage than good and the only reason to be here is for our jobs." This was a cynical, if not entirely honest, confession, a virtual cross-section of life here amongst humanitarian workers.

One problem I have noticed in many NGOs and governmental organizations is that age discrimination is quite frequent. The under forty corps of workers easily forms 80% of all organizations here, and these individuals are some of the hardest working bunch of people I have seen. Most of these relief workers put in fifteen hour days, six to seven days a week, while their supervisors are often sitting in the air-conditioned offices, pushing paperwork, yielding huge salaries, and setting off to frequent meetings and dinners while also hindering the actual progress of these underlings who see quite clearly, what needs to be done today. There is a definite air of distress amongst some of the forty-plus year olds who demonstrate an inability to handle criticism of their orangizations' mandates. As I work between several agencies it became quite clear to me that these managers are here to make sure things do not get done too quickly, and sometimes it would seem as if they were sent here to ensure tasks do not get accomplished at all. The younger workers in these organizations are energetic and realize that too much thinking about what to do only leads to more meetings, discussions as whether to have a steering committee or not, should this email be copied to the minister and what about that meeting to have a meeting next week? At the end of the day, nothing has changed. I have seen these younger workers move mountains only to have their supervisors come in and take credit for the work done or to take the work of those who are effecting positive changes and effectively destroy months of operations. It is disconcerting to see such behavior where collaboration has little to do with relief work and where defiance of those who attempt to co-opt your work becomes a life-saving technique. As another aid worker told me, "I now have to stop communicating with my superior since I have figured out he is only going to undermine what I do." And this person's remaining weeks in Haiti have been dedicated to push through as many actions as possible while the superior will hopefully be busy taking credit for someone else's work. As many of these humanitarian workers' time in Haiti draws nigh, there is often the realization that nothing has been "accomplished." In some instances the younger development teams who were initially told that all their efforts were not welcome are suddenly told to create something, anything, so that the management can stick their name on a project before these teams leave the country.

Egos are almost as huge in the relief business as are the salaries. One aid worker told me that many are earning as much as $10,000 per month here. I was astounded and he said, "But Haiti is like one of the top destinations." He was not speaking tourist destinations, but disaster relief destinations, a feather for your cap after East Timor. While not all aid workers are making this type of money, the argument many provide is: "why not?" In this business, you can have no family or personal life and money is one of the positive factors for living in a virtual bubble, deprived of any form of home for years on end. Aid workers live in a world of intense work days and little to no steady social contacts as many are constantly thrown from country to country and those who stay on for several years, are contractually refused contact with the rest of the world here. I was informed recently that should I ever take a contract here I would be subject to the lifestyle of these aid workers: no more tap tap, no more motorcycle, I would have to move from my family's home into posher surroundings, and well it would mean, the end of the world as I know it.

These aid workers, it cannot be underscored enough, are highly functioning people able who carry out all sorts of tasks conterminously, all incredibly well. They are able to reason and come up with counter-arguments to their reason only to find a third and fourth manner of getting something done—that is before their overlord tells them to go to a meeting or to write up the minutes to the previous meeting. Most of these workers smoke heavily and then the evenings are spent catching up on sleep or finally eating a meal and drinking and smoking. These are driven people whose only release after a day of non-stop work might very well be a critique of their day's work or a night on the town, at a club in Petionville.

I was treated to one such club recently: the Quartier Latin, a posh bistro with an open garden, a wooden arch in the courtyard and underneath this arch, a full salsa ensemble every Thursday evening. There were easily one hundred people dining and dancing, the menu prices all in US dollars and nothing on the menu was under $10. Not only would few of my friends from New York be able to afford this place, but very few Haitians would have economic access to the Quartier Latin. The place was full of NGO and UN staffers. I have made lovely friends in these organizations and they are extremely perceptive individuals. After I had just entered the premises and sat down, one friend looked at me, or rather through me, and said, "You are freaked out because this place is so expensive, and here we are in front of an IDP camp." He read my mind. But my concern was not only the IDP camp which is Place Boyer, but the entire idea that I live ten minutes away on foot and this kind of place was surreal to me. I missed the mice in my bedroom and the annoying neighbors who awaken me every morning with Jesus—either the spoken words from the radio or music thereof. I ordered a lime soda and my friends tried to buy me dinner and I wouldn't let them—not because I wanted any sort of solidarity, but I honestly have become so used to eating every other day here that I rather enjoy just drinking juice or water at night. Of course they thought I was reacting out of guilt and it led to a revelatory discussion.

One friend who works with agriculture in FAO (Food and Agriculture Organization) told me, "I don't feel guilty. I work very hard, I give all I can and work long hours to help people, and then I enjoy myself when I am not working." He, of course, was absolutely right in theory and though I had not refused eating dinner out of solidarity with those in Camp Boyer, I did nonetheless need to hear these words. The importance of working hard, of being proud of one's profession, the acknowledgment of giving to another (albeit an unknown, random other), and the recognition that at the end of the day, you deserve to have fun, to relax. This is an attitude I rarely find amongst most professions, and certainly least of all academia where there is this almost self-loathing attitude, if not entirely masochistic and competitive, with little communication about one's actual work and more competitive suffering with people talking about how much one works. "Je suis débordée" ("I am overwhelmed with work") is the only phrase I have heard from certain of my more insane colleagues back in the world of academia in Montreal. Never had I a discussion with these allegedly "overworked" colleagues about their actual work. I was only given the litany of updates about how much work they actually do. With these aid workers, however, I found their insightfulness and self-critique astounding in terms of coherent discussions about the theories and practices of development work and neo-colonial ties to dependency. It is clear that such ideas are the fertile ground for the necessary changes in the field of development and relief work and these are the actors who should be positioned alongside their Haitian peers to bring forth such dialogues. However, there is a dead body in Haiti and it is that of the model of development which is based upon the central premise of neoliberalism: that money solves all problems.

Money is going to solve none of Haiti's problems. Haitians and these development specialists know this. What is working here are the educational, ecological and organizational models for turning their system of dependency into a structure of self-sufficiency. Most NGOs are not working with the government, hence they create parallel entities which waste valuable time and resources replicating and squandering efforts, human resources, time, and materials. Other NGOs have tried to work with the government but have not come up with a structural model as to how to get things done, how to move from idea to word, from dialogue to action. The reality is that most of the NGOs are caught up in a business model dating back to post-war America, spending their days in meetings or writing up a brief about the meetings they have just spent all day attending. Communication is important, for certain, but too much communication risks being the end all of development work and there is often a fine line between too much and just enough. Might there be a science to communication or is it more like *feng shui* and astrology? A bit of random hocus pocus, the Kierkegaardian leap of faith and it all seems fine. Why can't NGOs function like *Chelsea Lately*? That television show in all its apparent unpreparedness comes off perfectly, no matter what. We have heard the clichés and indeed if "less is more" and "language is a virus," then perhaps NGOs ought to communicate and meet less, listen and act more. Again, one of the highest praises of Sean Penn's and Alison Thompson's work is that they listen to those with whom they work.

The other evening on the way home from MINUSTAH, I took the escort car service as I do when I work late on a research project I have been developing for UNICEF. I was given a taste of what life would be like from "the other side." In riding home we passed all the local transport vehicles, I saw people on the tap tap and I immediately missed being there with them. On the UN vehicle my hips were not crushed by others, my feet not stepped upon, and there was no sprint to catch the transport. Instead my body was cushioned by UN opulence: plush bucket-seats, radio, radar, bullet proof glass and I imagine there must have been an eject button. Still, I missed the tap tap.

I really enjoy the people I have come to know in these organizations and it is difficult to know if the "other side" is always devastated by the efforts of these organizations. However, the experiential evidence from many Haitians has taught me that most humanitarian efforts here are detrimental to society. The intelligence which guides people here also allows them to realize the destructive ways of the organizations which they represent and conterminously forces them to confront their ineffectiveness in changing any of it. These people have jobs and are mostly happy to have them, but many express distress in the situation about not having the ability to create jobs for Haitians because the structure in which they work is really about manifesting a longevity of the organization for which they work and not about changing the structures in which Haitians exist. Most of the jobs for Haitians created here since the disaster are under "cash for work" schemes which are rightfully scorned by these workers: "What a name for a job!" one aid worker told me. "Of course you work for money! Why not call it a fucking 'job'?" Such observations are everywhere to be found, but the ongoing "cash for work" schemes and appelations continue while long-time, real jobs are few and far between. I am now asked by every fifth Haitian with whom I have a discussion if I can help them find a job. I showed the server, Diruvela, in the street restaurant facing MINUSTAH my visitor's badge today, I told her, "I am a volunteer worker here and I really do not know how to help you get a job at the UN." I wanted to help her but I was aware that I could not.

Recently, in a discussion with a development worker, I suggested that the NGOs need to engage Bill Gates and Richard Branson to get jobs developed here. And one stared at me and repeated, "That's a really good idea." Well, ideas are a dime a dozen here and what is needed here now (and yesterday) are jobs. Or as Keenan Thompson's *Saturday Night Live* character, Oscar Rogers, would repeatedly yell about the US economy: "Just fix it!" What seems to be holding back relief work here is the actual "relief" part of the business. The work is everywhere, that is if you are in the business of relief work: the cars, the houses, the swimming pools, the salaries of honest people who are excellent at their jobs. But the indicator of success seems to be broken. For where are the checks and balances, where is the self-evaluation for one simple question: "Are we helping Haitians?" Nobody has even asked what Haitians want with the exceptions of very few NGOs. This is the question I rarely see asked, or for that matter, answered.

In a post-disaster paradigm, the interests of the local people should be central and questions should be put to those coming to impose their notion of humanitarian relief. Now the forces have shifted to business as usual and finding ways to stimulate job creation and the Haitian economy is simply not on the table. We need to ask ourselves more questions about the projects we are proposing and realizing. Is the continual launching of new programs to reforest, to aerate terrain, to create recycling programs, to maintain x number of hospitals, and so forth, the answer to Haiti's problems? Or might these efforts be incredibly useful if not even essential but sorely in need of an accompanying scheme of economic development? Another way of thinking development would be to provide Haitians with regular jobs that they go to every day, and not a 20 day "cash for work" program aimed at their picking up plastic bottles from day to day whilst they wear a t-shirt from a Bible Camp in Arkansas. I often think about the humiliation that Haitians must live through on a daily basis as the masses wear mostly American "hand-me-downs"—clothes that fit badly, broken zippers, and t-shirts decorated with the signatures of brands and places with which Haitians have absolutely no identification or exchange. And they are bored to death in these clothes.

I waited for the UN car this morning instead of taking the tap tap since the weather is scorching and I wanted to wear my skirt one day. As I live on a rock road far from Petionville center, walking so many kilometers on rather large rocks in heels is no small task. So I awaited the UN car unsure of the choice I made to take this car. I love my liberty and especially the ability to take the tap tap everywhere I please. As I emerged from my house, onto the steps near the road, I found a man in his early thirties sitting on one of Haiti's typical public sculptures, the unused motor. I rather loved his bright blue socks and lime green shirt. He was silent, staring at me from time to time since in this neighborhood I am the only non-Haitian. As people walked up and down the streets, mostly parents with their brightly-dressed school children, I stood on the top step just appearing at the street level and I was the object of curiosity for a good fifteen minutes from each and every child who passed me. A bit bored of the side show, I spoke to this man, Willyo, and he explained to me about the fact that most all the schools were open except for those which were still not re-situated. He indicated both schools were nearby and we discussed the passing tap tap entirely devoted to collecting school children.

Willyo offered me a seat on the motor and I declined and instead I asked him if I might have a picture of him. He obliged, stiffening up and changing his posture completely. He moved in such a way that I could no longer see his brightly colored socks and his faced became less relaxed. So I asked him, "Can you leave your left leg down and your right leg back on the motor?" He was sort of the way I first saw him, but not quite that same way. Just as in Heisenberg's uncertainty principle, I had, by virtue of my asking Willyo to pose for me, changed the "natural" position in which I first found him.

The Poetics of Seeing

"You can take her out of New York..." or so the aphorism begins. But it was only Monday that I realized why I love bargaining so much. And the answer has nothing to do with that old New York tradition of being stuffed into someone's flat with a dozen or two others humans, inevitably your body pushed up against the kitchen stove, and all in attendance are swapping stories of who has the cheapest deal in apartments. Going to parties in New York City is a task of pure daring mixed with resilience in that you simply must be prepared to find out that you are paying way too much for your cockroach-infested shoebox with a window looking onto a brick wall. And of course, you find this out as you drink a Corona in an apartment situated in a better neighborhood, with a functioning intercom, and with the absence of that want-to-be musician neighbor practicing "Baracuda" fifty times a day. Of course, the storyteller of this great coup in real estate informs you about her connections in getting the bargain, punctuating the entire narrative with, "It was just luck." Because of this "training" I received in two decades of living in New York, I thought bargaining was some form of intrinsic, pseudo-psychological competition that drove people not only to bargain harder, but to boast their stories of how little they paid for a suit or where to find the "best deal in the city" on winter coats. However, a few days ago as I haggled over the price of my lunch, I realized why I bargain. And the reason was entirely linked to the human condition, not at all related to the propriety of bragging powers.

In Haiti, the word "blanc" is used not only to refer to people of European origin—it is used to signify wealth, the upper class, a foreigner. Being "blanc" is applicable to extremely dark-skinned Haitians who tell me that they could never take the tap tap for fear of class reprisal as well as the Sri Lankan UN guard. And being "blanc" does not exclude one from being Haitian but it is one measure of belonging to society. And the signs of belonging are multiple and they are precisely executed through many types of performances: being able to speak Kreyòl, being able to know the right price for just about everything in the market, and having the ability to be angry in one minute at the guy on the corner blocking traffic, but as you turn a corner—oh, it's your friend—and the scorning hand gesture turns quickly to a wave and sincere smile. There is a lightness to social relations here that is refreshing, despite the ongoing situation of desperation. People nonetheless manage to maneuver the terrain of devastation and light-heartedness with no problems of dexterity or translation.

I was taking a moment to make phone calls yesterday and I took advantage of the light breeze coming through after several days of stifling heat and humidity. Walking up to the corner of MINUSTAH's outer wall, I noticed a series of toilettes hoisted high on platforms, entire bathrooms exposed outside awaiting, I presume, their eventual installation. I spoke with friends on the telephone and paced. Between phone calls, two of the Haitian staff taking a break smiled at me. One said, "Are you French?" "Un, no," I replied, perplexed why he would have assumed this since I was speaking on the phone in Spanish and I did not know these men at all. The other gentleman said, "It is just that you look like the French woman who works here in our office." I had never seen this woman but I became uncontrollably mischievous and said to them, half smiling, "Oh, no! Don't tell me you think all non-Haitians look alike!" The men burst out laughing so joyously that I joined in as they both confessed to thinking this.

But this is what we do when we do not know what to make of the other. After all, as I stood this morning waiting for a vehicle to pick me up, I was once again the center of scrutiny for dozens of passers by—from older parents to the very young children dressed in bright orange jumpers and pants. It was clear that these people had never seen a person who was light-skinned sitting in their neighborhood. People had this expression on their face that made it quite clear that they didn't know what I was doing. Today, I even sat on the motor upon which Willyo sat yesterday. I was "out of place," but there I was in my place, my home, my new neighborhood. Is it racist or racialist that people would look at me, gawking candidly, wondering what on earth is that "blanc" doing there, sitting on that car engine in her yellow shoes. Ok, I am ad-libbing here a bit; but these are my subjective interpretations of some of the various facial expressions I witnessed during my forty-minute wait for the car this morning.

Yesterday, as I obsessed over the cranes moving the containers, I was likewise out of place—even within the walls of MINUSTAH—simply because I was a woman (still in skirt and yellow shoes) showing interest in this displacement of containers. I have a "thing" for cranes and stop all that I am doing to observe and photograph them. I cannot help but fascinate over the gradual moving of huge objects as if at that very moment we are seeing the shifting of the earth in relatively tiny blocks. Hours later a building "magically" changes—another level is added, or a tower is erected all in the silence of this slowly moving arm from above. The crane is this mute creature that displaces space in a time of the everyday such that we can work or live directly next to a building being constructed and never pay attention to the process. Time is often eclipsed by the quotidian running to meetings and taking care of errands. Then one day, that empty lot next door is "suddenly" a building and we realize that we do not remember the time in between. Observing, even noticing metamorphosis and difference might actually be those moments of breaking the patterns of the everyday which mark progress through the manifestations of the completed project, never the slow process of one block placed upon the next. We are trained to see goals and to discuss our successes. Rarely do we share the pleasure of the process and the passing of time as a non-event. Hence, I celebrate this particularly human, if not flawed, act of noticing, staring and reacting.

The passersby this morning noticed me and they made decisions about what I represented to them as their fixed stares clearly indicated. One man kept looking over his shoulder at me as if I were a demon, another man looked at me as if he could not trust me for sitting upon my motor. His brow curled and he pulled his child alongside him, quickening his pace once he noticed me. Others would just pass quickly and laugh, and one little girl with closely cropped hair just lifted her hand, waved and smiled. All forms of communication because this woman was out of place, or perhaps, because she was in *their* place. The only physical detail that highlighted my presence was my skin tone and this, inasmuch as it is a somatic fact, is also an inevitable aesthetic marker of difference. The same way that some people can recognize fake Louis Vuitton bags from the real thing. Perhaps for me, coming from a place like New York, there is no big deal about being a different looking person in a new part of town. But in my neighborhood of Port-au-Prince this was not a daily occurrence and so even if I was used to perching myself on a motor to watch passersby, it did not mean that those strolling by would embrace my presence as coincidental. I was a small meteorite for many.

I used to find such gawking unacceptable when I lived in North America where the object of gawking was usually the dark-skinned or amputated other. But then there were as many instances where I too was the subject of scrutiny, children in my neighborhood growing up did not understand if we were African-American, Indian, or Cambodian. We were, in fact, not Cambodian, but the refugees from Cambodia in the mid-1970s left this new vocabulary word adrift the mouths of fifth-graders and their parents whose only "insult" to me and my brother was to distort our family name, Mankodi, and call us either Cambodi or even a variation on the word for "commode," we were labelled "Commodi." But being the subject of such gawking this morning, I began to understand how primal this function of "noticing difference" is to the human condition. Perhaps this is more fundamental to discussions of difference within micro-cultural and intra-national settings where individuals struggle to open dialogue, politicize the need for certain equal rights, or merely to vocalize that certain forms of equality be recognized at all. Such exercises of dialogue, jurisprudence, and media spectacles, over time, render difference in most every context, negligible. And we return the ability to recognize fake Louis Vuitton bags or simply not to notice what the man sitting next to you on the subway looks like. Sometimes we stop noticing altogether. The unconscious of skin tone for many of us in places like New York City, where green is the symbolic interlocutor of place and status, is a privilege confined to the five boroughs, some might argue. Yet, are we not all privy to make these distinctions? Do we not approach the one person on the block who (we think) looks like she might know where the nearest mechanic or shoe cobbler is? What makes us ask her, specifically, and not another?

So I haggled over my lunch earlier this week, reminding the owner of the street restaurant that I saw her charge Haitians 100 gourdes for a full meal. I said to her as she sat on her stool, cleaning greens and talking with her friends who were likewise cleaning greens, "I come here every day to eat and you charged my friend 125 gourdes for his meal the other day. And you charged me 100 gourdes. So, I would like to know if I continue to eat here, will you charge me the fair price, since I do not eat meat, 70 gourdes?" She smiled, let out an accepting laugh and said, "Oui." I was, of course haggling over dimes, and I thought to myself: "Is this the New York coming out of me?" And then I realized that I haggled simply to be like the others, to be treated as the other Haitians with whom I eat, live, ride the tap tap, and communicate. Why on earth I had not realized this before escapes me. Perhaps the financial struggle of living in New York City for so many years tricks the brain of the struggling New Yorker into thinking that everything is really about money? Indeed, the reason we sit in those late evening East Village parties, crammed into bathrooms and tightly-packed kitchens, is to know that we are equal to the next person. We are reassured by such symbolic acts: often times the only real measure of equality is evidenced in the price we pay for things. Words often cannot make us feel equal—they can sing and portend equality for certain. Only actions can manifest equality and in the scale of human experience, money tends to be the marker of individuals' perceived self-value, amongst other vectors of meaning and poetics.

Nonetheless, difference creeps back into my vocabulary and vision. I cannot deny that I inevitably do notice height, size, colors and shades. Yesterday as I tried to synch my iPhone to a computer I was using, I scanned the cafeteria where I was working for my iPhone. I noticed two bluetooth devices, one which carried the name of my son who passed away three years ago. I freaked out thinking to myself, "Surely, I did not name my iPhone after my son!" I would never do that. Then I realized I had not yet activated the bluetooth on my phone, so this device could not possibly be mine. I looked up and thought many thoughts, none of which I could put into words here. I muttered to myself—something I rarely do—and stood up and looked around the room for someone from India who might bear my son's name. I found two men who looked South Asian and I said, "Excuse me, what are your names?" Very friendly they were indeed for not finding it at all strange that this woman, whom they had never seen, approaches them asking for their names. They told me their names. Not having realized they only pronounced their surnames, I said, "So you are not Umesh" and I started to turn away. Then the gentleman on the right interrupted and said, "But I am Umesh." I felt relieved to know that I was not nuts, but also sad because I suddenly realized that I had put myself in this awkward position. I truly didn't know how to tell these men why I made such a dramatic entrance on their coffee. So, I told them the truth: that my son's name was Umesh as well and that I found his name on the bluetooth waves while trying to sync my computer and phone. Umesh was thrilled that my son and he shared the same name and that our families came from neighboring parts of India. So he asked to see photos of my son, and I showed him and his friend my iPhone pictures of my little boy. They were thrilled until I announced that my son had died. Then, seeing their sadness, I too became sad. There I was chasing this virtual name to verify if I was mad or not—to verify if my son had materialized in my mind, on a bluetooth wavelength, in the body of another human or as a dragonfly. There is a poetics to how we conceive the physical world and mine is still under construction.

Celebrity Rehab

I generally consider myself fortunate not to own a television and though I am not one to use the word "never" with any frequency, I can fairly say that I will never own this instrument. This desire professed, I cannot deny downloading my sinful delights from time to time which allows me to selectively access media while being shielded from seeing even a momentary commercial blip of shows I deem abject such as *Dancing with the Stars* and *Survivor* and just about every reality show whose vast distance from "the real" enables nostalgia—as Jean Baudrillard foretells—to "assume its full meaning."

[*Nota bene*: There is one exception to my appraisal of reality television—I have recently discovered Kathy Griffin's *My Life on the D-List*, an alleged reality show which is more of an ethnography of reality television via a brilliantly comical critique of all things Hollywood. If you have not seen Kathy Griffin imitate Whitney Houston from *Being Bobby Brown* or allude to Gayle's and Oprah's lesbian love affair, then you have missed one of the best deconstructions of American culture and television.]

When stuck in an airport or restaurant, it is inevitable that I am forced to hear the passing sounds of these horrifying productions of "reality" television replete with giggles of contestants who think Africa is a city and whose conception of the world begins with Disney and ends with MTV. I inevitably become mesmerized—perhaps this is where the term "stupefied" would fit best—by the spectacle from which I avert my attention. I remember one television show years back where the contestants had to eat a series of insects for competition. Apart from being entirely revolting to watch, I could not fathom a culture where such spectacle would not only sell expensive commercial air time, but I also could not imagine that such fodder would accumulate millions of spectators to merit the price tag for Campbell's Soup and Procter & Gamble investments. Then there was my five-minute encounter with *Survivor* which left me so enraged that I remain to this day dismayed that such a show was aired for a pilot, much less that it still continues to be aired ten years later in the United States. This is a television show whose essence harbors the Gestalt of pure fascism. Where else can you watch a production that makes light of real life dangers and trivializes economic devastation and the precarious quotidian struggle of "survival" by turning it into a game whose goal is to entertain?

Here is my fantasy which, should ever a Hollywood production company grant me the possibility whereI really would take exceptional pains to produce my own version of *Survivor*. The scene opens with the group of

Americans and Canadians (let's go wild and mix it up a bit) who are selected to participate in this survival game.   The sun is rising over a Vancouver airstrip and the contestants' luggage is loaded onto the plane and they depart.   Our future heroes then share their hopes and fears regarding the competition and the plane lands one an island somewhere in the South Pacific.   The contestants are then transferred to a helicopter where they are flown to a deserted island, miles away from human life where they will have no contact with any technology or communication. They are then read the rules of this "game" and the announcer and camera crew get into the helicopter and depart. The contestants are then left on the island without any cameras, forever.   The credits roll and the contestants will stay on their island paradise being denied a second installment to their "survival."

In Haiti, as in the rest of the world, survival is far from a game.   Real survival is never a fifty-minute narrative about a school teacher who is struggling to pay rent and child support in San Francisco or the rickshaw driver in Mangalore whose feet are torn apart from running barefoot on the streets. Survival is not a spectacle in its essence as this act of "just getting by," rests forever on the precipice of "not getting by." There is a hair-thin distinction between these two valences and for those of us who have been down and out, we are aware of how the world looks from the real-life version of "survival" where there are no confessional booths into which to decry other "players," certainly no camera to capture one's thoughts. Survival is a personal struggle that is felt and lived by the individual—it is not the stuff of television spectacularization. Who the fuck cares what the poor man who cannot find a job thinks or feels? If he is not a fallen rock star or a sexually-frustrated housewife from Atlantic City, then there is nothing really to hyperbolize or render commodity. This is the truth of the lived reality of real suffering: few people from outside one's own circle of family and friends truly care. Sadly, ours is a world where certain types of people have more access to claiming the posture of suffering and thus they recount their misery to the camera. But let us be honest here, we are given theatrical miseries, nothing akin to survival in its more primal meaning, as we witness the "trauma" of certain members who had to vote Jake off the island.

Simply put, suffering is accessible only to very few because suffering today is a privilege of performance linked to the media theatre. Certainly the heterological discourses of history have always embarked upon certain tragedies as "more severe" than others, despite the body counts never quite rendering justice to the words of *Sturm und Drang*. Those who survive certain devastations suffer inevitably—they suffer for having been at or near the scene, they suffer for having witnessed and felt, and they suffer so deeply for the losses in their lives, the loved ones taken from them for no logical reason, and they suffer even for having survived. Death is by its very nature always illogical to those who survive it. And it follows that the survivor speaks, history "records" (what a horrid cliché) and media enterprises worldwide, as if taking their cues from the very machinery that sells the seconds of air time to Pepsi Cola and Nike, promulgate the deaths of approximately 200,000 in Haiti as less significant and more natural than the deaths of 2,976 in New York. Death is somehow more acceptable for the western subject to witness when the bodies of those lost in a hurricane, earthquake or mudslide do not have beautiful houses and high-powered jobs. For these spectators death is extricated from their reality as if the fact of having a desk and a cubicle magically removes death (even nature) from the everyday. Yet the media pageantry of death—not the reality of course—is that certain deaths are more terrible, more unjust and even more preventable than others. It is through the trope of tragedy that the contestants on *Survivor* enact what could not be further from tragedy, but which evidences the apparati of *real tragedy* (ie. no food, no lodging, no job, no money, colonial invasions, etc) turning this scene of dire circumstance into a spectacle that only a western subject could masturbatingly call "survival."

Western media often takes this fundamental shift between "real survival" and "media survival" and spins the fabric of neo-colonialism distancing the real terror from the fabricated terror: as our military forces from many western nations were killing people in Afghanistan and Iraq, our media was pumping the airways narratives of the tragedy of terrorism, underscoring the deaths of the European of North American subject (9/11 and 7/7) for whom death is always more tragic, simply because these victims had more "success," more material wealth and hence, more to lose. This is not to say that wealthy westerners do not suffer, but there is a notably exaggerated focus upon the threat of Islam in western public discourse and media while there is extremely little mentioned about the western violences against the people and regions our armies are killing through the support of despots, covert actions, and the counter-insurgence operations used to overthrow our then enemy of our "new friend." Very little time is spent interviewing the wives of fallen Iraqi or Afghani men, there are no articles that list the name of "Iraqi personnel killed in Operation Iraqi Freedom" and much of western media has allowed itself to get entangled within the narrative of "saving democracy" through the unfortunate contrivance of "embedded reporting" rather than to question the typical vehicle of colonialist rhetoric. The message could not be clearer as the images of those Canary Wharf and Wall Street bankers became the catapult for launching the true figure of survival: the western subject who is potential prey at any moment to the evil deeds of Muslim fundamentalists. Little serious media coverage over the past decade has been given to the terrorizing actions of western governments and military. There is a new opiate of the masses and it is no longer the church: it is reality television, shows like *American Idol* and pseudo-political talk shows whereby "truthiness," as Stephen Colbert has shown us, means that the subject no longer needs facts, she only needs to believe something and this fictional belief becomes the paradigmatic basis for all reality. Vote for your favorite idol and vote off the person whom you think should be kicked out of the house. This is the vibrator version of "democracy"—all in the privacy of your own home.

The conterminous network spectacles of "surviving" on a fake island and surviving in Baghdad worked in perfect union within cultures who took more seriously the result of a fire-making contest in Palau over the innocence of many of the 104,595 killed in Iraq since the beginning of the western aggression. What is even sadder, is that many subjects of the occupying countries tended to be more in touch with the events of "reality television" than they were familiar with the fact that by 2007 "53 percent of Iraqis say a close friend or immediate family member has been hurt in the current violence" in Iraq.[11] The word "reality" thus takes on a biting

---

[11] "Voices From Iraq 2007: Ebbing Hope in a Landscape of Loss." By Gary Langer. March 19, 2007. ABC News.

irony whereby we are forced to admit that reality television has as little to do with real life as the Kardashian family drama only "keeps us up" with the narrative being spun. Reality is in free-fall and reality television is more heavily scripted than the sitcoms and drama of night time television.

For people here in Port-au-Prince, the sky-rocketing prices of gasoline mean for many that they simply cannot get around. The impossibility of finding jobs means that most people grow increasingly thinner and weaker. There are no confessional booths wherein the people say what they think of their lazy brother-in-law who won't help out with housework or the sister who works at MINUSTAH and who does not help the rest of the family out with expenses. What matters is the order of the day, usually that of unemployment and lack of any infrastructure within this country. This is reality and it is simply not televised.

Recently there is a new wave to reality television in North America and I am curious as to how many people are aware of this shift. When relativity television "began" (though this beginning is arguable if we are to look back to its precursors such as *An American Family*, 1971), a sense that no matter how tacky and tasteless reality television got, there was the silver lining of democratization: now everyone, just like Nicole Kidman as Suzanne Stone in *To Die For*, could have her few minutes of stardom. Many of the no-names of Middle America became forces in the entertainment industry, hosting their own shows, selling out concerts and making music videos, and becoming household names extending far beyond five minutes of fame. This media experiment cut through the perceived elitism of success and put the judgment of quality and fame directly in the hands of the people.

But who would have thought that the undercurrent to the success story would ever have been the "fallen star," the infamous celebrity who had let herself go to drugs and/or alcohol and/or sex addiction? And now she wants to "come back" and must pass the test of public approval or censor. Usher in *Celebrity Rehab* and you now have the celebrity rendered "talentless has-been" for whom the gong awaits the final screen call. Even when not a specifically aired television show, we are reminded constantly of that "fall from grace" as the BBC announces "Woods set 'to take more time off'." With these celebrity reality shows which have been in circulation for many years, stars and former stars have to face the virtual audiences around the globe in order to pass through the obstacle course of public opinion as their lives are displayed in gruesome detail to the point that much of the televised audience is either too young to remember when these actors were celebrities and/or the behavior is so trashy that the viewer forgets that they are watching "stars." With the back and forth of former lovers, Tom Sizemore and Heidi Fleiss, what are we to think with lines that audaciously proclaim fame while the content staunchly defies it: "I'm Heidi Fleiss and I was the greatest madam that ever lived."

If I did not suspect that the sound bites were better than the actual continuity of narratives, I might also be hooked on these shows. However, I am only too aware of the dangers of such "reality" vehicles and I choose to treat them with extreme caution. The leitmotif of *Celebrity Rehab* is that these stars ostensibly have as much agency to make their return to the limelight as anyone else; but the camera tells another story. The washed-up stars are not doing these reality shows for any other reason than they have hit rock bottom—especially, the economic rock bottom. This pseudo-reality television show of *Celebrity Rehab* is nothing other than the most real vehicle of television: that of the ex-celebrity whose aged body and drug use has gotten the better of him and this mere fact could not be more vulgarly acted or scripted. The trick played on the audience by the producers of this show is to make us part of the "re-legitimation" of these stars, since most spectators react to these people, not as stars, but as characters in a Bildungsroman. The spectators' role is to witness the "return" of the faded star, to observe an auto-destructed Nora Desmond as we are simultaneously denied the voiceover role of Joe Gillis. Our task as spectator is to take in reality television as its excesses spill over into the more acceptable domains of television and become re-legitimated as "real life," because as Kathy Griffin reminds us, "Oprah tells us so." Indeed, Mackenzie Philips is irresistible as reality television, not because she confessed to having sex with her father, but because she managed to get Oprah Winfrey to extract this narrative from her above and beyond her *Celebrity Rehab* stint. (I now understand Griffin's obsession with American media—just when you think you have "seen it all," you so have not!) What is fascinating with this deviation of reality television is that it is as sad as it is empowering. Yet both valences of "sadness" and "empowerment" are equally perplexing for we are not quite sure if it is the viewer, who feels "sad for" or "empowered by" these stories, or if he concedes to the star either emotion. Ultimately, these are personal and real stories of addiction rendered circus attractions because of their power to signify the real explicitly through the mouths of those fallen idols.

I take in media from time to time while in Haiti and most times it is the necessary relief to a heavy day of even weightier subjects. For instance, I laughed to the point of tears when I read that the US healthcare bill was delayed by "worries" that pedophiles would have access to Viagra. But there is another side to this paradigm of cultural and media extremity—one of true degeneration. The media circus is self-perpetuated and amassed and we are the agents of this creation. As such, we buy the papers, we roll over to these websites, we turn on Fox and we feed the fires of *Celebrity Rehab* by tuning in and making it part of our weekly television habit.

People discuss Kim Kardashian's sex video or they share stories from her television show because as the title tells us, we are implicated in this "keeping up with" the Kardashians. But there is a point when our individual ignorance about the the rest of the world is negatively reflected in our hyper-knowledge of the minutiae of reality television and superstars' lives while, ironically, so many people's individual realities are absorbed through the television reality of someone else's life.

We are all humans and certainly we can agree that the onetime celebrity suffers just as the unknown Haitian who cannot get a job. The suffering is different, of course, as all suffering is. But what does the spectator get out of reading or watching this suffering? Are these revelations rhetorical or spectacle, or both? Is the epistolary nature of the series that chronicles the "fall" or "comeback" of the star set to encourage voyeurism or to garner understanding? In the end, there is a point when our watching reality implicates us in *not living* our own realities and in surrendering our agency to the exploitation of the here and now through media. At the risk of sounding like a purist, I cannot help but notice what seems to be a direct relationship between our obsession over that which is so wholly unimportant while we maintain a cultural and mediatized deflection of the central questions of life and death. From the pre-emptive war on terror that continues under different monickers to the telethonesque obsession over Haiti throughout the second half of January 2010 that had all but vanished in several months later, it would seem that we are incapable of taking anything seriously. Most prominent in the cartography of our humanity, we are in need of a *Reality Rehab* whereby we are all dropped onto the island of my version of *Survivor* and made to look at the very real consequences of our political and social actions on both the micro and macro levels. Or at the very least, it might just be time that we learned about the everyday lives of people who have no running water, no constant electricity and who pay $5 per gallon of gas while living on under $2 per day.

Life is here, in front of you, behind you. Touch it. Live it.

iPhone Ergo Sum

I had a virtual crash of sorts on Monday—and this event forced me to wonder how much the technological and the somatic might be related both in my own life and a larger cultural nexus of information, desire and notions of self-fulfillment. After my Internet service had been disrupted by the charmingly unreliable Voilà (but their operators are so polite) since Saturday night, I spent many hours with these people on the phone from Sunday morning through Sunday afternoon and again on Monday morning. At a certain moment, I doubted the problem might be my mobile phone carrier and I thought it may just be my beloved iPhone. Indeed, this new addition to my life has had me telling students recently that I would reconsider my impending marriage to my iMac and instead elope with my one true love, my iPhone. Hence I wondered: had my iPhone betrayed me and dumped me for a netherworld?

In my attempt to supersede Voilà's lengthy response from technical support, I went online and found the new hack upgrade for what is called in the hacker's universe a "jail-broken iPhone." I found this new software, prodigiously called Spirit—and yes, I did the unthinkable, unconscionable act: I clicked and downloaded. Regretably, I did not do have that knee-jerk pause before clicking the installation icon, nor did my brain preview what horror was soon to befall me as I merrily proceeded to click yet again and I installed Spirit onto my already "jail-broken iPhone." The result of this act of freakish wanton certainty that nothing could possibly harm my iPhone was that I had unwittingly put my newly pronounced fiancé, frozen and lifeless, into a coma. What had I done to my betrothed? Nothing I tried would make it breathe again—I had delivered the poisonous apple for which there was no magical solution, no soft kiss delivered by a prince or princess, no secret potion brewed off in the mountain caves of an outcast sorceress, no elusive spell to make my iPhone awaken. It is simply gone (for now).

After contacting the person in New York who sold my iPhone to me, Xin Hu, I found out that I should not have upgraded since Spirit was a jailbreak (and I had already jail-broken my phone) and that an unlock for Spirit would not be out for a few more weeks. In short, I would have to wait for the unlock for Spirit in several weeks' time. I am still attempting to recuperate this iPhone as an iPod Touch until the unlock is released and this ordeal is causing me to become more a computer geek than I had ever hoped never to be. Finally, after trying various Windows platforms which have compatibility issues in recognizing the proper version of iTunes, I found someone with a Macintosh and was able to perform the necessary repairs to render my iPhone, for the next few weeks, an iPod with at least the capacity for Skype and WordPress. The crash of my iPhone resulted in the loss of all my music so the iPod function of my mobile is in name only and my iPhone is now a transvestite of technology. I am somewhat resigned to the fact that I can now return to my picture-taking and video-making in addition to my work here with child trafficking and permaculture.

However, my reaction to this lack of iPhone was not pleasant and I have pondered my reaction to this technological absence over the past few days. I think the best term to describe my reaction to the reality of my iPhone's coma would more accurately be called a "meltdown." Embarrassingly, I became emotional to a startlingly degree—after all, this was just a phone with a software problem whose resolution was a few weeks away. Nonetheless, I could not resolve being without this instrument for several weeks and I panicked: I wondered how I would function for I could no longer write my articles without being on a borrowed or rented computer which is a near impossibility here given my work schedule. I also could not check my emails when I fancied, and worse, I could no longer take any photos whenever I found something that I deemed photo-worthy. None of this is tragic, none of this is really even urgent. So, why on earth would this drive me to the brink of tears? Why would such a small tool wield so much control over my life? Or more directly, why would I let such a tool have so much importance? Perhaps you can relate when *x* apparatus died— your juicer, your razor, your car, your winter boots—and you too have found yourself in this space of *"But what shall I do now?"*

These are questions that are as much of the personal order as they are of the cultural. Clearly, I had no problem *not writing on* this device before I purchased it, nor did I miss taking photos or making videos at any given moment. Before the iPhone I would simply live with the fact that my computer or camera were in my home when I walked past something I thought might be worth capturing. What is it about this delicious compact nature of the iPhone which has applications for most everything (even a flashlight which I must use to descend these very dangerous stairs near my house each night) and which has the "power" to leave a grown adult on the board of tears when its software goes on vacation? As much as I love writing every day, I also love yoga, cooking, long baths, gardening; yet, while I can live without most of these events on a daily basis, the coma of my iPhone brought out the beast within. I am very conscious of the various addictions "out there": the Internet, television, cocaine and, well in western culture, it seems we have the ability to turn anything into an

addiction.   Yet, I did not have withdrawal symptoms for my inability to
take baths or for the absence of a kitchen where I currently live—I do not
get the shakes or the "I have to write an article now, God damn it!"
bitchitude.   Before January, I utilized my computer by setting time aside
for this and when I was far from my computer, I took notes and accepted
this reality.   But when my iPhone succumbed on Monday afternoon, I
became sad, angry (that I uploaded the wrong software on my hacked
iPhone), and then I felt slightly out of control over my life.

I don't know if this emotional reaction was a reflection of my wish to
have control over not only what I do, but moreso to control what I should
not have done.   I strongly suspect that I was annoyed with myself for what
I should have done and did not (ie. not having read up on this new hack-
ware, not having done my normal reading and posting on blogs and boards
to ensure it was a stable version and suitable to my already hacked iPhone,
not having thought more, and not having stopped myself from that final
click).   Yet for the following twenty-four hours I manifested a will, of sorts,
to control time, to control the past and it manifested itself through my
being quite distraught.   How often we observe time as if in slow motion
and wish to ourselves that we could have stopped ourselves from pushing
that button, almost like watching a bad horror movie for whom the wrong
choices we foresee just in the very moments the badly-scripted actors are
entering the clearly haunted house.   And with a similar attitude that I
maintained while watching the babysitter pick up the phone in *When a
Stranger Calls* wishing she simply would not have answered the phone, I
would run through my mind to that precise moment when I iSlaughtered
my iPhone repeating to myself, "What on earth was I thinking?"

Logically, I know this not to be the case: it is a truism that we cannot
control everything in life.   There are simply things that we do not and
cannot control regardless of the multiple pop-psychologies out there that
portend a fascistic will to self-manifestation with theories that the subject
can control all life.   Such philosophies are often banalizations of
transcendental or Sufi philosophies, with the metaphoric notion of selfhood
and corporeality being effaced by new-ageisms that forget that indeed
death is part of life and that self-will does not control or influence all
exterior forces.   Certainly we can influence the price of certain
commodities, we can often influence that we are given a raise or not, and
yes, using a seatbelt can statistically influence our chances of survival in a
head-on collision.   But, I am at a loss for words when confronted by the
arrogance of anyone who claims we control everything—sickness, death,
loss of love.   These are things that simply "just happen" and as much as we
can eat properly, exercise, show love to our fellow humans and not smoke,
none of these actions are guarantees of anything.   Life happens, and thank

goodness we do not control it all. Yet there I was overwhelmed with emotion before a lifeless iPhone, unable to fathom how I got from January's posture of "I'll never own an iPhone" to this, my pitiful demonstration of dependence on this instrument I had so grown to love.

Let's chalk it up to a transference of emotions onto a machine: it felt for a moment as if I didn't exist because I could not produce my articles, I could not make my films and shoot my pictures, I could not even look at special photos from time to time which force me to remember that I have a past, that I am loved. It was as if the coma of my iPhone implicated me in a free-floating loss of self, an amputation of some part of me and that for however long, I would have to be in that search of myself, albeit my new self, *sans* iPhone. How was I to reinterpret myself to myself in this endless act of self-recognition that to varying degrees most every human today surrenders, in part, through technology. Where had I lost my personal time within that time lost on the recovery mode screen of my iPhone? It was as if both my iPhone and myself were stuck in recovery mode together.

We are technological beings (whether or not we admit to this is another story). We use technology in just about everything—from the grinding of grains into flours, the purification process of water, our sewage systems, eyeglasses, contact lenses, artificial hips and amalgams in our teeth. We are products of technology and we generally live quite seamlessly with these material realities. Yet, the invention of the video game has had psychologists popping up all over television for the past twenty-five years as they are interviewed as to the links between aggressive behavior in teenagers, the Columbine shootings, and the various forms of social and psychological alienation imposed by such gadgets. Internet dating is another monster of addiction therapy that is coming to the fore in serious discussions of sociability as a friend recounts to me the story of her law partner who had missed so many days in court due to her Internet dating addiction that she was eventually arrested and eventually disbarred. And the "sex addiction" could not be more painfully ironized through the actor of David Duchovny who plays an alleged "sex addict"/womanizer in *Californication* who last year went into rehab in his real-life for sex addiction. Is this art imitating life, life imitating art, or art imitating life imitating pathology? It would seem that we are a culture where addiction, even obsession with our pathologies, would seem to be our "normal" and where trite notions of "the normal" seem mostly to exist in Hollywood cinema. Or do I exaggerate? Ultimately, I do wonder if in the west we have not created a culture of addiction which attempts to look at symptoms (ie. sex, the video games, the Internet, my iPhone), rather than look at how these tools or acts might just be part of a larger process of possessing things that we have long avoided analyzing due to our, preoccupation with "loftier" tasks such as industrialization, wars, political malfeasance, and reality television.

Jean Rouch's *Les Maîtres fous* is a controversial film for its examination of the Hauka, a religious movement which emerged in the early 20th century during the French colonization of Central and Western Africa, originating in Niger. This movement was characterized by rituals of transe in which the colonized subject would become possessed, his eyes would roll back into his head, his mouth would foam, subjects would engage in forbidden acts (ie. consuming the flesh of a dog), and the body would contort, jerk and even assume the role of the French colonizers. This film was for many years the subject of debate, but it seems that much of the debate was based on misinterpretation of Rouch's experiment being one of experimental spectatorship and of the obliquely worded opening titles from "the Producer" of this film to forewarn the viewer of the "violence and cruelty" therein which show how "some Africans represent our western civilization"). Certainly the experimentation of Rouch's project is interceded by the narrative which warns of "cultural shock," meanwhile any alarum regarding the "western civilization" of French colonization was discretely absent from these titles. And herein, Rouch proceeds, with his non-synchronous sound film which narrates the events of a Hauka transe, to leave all interpretation to the viewer of Rouch's images, to the auditor of his words, forcing the spectator into the transe of these actors. Originally considered a racist depiction of Africans, *Les Maîtres fous* is now considered to be one of the best depictions of French colonialism on film as this narrative brings together the processes of colonialism, decolonization and transe through these Sonhay actors. The spectator is forced to see interpretations of an off-camera violence, through this on-camera ritual in reaction to the cruel realities of French colonialism not present on the screen. The transe for the Hauka was a means of dealing with the colonial powers and oppression. Transe has always been a necessary practice for individual ethnopsychoanalysis which, as crazy and obsessive as it might look, allows the subject to continue her life and to incorporate her subjectivity within a certain community.

I query if the use of my iPhone might not be an instrument/act of trance, a cycle of release for me from my exterior world as this gadget allows me to express myself through my intellectual efforts of words, to maintain contact (albeit superficially, via email) with friends and colleagues and it affords me the ability to capture a moment I deem interesting, personal, or anything in between these two valences for more artistic productions. For many people the iPhone enables the subject to be able to do so much within a light, tiny framework which is portable and negligible. It is undeniable that I felt, for a moment, all powerful when I realized I did not need my iMac at my side in order to get work done. And because of the excellence of this device, I must confess to having felt a momentary twinge of superiority, simply because this little gadget does almost as much as my much larger and heavier laptop. So somehow this superior function and form of the iPhone was translated to my own self, my own body. It is as if I have entered the anti-phallic stage of history where bigger is definitely not better; in fact, bigger just makes you feel more immobile. Perhaps what I love most about my iPhone is that it is so small that it feels magically invisible when you do not want to see it, and then, conversely, there it is there within a flick of the wrist. The magic and sorcery of many trance ceremonies might actually not be more complicated than this fetishism of technological time and being. We usurp a temporal narrative within our physical space of life, our existence, and from within our bodies we make emerge narratives, ideas, dialogues, recipes, yoga chants, and so forth. Our being is wrapped up in our conception of ourselves in this momentary intersection of our reality with an other. And so our postmodern totem is no longer twenty feet tall, but is instead pocket-sized.

Tuesday night I treated myself to a Thai dinner after spending months here eating every other day, for what would translate to approximately $1.50 per day. After the most expensive Thai food I have ever had in my life, I became violently ill. I was out of sorts on Wednesday and returned to earth Thursday, reborn, refreshed...still without my beloved iPhone. Since this revitalization I have been wondering if my illness might have been the somatic reaction to the psychological trauma of my iPhone coma, or rather if I brought on my illness through psychosomatic manifestations? As much as I wish to doubt this being the case, I cannot say for certain this is not. I think those of us who depend upon technology to produce our thoughts, in many respects, are part of these mechanisms. Not having a computer or an iPhone is like the painter without her paints or the cook without his knives. And I do know people in both professions who need to practice these arts on a daily basis. Yet the techno-pathology in which much of our culture is invested poses certain limits to the notions of use versus abuse, utilization versus addiction. Certain measures of the self are necessarily caught up in the exteriorization of technological productions. Even these words that I write might just be the vehicle through which I create myself and without such a machine to aid in this creation, I simply do not exist.

Existence perceived in this way fits into a very Cartesian methodology of course. This machine allows me to escape the every day as I toil over words, produce elusive thoughts—words which no longer embody "the real" and on paper—and then string these thoughts throughout this virtual world where meaning is hopefully inflected, frozen, and undone all at once. There is a paradox in that despite my possessing the most "normal" and banal of contraptions in this iPhone, I am somehow able to express my difference as a human. Through such a normative medium, I am undoing any normalization of myself, escaping all conformity and creating something that is *both outside of yet akin to* myself. There is a trap within such technology as the age-old dichotomy of nature/machine no longer exists and we are held hostage to the temporality of our existence through a device which is both outside the body, yet the machine forms a part of us.

In *Being and Time*, Heidegger develops his "existential analytic" of these very two concepts, Being and Time, wherein he argues that in order to represent experience, it is most important to find the being for whom such representations of experience might matter. Hence his *Dasein* (literally "being there"), references being for whom such being is crucial, for whom being is a question. Heidegger views *Dasein* is that which is thrown into the many possibilities of life and through which one seeks responsibility for one's own existence (hence his notions of resoluteness and authenticity), such that the subject quests for the escape of the vulgar through authentic time.

Perhaps there is a vulgarity in the iPhone or the fact that I am even writing about my strange relationship to this piece of technology post-vomitorium Wednesday. Yet, I cannot escape the reality that while I write this, the lifeless body of my iPhone rests "happily" asleep and in another dimension in its transvestite life as an iPod. Or in a parallel universe, perhaps I ought to have married my iPhone while it was still alive? Perhaps this level of technological "understanding" will be the impetus for future declarations of love and creation where the *Dasein* of the iPhone is a phenomenological experience of intentionality and of where the self as perception and the self as construction are merged through this intermediary that is neither human nor beast, neither mother nor priest. Before I bought the iPhone, I was not at all interested in having a little device that had the potential (as I had witnessed with friends) to become an addiction, if not an obsession. And now having this instrument, I realize that this glean in their eyes was neither addiction nor obsession—it was pure contentment in—if not dependence upon—an object.

And so goes the story of our culture which warns of such proximities or "repeated uses." While I am mindful of this relationship that our culture maintains between use and abuse—albeit a constantly changing and contradictory shift between these two distinctions—I cannot help but find what is troubling is not the occasional case of addiction, but rather our societal preoccupation with the good use of technology. I have gained a deep appreciation for this tool in its support of the WordPress app for writing this book, Skype for my rare moments to call friends, and for checking email. I have likewise gained enormous pleasure out of new applications in all their use or frivolity—especially the cat meow piano. Surprisingly, I have used my iPhone far less while in Haiti than my normal quotidian use of my computer back home. Nonetheless, my iPhone has become this object through which many of my thoughts and visions are recorded and it is currently my vehicle for sharing my being with others for whom [my] being and narrative matters. I do not pretend to be wholly united with this piece of machinery; conversely, I cannot attest to being entirely untethered from it either. There is a point in which our reliance upon technology is simply, for lack of a better word, "natural."

On Love & Other Vicissitudes

Now that I have lost the music on my iPhone, I have had these lyrics in my head from Jay-Z for several days bouncing about my thoughts and could not resist recalling them yesterday morning:

Yeah Yeah What we talkin' bout real shit?
Or we talkin' bout rhymes
You talkin' bout millions Or you talking' bout mine
What we talkin' bout Cuz I ain't got time
For what people be talkin' bout all the time
What we talkin' bout fiction Or we talkin bout fact
You talkin' bout fiction? Hold up pardon my back
I'm talkin' bout life And all I hear is
Oh yeah he keeps talkin' bout crack
I ain't talkin' bout profit I'm talkin' bout pain
I'm talkin' bout despair I'm talkin' bout shame...

As I repeat the words in my head, I realize that Jay-Z's song is very much engaged in breaking down the pain of the past by reacting in the present as he invokes us: "[to] talk about the future." Jay-Z offers us the "Blueprint" of our lives, admonishing us to cast out the past and to write our future in a present of creation, collaboration, and love.

As I listen to Jay-Z I realize that his words resonate for me here, amidst this extremely rich and loving culture of Haiti which shows great care, concern and sharing within the setting of terrible poverty and quotidian dangers. Poverty affects most all interactions here and resultantly people in the most devastating moments of this country's recent history are imbued with lightness and love that can be felt pretty much everywhere. Riding back to Petionville with a friend Monday night, we witnessed what could have filled a two hour movie which I compared to Scorsese's *After Hours*—the Port-au-Prince version. I cannot properly describe the events of that voyage because they merge together in a manner than robs the narrative (and time) of linearity, but the recipe for this night would include the following ingredients: flood waters of two to three feet, tap taps stuffed to the water's edge, a behemoth hole in the middle of road and a river suddenly appearing before me as if I were witnessing a biblical story come to life, and the joy on people's faces as they jumped over obstacles to avoid the waters as they would exit the tap tap. One woman exited her tap tap in what were, at the beginning of the day, white pants which were now disfigured by mud and rain—they were everything but white. She was laughing and overjoyed as she left the tap tap and I was overcome with this feeling of witnessing some sort of super-human feat. Indeed many people in the west would have simply been upset by the fact that their clothes were destroyed and my brain could barely piece together the array of images in all their technicolor emotions that swept across the rain-filled streets between MINUSTAH and Petionville.

How to describe feelings of love and other emotional textures whose vicissitudes seem to be un-representable at the very moment of enunciation? Words fall flat as they can only mean a very precise thing at an even more acute moment in time. Words can define and delimit what we wish to represent, but they often skirt around meaning as the directness of language can often kill the exact feeling we are attempting to convey. The problem with language is that it is aporetic and one is left struggling with how to represent without losing your subject while likewise not over-investing meaning in it. In matters of love, at least, this is my experience —language can simply be too much or too little. What Roland Barthes writes of the language of love can easily be applied to all sorts of emotions which we evidence through performance and words:

> To try to write love is to confront the muck of language; that region of hysteria where language is both too much and too little, excessive (by the limitless expansion of the ego, by emotive submersion) and impoverished (by the codes on which love diminishes and levels it) (99).

Similar to the communication of love, other emotions are likewise invested in the complexity of language's paucity or excess. It is the medium which becomes problematic due to the way in which emotions arise, change, and refuse to remain stable. Language can simply never be enough and in the challenge to represent exactly what one feels, the risk is that language overwhelms and even perverts the emotion being described. Words are used to represent order and to give a semblance of control over oneself: after all, if I can explain myself to you then I must know who I am, right? Language is often a trap as it forces us to box up meanings, check off adjectives and conform (or not) to social strategies and codes. Language obliges us, in a split second, to concede or refuse a word. As I have always refused the use of "white" and "black" when referring to people since no such skin color exists, I am aware that people do not always understand to what I am referring and these words, despite being wholly inaccurate and archaic adjectives, lock people's minds from hearing any modification to newer referents or more liberatory ways of thinking about our collective humanity. There is a societal push to speak the same language as other humans and because of this reality self-invention is not so much frowned upon as it is simply elided.

Certain modalities of language are not only acceptable, they are often contrived discourses of the self wherein each narrative reveals a family or cultural posturing of something—of success, of happiness— to where language often acts as a surrogate to *real* emotion.   We no longer live happy, fulfilled lives—we must go on television or YouTube and profess these emotions, we affirm in our okcupid profile how happy we are, and we expose our most superficial non-achievements as actual achievements. In the end, people speak the language of emotions reacting to these emotions with platitudes of success and structure which lends credibility to the fact that x must really be successful because she landed a job in c.   To be fair, we approach many of life's tasks as if a goal which must be accomplished in a certain order and rigor simply because we are taught to think of our lives in terms of dates, degrees, titles, and educational expertise.   We are programmed at a young age to organize our time, prioritize tasks, accomplish certain feats and all these acts cumulatively we hope will eventually lead to "achievement."   More paradoxically, even talking about achievement has become in and of itself an "achievement" simply because our societies are caught up in the task of planning successes whilst the work of this success, the actual "stuff of success," remains linguistic, an idea which lasts more time as pure discourse than it ever existed in action.   And at a later point in life, these benchmarks of "success" become salaries, neighborhoods, types of car owned and where our children study.   Success is more about the narratives we tell than the happiness that many in our societies can and do extract from their work.

Rarely do we question these notions—the fact that "success" is not all that it is cracked up to be and that maybe we ought to be worrying about what we want to do, rather than what "seems" successful. For instance, I have friends who tell me of their child's future achievements before this child even has expressed any interest in going to x university or in studying y subject. Success in the west is a pretense and a prerequisite to discussing one's child and like the pre-emptive war on terror, it would seem that even happiness and success exist mostly as pre-emptive. We await our own happiness and success by creating this reality through language, so much of who were are—our happiness or disappointment therein— is based on this measure on who we were *meant to be*. Or so we wish to believe. And the result is that we are put on a track for our life as productive humans who will become successful lawyers, economists and artists.   Success has become the stranglehold of identity and I have witnessed our societal drive to embrace success as a panacea for human relationships and love. Indeed, I have witnessed many a parent talking about where her own child will attend university and what she will study while the parent has ignored the very voice of this young adult who expresses opposing views. Regardless, she will be a success. Through language we express who we are in relation to the exterior orders of things—valences of success, notions of happiness, desires that we seek to realize, and the people to whom we represent ourselves.

James turns to me and says, "You know you are very direct." Knowing this about myself, but not knowing to what he was referring, I turned to him and asked what he meant precisely. He replied, "When, I barely knew you you told me in a matter of fact way that your child had died." I responded to this by telling James that I did not feel that life's details needed a prologue, be it about announcing one's sexuality to family or to telling friends that you are left-handed. All these qualities are as natural as the next, all are incidental or central parts of life and for me I cannot begin to put precursors on what is a biographical element, as if a specific detail must only be presented after reaching "level three" of friendship status. "I might shock people at times," I told my friend, "but who is to say that those people living in Toronto with a wife, children and a Volvo might not shock or revolt me?"

Sunday morning I was involved in a discussion that has affected my entire week to the point of tears and confusion. Julia, a French woman working for the United Nations, told us about her having removed bodies from MINUSTAH in the weeks following January's earthquake. She described in painful detail how bulldozers took loads of bodies and dumped them into mass graves describing how rubbish trucks would pass through the streets as bodies were not only loaded into them, but she recounted how the jaws of these trucks closed in, crunching the bodies. She looked up and said, "And I was like, 'OK, this is a dire emergency—it is what has to be done." And I just continued on to the next body." Jennifer, a Haitian specialist in public health, then shared how she saw certain images on the television and said that such treatment of the dead represented the loss of humanity for Haitians. Julia strongly disagreed and said that there was no other choice—that decisions had to be taken to reduce the possibility of disease and epidemic. Jennifer rephrased her point: "I am not saying something should have been done differently. I am saying that this treatment of the bodies indicates a loss of humanity—to be treated like rubbish is simply dehumanizing." The discussion continued as it became clear that both speakers were correct in their ideas of practicality and public health. This discussion underscored that at times, doing what is necessary can provoke dehumanizing, albeit unintended, effects. Reality can be unavoidably harsh and our making sense of this violence is often equally as violent.

I happened to hear many stories of the events on and after the earthquake this past weekend. These discussions forced me to reflect on my own description of the death of my son and how western narratives of loss are often either warmly embraced or stiffly refused, rarely with any emotion in between these two polarities. I was simply unprepared for the completely thoughtless comments I would be told after the death of my child from, comment made by individuals whom I considered to be friends: one person told me that I ought to adopt a dog, another told me that my child's death was not as much as tragedy as the death of an older child, and there was even one who was upset at me because I did not answer her emails in the days following my son's death and she caste suspicion on my child's death (likely a projection of her own cruel childhood)! I was not braced for the cruelty and ignorance of fellow humans and it was not until I lost my child that I realized how false the fictions of community are where "everyone" comes together during a tragedy. What I found is that when a child dies, most people simply want to know nothing about it, as if hearing of this death were to set into motion the higher potentiality of this happening to their children. Many people step back in a selfish act of protection while the person for whom tragedy is real becomes isolated in this cultural refusal to accept death. Yet, mass tragedy sets into motion a space of normalcy for discussing catastrophe, such that certain losses seem greater than others simply because there is a social vehicle for legitimating these feelings because of the sheer numbers of people affected. After further contemplation on this subject, a part of me was upset simply because the space for discussing the recuperation and disposal of bodies was rendered more "normal" and socially acceptable than my briefly mentioning the fact my child had died. I grew distressed by this revelation: that closets are created by people who simply think that there are certain social facts you can state and other social truths that you cannot utter unless in certain situations and amongst certain people.

Why are cultural norms—from sexuality to diverse narrations of loss—imposed when culture is implicated in the inclusion of difference? For what I observe in this life, what people commonly call "culture," is an assumption of a hegemonic, dominant system which must not be questioned, put into doubt, or delegitimized. This notion of "respecting culture," smacks of myriad problematic historical positions which, need I remind the reader, were also enforced in the name of cultural normalcy, historical supremacy and racial purity. Scratch the surface of any culture and you shall find no monolith. There remain only fragments of multiple narratives many of which are absent from the scene of mass cultural representation: the atheist, the homosexual, the fornicating or the pot-smoking Haitian. All are absent from all public and official discourse. Yet, these are not cultural anomalies and they are every bit as central to this society as the omnipresence of Christianity in tap tap graffiti art wherein Jesus could easily be mistaken for a second-rate rock star.

What we cannot represent, due to those individuals whose interpretations of culture obligates our silence in an obedient "show of respect," necessitates an archeology of the senses—and of culture itself. Cultural hegemony is real *both between and within* cultures and we must constantly negotiate these spaces and fight against normativity, to fight against the silencing of dialogue. How certain ideas and practices are perceived usually fit into a continuum or they causes friction, falling outside the boundaries of the "normal" and clashing with the perceived "center." But are these schisms and moments of discord any more external to the integrity of culture than that which is perceived as essential to culture? Is there not a danger in perceiving culture as being unable to handle discussions of women's rights, slavery, homosexuality, and workers' rights such that these discussions actually threaten the grand stereotype propounded? Where do the margins evidence themselves if they are inevitably always left outside popular representation and other mimetic functions? In reality the lack of a constant and public discourse of these perceived "minor" identities simply does not mean that these identities are any less important to the cultural fabric or that they ought to remain silent in observation of those age-old bearers of power who must be protected. Instead the more marginal identities are often sacrificed for the sake of rhetoric in our inter-cultural refusal to accept difference.

I was deeply moved by James' comment to me for he reacted to the story of my son's death in a way that demonstrated shock. In all fairness, were I in his place, I would perhaps not know how to react to news from a stranger of her child's death, especially when mentioned dryly, as a matter of fact. But then there are moments when my utterances on this subject are more heartfelt, more steeped in the shit of pain, and again other moments when I just don't mention it at all. Each utterance is as right as it is wrong as language robs the presence of any unique or unilateral definition of identity. Indeed, I was expected to step into this space of the identity of loss, to uphold its fictions, when in fact there no such identity exists. Like all identity, even this is a fiction meant to be some sort of linguistic nostrum to death. It would seem that the only way to deal with death in all its messiness and dehumanization is to embrace the plurality of its pain. The truth behind mourning, like emotions, does not lie in its uniqueness or its monolithic formations, but instead such personal truths exist in all opposition to the perceived norms such that meaning emerges from the contradictions of these enunciations and not in their seamless renderings.

There is much about life and death that is both purely wonderful and dehumanizing as we stagger between the two in our personal and collective endeavors to communicate ourselves to others and even to ourselves.

So yesterday afternoon I went to the Bourdon Valley, smack in the middle of Port-au-Prince. This valley belongs nowhere near the garbage-filled streets of the capital and it harbors none of the rapidity of the tap tap-filled city. This valley is a magical space of green, semi-jungle and riverbed around which live various communities and camps. I visited a school established by AMURT (Ananda Marga Universal Relief Team) run by tantric yoga nuns from Spain and the United States. One woman, Lule, invited me to visit her community. Although I have worked in many communities and camps in my time here, I have never seen a community which is situated in such a beautiful space as this. The misery, nonetheless, is omnipresent in its physical characteristics; yet the people, like the woman drenched in rain and black-grey mud descending the tap tap emitting pure joy, are full of love and hope.

Shortly after my arrival, Lule brought me to a family in the next community where a wall had fallen Monday morning as three young people slept, injuring two and killing one, a twenty-two year old man. We arrived at a house and a family was gathered in a small room, a woman in her early fifties lying stomach down on the bed, overwhelmed with grief. For a brief moment, I saw myself three years ago as I felt her pain pass through me. The loss of her son was markedly present on her face and on the faces of everyone who came to share their commiseration. The mother was inconsolable. We sat with her, her relatives scattered around the room, all of us looking towards this woman's inclined body and Lola stroked her arm while humming verses (from where they came I cannot say). I was touched by this woman's loss and could not help but remark my own helplessness as I was rendered an observer which is, in and of itself, a liminal presence. There is nothing you can do as you watch a person in absolute pain and loss except to be present. Yet, presence does not correct the situation and dare I say it does not really lend understanding, for nobody can understand such a loss. And I, sitting there, having lost my own son three years ago could simply not understand *her* pain. It is unique and galaxies away from my own as pain, like love, is a feeling that is un-duplicable, un-representable through language.

The other day, I had an unexpected emotional reaction to my attempt to move from my home in Petionville to another more affordable room: I found that I could not leave my family to whom I have been feeling more and more attached. I was completely ready to make the move as I love them dearly, but the rats that I have encountered just above my bedroom, as a result of the kitchen left in ruins, has resulted in my not being able to sleep some nights. I have this Disney film in my head as the mice are having a huge feast, each one coming in, searching for food, dancing, eating again. So, instead of my announcing my departure, I surprisingly found myself asking Frantz to please ensure that the kitchen is cleaned up at night so that mice and rats do not come over for the grand buffet. I realized that this family and I have a harmonious relationship and I was not about to let a few mice (and more recently rats) get in the way. I sat under the almond tree yesterday and realized that I could not leave here and that I was undecided about my future work with the United Nations.

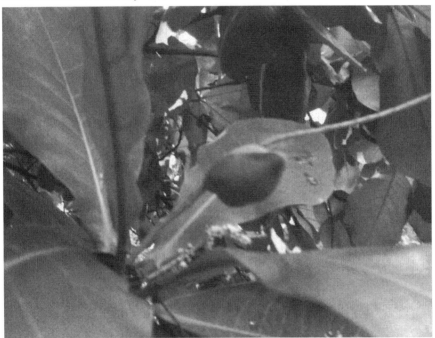

To be truthful, I have had a crisis of sorts over my past month's collaboration with UNICEF. On the one hand, I have been having these overwhelming feelings of disconnect because the politics of the United Nations is nothing less than problematic. Meetings about having the next meeting and operations that are based on revising the previous team's assessment with little actually being done began to wear on me. Even my presentation at the UNICEF offices after my discovery of three different instances of child trafficking left me in front of UNICEF's regional child protection specialist who shrugged off the incidents telling me to go to the police (from where I had just arrived). Once I was finally approached by one honest child protection officer in UNICEF I worked on several projects one of which was to prepare a strategic international research project that I have been invited to conduct. Though this is an excellent project which can change the fate of thousands of children a year, I am unsure if it is worth my working with MINUSTAH bureaucrats, some whose $19,000 per month salaries do not warrant their attachment to such a project of social justice in a country where my family and neighbors do not live on a tenth of this monthly salary in one year. The almond tree seemed all the more consistent in my world and while sitting under it these past few mornings I have come into touch with my sense of conflict about what I am doing in Haiti. While I realize that this research project will effect changes in social policy and jurisprudence, it means that I must stay many more months and collaborate with an institution which needs to be seriously restructured in order to bring about the necessary social and political changes here. In essence, I am split between my disgust for the politics of the UN within Haiti and my desire to change human rights law. This is not an uncommon dilemma, but it is not one I wish to approach now as I have left the fetid world of academia for not so dissimilar reasons.

The answers I seek might be the very same as those which my colleagues engaged in the discussion of the disposal of bodies in Port-au-Prince search out—the very same answers because of the uncertainty regarding representations of the death of a loved one or the death of many. Perhaps there is no right answer. And it highly probable that there are no answers only the extant possibilities of acceptance, love, and hope. I do not possess any answers and I am exhausted in my attempt to "do the right thing," as if there is one comportment, one way, one cultural norm, one form of doing. There is not. And while some manners are patently wrong, it is perhaps necessary to try and voyage within the error of possibility. Maybe the problem with attempting to precise the acceptable representations that will not offend or shock, or that will approximate the "appropriate" way to tell someone about a personal tragedy confronts more than just the force of language and so-called cultural conventions? Might there be something to our existential implication in this culture, of our just being present to listen, to help and to hold someone's hand? Certainly, we must attempt to build bridges across and through our societies, not in an act of defiance or belligerence, but in the striving for personal liberation that will have nobody apologizing for the kind of person one loves, for the way he tells of his wife's death or the factual terms of evacuating bodies that rests in perpetual contradistinction to those facts of humanity, now denigrated under the bulldozer's teeth.

In the end, the song by Jay-Z's "What We Talkin' About" repeats a hook that speaks to *the personal fears of and societal taboos* against representing the marginalized voices of this planet, speaking out against injustice, and ultimately stepping out of all sorts of closets through words that rupture, actions that breath life into the present, language which slices reality with discomfort:

> *They Talk, We Live, We see what They say, They say, They say*
> *They Talk, We Did, Who cares what They say, They say, They say...*

I was at the UNICEF tent Monday night during the first stage of a very big storm. The water came down in truckloads and everyone at MINUSTAH's Log Base was stepping from cinder block to piece of wood, balancing their weight on anything that was remotely dry as wires were soaked in rainwater puddles while ponds formed inside tented offices. Myriam, Gilles, and I were having a conversation about child protection during this storm: Myriam standing on a cinder block, Gilles on a higher mound of pebbles and I was on a wooden loading dock palette. At one point I remarked that this setting would make for the perfect theatrical scene out of a Beckett play. And indeed UNICEF in Haiti was just that.

Show and Tell

Gismaine greeted me this morning with her warm smile. As I was running off to work the other day she mentioned that she had not earned any money in two years. This morning I revisited the subject, asking her what she did before. She told me that she sold bags, then ran to her room and returned to the kitchen with a brown, vinyl, rather baroque handbag. She asked if I wanted to buy a bag (750 gourdes) and I declined her offer pointing to my bag, indicating that I had a bag but promised to find her clients. I would rather have been able to offer Gismaine a job, a permanent way of maintaining her life. Gismaine lives with her husband, daughter, and two other children who are not at all related to her. People in Port-au-Prince—even before the earthquake—live in combined families and these past months, learning who is related to whom has simply not been that easy for me. I have only started to make most of the family connections these past few days and yet, I am far from complete comprehension as the myriad histories, family lineages, divorces, children from a previous relationship, and orphan makes this what I initially thought to be a household of four families, more like a household of twelve families. Of course, when everyone explain how they are connected to one another, it became obvious and they look at me as if I am quite daft not to have gathered this before. Here people stay at the house for a few days, leave without notice, or many only live at the house in the day while working at night. I should not forget to mention that I have met most everyone at night in the courtyard when there is never any electricity (except for Easter weekend). The house gets electricity in the day so it is at night when I listen to these stories of complex family relations such that I wish I had that family tree from *One Hundred Years of Solitude*. Frantz has three jobs: as a bouncer at Café des Arts, as a technician at a telephone company, and he often takes up private security jobs. Frantz's wife's brother, Sanson, his brother, Johny, and another friend and neighbor also work at Café des Arts.

Frantz and his wife, Nathalie, rent a room to me which is located directly underneath the kitchen in a separate building from where they and the other families live. My room holds a bed, a small chest with a key which Frantz gave me to hold my valuable items, a candle inside an ashtray, and a wicker divan. The floor is concrete and even the bathroom is completely untiled. Frantz is the youngest of seven children, most of whom do not live in the house. Poussin, his oldest brother is a painter and he lives down the street. When I arrived Poussin told me of his plans to marry his girlfriend in St. Louis, Missouri, with whom he has a child. He is awaiting his visa to see her. So when I went to see Poussin's paintings the other week, I was surprised to see his girlfriend in his apartment. I asked her when she arrived in Haiti from St. Louis. She smiled and went into the next room. Poussin said, "That is not the same girlfriend." I replied, "Why on earth did you not tell me you had two girlfriends? I would not have opened my mouth. As a matter of fact, I would have told her to dump you!" Johny laughed with me. The second eldest and a horticulture genius, Johny lives in the house with his first girlfriend. He is a wonderful man— gentle, funny, and generous. He works at Café des Arts and whenever I am there at night working on a project, since I return home much earlier than he, Johny always takes me on his motorcycle home and drives back to work. It just occurred to me the other day, seeing him making yet another beautiful garden at Café des Arts, that Johny is an installation artist of plants and plastic bottles. Johny's work is beautiful and grotesque all at once, defying any strict norms of "gardening" as he perches plants in cut-off plastic bottles, in recycled Alaska powdered milk cans, and tied to trees as these plants' roots slowly embed themselves in the tree trunk.

I wake up each morning and jump into my clothes and, every third day or so, I wash my laundry and hang it outside in the vast courtyard. Since I am pitiful at hand-wringing my clothes, my jeans usually take too long to dry without smelling of old water; hence one of the children jumps onto the roof tossing my jeans onto the metal structure helping my jeans dry on the rooftop in record speed. I have brought a pair of jeans, six underwear, six socks, six shirts, a jumper, a skirt, Canadian army boots and yellow Camper dress shoes which are like trainers. I have acquired since arriving here, a coconut shell necklace, two plastic necklaces, and a Creole-French/ French-Creole dictionary. And I almost forgot that since I transformed my iPhone into an iPod Touch, I have temporarily obtained a street vendor's "Viva" mobile phone which I am due to return while he searches me a working second-hand phone.

I have recently stopped taking my malaria prophylaxis and I have absolutely no need for face cream with the humidity and heat here. On the ledge of my bathroom washing area are: soap, a toothbrush, toothpaste, dental floss, my personal soap, the soap which I use to wash my clothes, and a bottle of shampoo with my green Japanese exfoliating cloth draped on top of the shampoo to dry. There is also this small, white container that once held ice cream or some other food which I use to draw water from the large blue barrel to bath (or more literally "to take a bucket") every night when I return home. There is no running water in my house and Frantz or Nathalie refill the blue bin every ten days or so. My towel hangs from an unfinished, sealed water pipe protruding from the wall.

My life here is not really that different in complexity than it was before—in some ways it is much more calm and full of love, in other ways more frustrating and longing to discover some sort of logic between the utter madness of the international presence which shows resolve in doing absolutely nothing against the backdrop of the Haitian people's patience to

tolerate such political posturing. Amongst other questions... The street sprawling in front of my home declares a simultaneous calm and chaos and perhaps this street in itself best captures this city.

Gismaine's cooking in the early morning is a ritual which I have been missing of late as I tend to leave for work at 5h00. But her warmth and

dialogue, when I do stay home past 6h00, regularly keep me sustained in what is a recognition of life's rhythms within a space of utter calm and stark poverty. She is the true core of this household—she is by far the superior cook and she is the most loving person I have ever met. One day, many weeks ago, I asked her if she saw very well as one of her eyes looks always up. She said that she sees perfectly well. I felt uncomfortable with the fact that I had just asked her this question, thinking I had invaded her privacy. She just smiled at me with love.

The only pause I have taken in recent weeks is atop this motor, my "bench," the place I sit when I forego the tap tap and wait for the UN car to pick me up. It is from here that I watch the street (above) and the young children filing past me, the work trucks where a man drives six children nestled in the front cab, young women with vegetables in baskets on their heads, and the lone Digicel boy with his red frock covering his torso and a huge red telephone under his arm. People move past, watching the rocks in the road, ensuring their children avoid the passing trucks and cars, sometimes looking at me with every third person passing me a "bonjour."

This is my world as I live it, as I know it, today. It is a very imperfect world full of imperfect subjects like myself, all of us living in this city full of burning plastic and market slush that smells of death; yet this place feels paradoxically like the epitome of perfection. Vladimir Horowitz one said, "perfection itself is imperfection" and I am left to wonder if perhaps the contrary might also be true.

Mad (Wo)Men

Thursday I had meetings with Govinda from Tear Fund and Myriam from UNICEF. We went to Delmas to meet up with some of Port-au-Prince's top four communications and advertising agencies.   There are many external projects Myriam has brought to the fore as her work in the Child Trafficking Cluster at UNICEF the past few months: from bringing me on board with my research and practical work on child trafficking and this impending communication campaign on the same which will raise awareness of this enormous problem throughout the country. There are no proper statistics to date but most figures based on previous data estimate that there are between 2,000 to 3,000 children trafficked each year. From my own preliminary research, it is clear this figure is likely less than half the actual number of children trafficked and excludes more liminal practices of trafficking such as forced labor. So, Thursday was the day that four candidate companies were to present their ad campaigns to us. It was a day for us to decide which companies would be the driving force behind selling the idea that child trafficking must stop.

We sat down at the table and took index cards upon which we were to rate each ad campaign.   Afterwards we were to discuss which agency would receive the campaign. Group number one came about half an hour late and they made a powerpoint presentation from a Macintosh.   The presentation was nervously undertaken and the man presenting read words from the computer screen as if it was his first time seeing the this project. The presentation itself was well thought out and glossy, words populating the screen in various hues and tones. The message was of community, of coalescing various realities of the current situation of child trafficking. The linguistic messages presented on-screen went something like this: *there is a problem*, it is *us* and *them*, it is *slavery*, and it *robs Haiti of its most valuable potential*. The message was complex in its plurality but univocal and unambiguous in its moral stance accompanied by a presentation of the *soupe joumou* campaign.   *Soupe joumou* is a pumpkin soup that is associated with the new year; yet before 1804, Haitian slaves were not allowed to consume this favorite dish. Upon the abolishment of slavery, Haitians could again eat *soupe joumou*. Despite a torturous presentation by the young man who seemed unstimulated and relatively monotone, the campaign was well-conceived. The message was simple: selling or giving your children into *restavèk* or other forms of trafficking is akin to denying yourself the right to eat the *soupe joumou*. I was still uninspired because I did not feel that this group had their hands on the pulse of Haitian society despite the fact that this company was Haitian-run.

The second and third groups arrived late as well and presented their campaigns which lacked any visual development. These candidates were more unsure of the viability of Soupe Joumou—after all, how to sell a concept when the metaphor is largely unknown to Haitians? We definitely needed Dan Draper here at this moment since both seemed completely viable concepts—education about a facet of Haitian tradition and forgotten history alongside a clear message that trafficking hurts Haiti. But the proposed campaigns were flat. I mentioned to one of the groups that it was not far-fetched to present one historically unknown fact in place of another more cliché representation. To exemplify my point, I used an American commercial from the 1970s wherein Benjamin Franklin was represented not for his diplomatic and political work, but for his inventions and relationship to electricity. Govinda jumped in an added to this saying that he remembered the commercial and the image of Franklin flying the kite during a thunderstorm. There was this definite sense that Govinda's instinct to use a professional media company to do the work of NGOs was right on target: after all if you can sell Nestlé and Maggi cubes, you must certainly be able to sell the end to human slavery and exploitation.

Overall, I was underwhelmed by all the presentations until the fourth person walked in on time. She was a middle-aged German woman who had made Haiti her home for the past thirty years and she started her presentation with a historical exegesis of Haiti—from slavery to the recent laws proposed in Parliament on child trafficking, paternity and the government's need to abide by its 1994 ratification of the CRC (Convention on the Rights of the Child) by implementing stronger national measures to protect children. This woman made clear connections between what was needed to sell Haitians on the end of trafficking and *restavèk* and how to effect political change in the process. She had the entire campaign outlined in accordance with bills facing the Senate in the coming months and each message was presented to encourage Haitians and the government to move forward: from signs which push for votes in Senate on the new adoption law recently passed in parliament to the impending ratification of the Hague Convention which would be signaled by billboards asking for government support, to thanking the government after its vote and pushing for further measures, to encouraging Haitians in the countryside to get involved in a caravan to encourage local leadership and vigilance against all forms of trafficking. This woman was fiery, knowledgeable and she deeply understood what was necessary to get all Haitians—to include the older generation of *restavèk* abusers—on board. She exclaimed, "We cannot go through with a campaign and tell Haitians they are all guilty and terrible for what they are doing. We need to give them a way out—to understand that this is the past and now we are moving into the future, a future free of trafficking and *restavèk*, a future where they too can construct and feel good about themselves for making that change." We had found our Don Draper and she was smoking at this game of "mad men."

After the conclusion of all four presentations, we discussed who we thought was best. Govinda and Myriam suggested using candidates one and four together—one to do the more formal advertising campaign on radio, television and visual media, and the other to conduct the more grassroots level media campaign with a spokesperson who would become the face of anti-trafficking measures in physical appearance around the country, giving public lectures and doing radio spots and to sponsor the local caravans of consciousness-raising. Another person from MINUSTAH and I were in favor of giving the entire campaign to this last group as their passion and experience seemed to win us over. The final vote was to hire both groups one and four. Myriam and I were elated that this campaign together with the research project would leave Haiti in an entirely different position vis a vis human rights by the fall.

The next day, Myriam's last day at UNICEF before leaving Haiti, she found that the management which had been harassing her for weeks, was continuing its work to destroy all that the twenty and thirty-something staff at UNICEF had been working on since the earthquake. I had witnessed the harassment, the denigrating behavior of the head of Child Protection who used condescending hand gestures to command her staff about the compound, whose comportment resembled that of a prison guard much more closely than that of the head of a Child Protection unit of the United Nations. Over the course of several months I witnessed Caroline Bakker bully and harass Myriam, I witnessed her obstruct information from several protection officers who were attempting to find missing children at the Haitian and Dominican border, and I was at times on the receiving end of this person's attempt for work on child protection to be completed. After Myriam had asked me to work on a research project authorizing my access to MINUSTAH and the tents in which to work, Bakker on several occasions attempted to stop all progress on this project. But Myriam suffered the brunt of what was nothing other than professional misconduct as just a two weeks before leaving Haiti, Bakker had told Myriam that she must stop all work in child protection and instead that she must devote the remaining time to administration, booking cars and organizing the hotel for New York's UNICEF representative who was due to arrive. Myriam's desire to have a child trafficking cluster workshop to focus on the output of this groups work over the past three weeks was also cancelled. Myriam was relegated to "gopher" and Caroline was more than happy that all of Myriam's work in child trafficking cease. Myriam's immediate supervisor, Henrik, who left the week before, told Myriam, "I know you are having fun working in child trafficking but we really must do other work." The sad irony of this statement was that Myriam *was hired to work specifically on the issue of child trafficking.* It was both a paradox and a grave frustration that she found herself being discouraged by her superiors from carrying out the work for which she was hired to undertake. Instead, she was told book appointments, cars, rooms and every task that was beyond her terms of reference. The hope, of course, was that Myriam would do the job of three or four people and have no time for the work on trafficking. Myriam did all the tasks demanded of her and was harassed precisely *for doing her job.*

The new head of Child Protection at UNICEF arrived this week and Myriam soon found out that this new head of Child Protection, Beth, and Caroline, two women of the approximately the same age, had organized a cabal as they proceeded to criticize Myriam on her last evening at Log Base. They met with Myriam last night and Caroline took out the weekly plan that she had made for Myriam last Friday and said, "So, you have not completed all the tasks I had asked you to do," and she went down the list of all the secretarial chores that she insisted Myriam do instead of her work on child trafficking. Indeed, Myriam had missed the minutes of the last meeting, and because of this she was forced to give a *mise à jour* (update) of every minute she passed the previous seven days. She had to justify every action that she undertook instead of booking a car when in fact she had done both, booking the car on moments stolen from meetings as I had observed on Thursday. This was harassment of the first order.

There was also the suspicious sabotage of the cluster meeting the week before where Myriam, Tearfund, Terre des Hommes and IOM had voted to have a steering committee on the Chick Trafficking cluster.   Shortly thereafter, Myriam received dozens of emails and phone calls from Henrik telling her not to do this. Paradoxically, she was hired to do exactly this and to ensure that the cluster's work would go as smoothly as possible while advancing ideas and putting them into action. Myriam was being given mandates not to do her job and was reprimanded during a good half hour last night by two woman, one of whom had pressured her over the past month to give her friends at Heartland Alliance a contract to control the cluster and the safe houses while also telling Myriam to stop all work on child trafficking. Additionally, Myriam was told by Beth, the incoming head, and Caroline this: "After you leave here, you can no longer do work on these issues." Shocked, Myriam replied, "But of course I am going to continue work on child trafficking—if UNICEF does not want to sponsor the research on trafficking or proceed with the campaign on trafficking, I will go elsewhere." Caroline said, "Myriam, you are headstrong, but you are not authorized to do this work outside of UNICEF." The message was clear as these women worried Myriam would get more done outside UNICEF than inside, that her work would evidence the gross incompetency of this structure that I had observed the previous months.

Myriam's work in the past few months in Haiti has resulted in the creation of: safe houses to secure trafficked children in the first weeks after their being found; a concerted effort between the UN, the BPM (Children's Protection Brigade) and the border patrol was coordinated; the identification of victims and legal support created through the BPM; the creation of family tracing and reunification and interim care; the passing of three important child protection measures in the Parliament and the consideration of the ratification of the Hague Convention; the creation of a media campaign against child trafficking and her inclusion in my work on the research of child trafficking between Haiti, the Dominican Republic and the United States; and the collaboration with Haitian judges and lawyers regarding the amelioration of the systems for prosecuting those involved with trafficking. Myriam was asked not to do this work in various direct and indirect manners—in writing and orally, through her being bombarded by menial tasks for which she was not mandated to undertake, through insult and intimidation, and through direct sabotage of her efforts to create efficacious communications amongst all groups in the child trafficking cluster.   Likewise, there was a clear alliance between Caroline, Henrik, and Heartland Alliance as there was a push for funds to be given to Heartland Alliance, an NGO with far less experience in child protection than any of the other cluster actors of Tearfund, IOM, and Terre des Hommes.   Myriam just found out mid-week that in fact before Heartland Alliance had proposed safe houses, UNICEF had already been working with a Haitian NGO which has had in place a system of safe houses. UNICEF's child protection head, Caroline Bakker, we discovered is friends of the aunt of one of Heartland Alliance's workers and Caroline has used every form of intimidation from outright censorship to castigation to humiliation to ensure that there are no democratic discussions and votes within the cluster. When Myriam reminded Caroline that she was hired to work on child trafficking stating that Caroline had only put secretarial work for her to do this week, Caroline responded, "Well, you know why we had to do that." Of course Myriam knew—she got results: she gained momentum and cooperation within the cluster, suggested a steering committee, and gained support from cluster members regarding necessary decisions. It was clear that these heads of UNICEF were not interested in reducing child trafficking in Haiti. But the real question is why?

This is the face of UNICEF where younger human rights experts under the age of forty are squeezed dry, working eighteen-hour days under people who are P5 (usually P5s are well into their forties, if not older). I fondly remember Myriam always saying, "I am only P3" on the days when she was stressed, repeating this chorus as if to emphasize the dehumanizing nature of her work under the oppressive force of the two P5s making her work difficult. With per diem and "hazard pay" many higher level UN staff member on consultation contractions such as the P5 are making $19,000 per month. The combined forces of fifty-something P5s working against younger P3s such as Myriam and her colleagues who complain of harassment are ignored by UN agencies such as UNICEF. The P5s receive their huge salaries, are invited to stay on and are rewarded for acting in collaboration with a huge monolith of those local and international mechanisms which abuse human rights, throwing sticks in the wheels of progress since the longer they stay on in Haiti, the longer they earn their huge salaries. Today Haitians are still find no work while organizations such as UNICEF and most every NGO exist for the purpose of furthering salaries. The recipe is simple: do as little as possible while giving the appearance of doing a lot and you will guarantee your tenure as P5. The lessons learned here are tragic and my stomach turned as I watched the sadism over the past months seeing Myriam contemplate never returning to the humanitarian sector. There is little that human rights workers at the UN can do to receive help in such treacherous working conditions.

I have collected stories of abuse from El Salvadoran and Jordanian UNPOL officers who told of those coming from poorer nations stationed in the most squalid of posts in Haiti while their colleagues from richer nations get the more posh assignments. A colleague in UNDP told me about being asked to sign checks for projects whose completion he had not seen. When he asked to visit the projects to verify their completion his superiors prohibited him from so doing and pushed him to sign the checks. Because of this pressure, he resigned within his first week of being in Haiti. Likewise, UNICEF emphasizes children's rights while ensuring that none of

these rights will be upheld through the installation of a class of incompetent managers who have little knowledge or experience in the fields of children's rights and trafficking. However, there were great pains taken to ensure that one of the UNICEF tents was equipped with two ceiling fans, each possessing the additional feature of ornate faux-Rococo styled lamps. This kitsch above my head distracted me as Myriam and I discussed the next steps for the research and trafficking campaign. I kept wondering why the priorities in lighting fixtures at UNICEF were visibly prioritized over employing a Haitian information manager or a logistics manager. Nothing made sense to me in this bizarre melding of corruption, incompetency, abusive management, and tacky decor. From *Mad Men* to "mad women" all in the course of 48 hours and UNICEFs final statement to Myriam was that child trafficking is simply not a priority.

Don Johnson

Have I mentioned that I live with Don Johnson? And I don't mean the Don Johnson with the white Italian sport coat, t-shirt, Ray-Bans and slip-on loafers. My Don Johnson is the son of "Don John" AKA Johny, brother of Frantz. Johny has three children: a daughter who lives in the province, Don Johnson who is ten years old, and Siara who is two. Each child has a different mother and Johny cares for each of his children raising them in his home: Don Johnson, Siara, and Don Johnson's older sister (who is not Johny's daughter), Stephanie who is 17 years of age. To describe the kinship ties in this family would be difficult because each time I return home, I find another person visiting their child or a child visiting a parent, ex-partners abound, and I am left astounded as to how peaceful this entire family is. In the United States, the reason why shows like *Divorce Court* thrive is both because they are incredibly trashy and violent and more importantly, because they represent the nastiness of divorce which is part and parcel of western culture. With the complexity of kinship creations in Haiti, I have yet to see a *Jerry Springer* moment in Haiti since everything seems to flow, despite the superficial complexity of personal relations.

Here relationships are formed relatively easily and then people either stay in these couplings, they move on to other lovers and sometimes have other children in these new relationships, or they stay in longterm relationships while engaging in secondary relationships. For all the talk of Christianity here, however, most of the younger families are created far from the narrative of marriage and the church. The underbelly of these social patterns reveals a remarkably high birth rate despite a particular couple's personal stability or ability to financially take care of one, much less several, children. The critiques amongst Haitians of those who have "too many" children after whom they are simply not able to care are numerous. Tap taps are abound in discussions of men who abandon women to run off to another woman who then have more children and of women who abandon their child and so forth. The recent Paternity Law will likely change this pattern as this law will force men to assume their role as parents and hopefully grant greater rights to these children to be raised within their families rather than abandoned as is the case with many whose mothers can no longer provide for them.

Johny, like many Haitian men, is the ideal father: he raises his children and the children of others, he works hard to pay the bills and is always ready to help others out on any project. Yesterday as I was waiting for my car, Johny came out to the curb to fix his motorcycle and announced that he would take me where I needed to go when his motorcycle was finished being repaired a few moments later. Johny and I spoke of events in the neighborhood and the family when I told him about little Sanson flirting with me a few nights prior. Johny states matter-of-factly, "Yes, he is a boy. I am a man." And certainly, Johny is very much that as he returns to say goodbye to Siara and Don Johnson before heading off to work.

On my way to the town center last Saturday I passed my neighborhood barber and had another Creole lesson with one of the apprentice barbers who sat down in a chair and wrote out vocabulary and grammatical structures for me. We spoke of the problems with MINUSTAH and the NGOs and all the barbers were rather shocked by my critiques simply because, as they told me, it is what most Haitians think and share amongst themselves, rarely with foreigners. Here in Port-au-Prince there is a palpable distrust of the rich UN worker who frequents restaurants that cost $30 US and upwards since they ostensibly are here to "help," or so the meta-narrative goes. And yet this distrust is not uniquely directed from the Haitian people—MINUSTAH staff from NGOs frequently attest to their presence being wholly unnecessary, they are cognizant that most people are here to "help themselves." In my research for this book I hear such admissions on a daily basis. So this double-edged sword of the foreign mission worker is troubling since everyone knows the dilemma yet nobody does anything about it because economically it is not in the individual's or organization's best interest. There are scandals brewing in most every NGO and UN agencies, yet there is no body of surveillance or system of checks and balances aside from one worker I met from RedR whose mission in Haiti was to investigate sexual abuses *by humanitarian workers*. There is no manner of deciphering where one mission is heading in the right direction, or another in a very wrong direction. In fact, I would just state flat out that the notions of "right" and "wrong" are completely absent here. The idea of a mission here is to continue despite the fact that most people find the mission they are on redundant, useless, and/or a waste of time.

So the barber wrote out my vocabulary and grammar list for the day and after our conversation added: *"Mwen ta renmen tande 'w"* ("I like listening to you") and he wanted to meet up again to talk. Many Haitians are aware their educational structure is lacking and thanks to the influence from their parents and grandparents the younger generation, void of much historical and philosophical contexts, have the narratological context of family stories and those of older generations to know that they need to know more. I have had many Haitians tell me, "I would like to be your student" to which I respond, "We are each other's student." Learning here is transparent and a great refresh to the stultified halls of western academia (*kaching!*) which leans upon self-aggrandizing structures of auto-referentiality. I must confess I am more comfortable learning on the tap tap than in the underground grotto of a Jean-Brillant building whose legacy means nothing to most of Montreal today. The halls of the tap tap are alive and underpinned by the toxicity of the NGO-ification of Haitian society, but it is through honest discussion of this toxicity that Haiti will emerge.

I move from the barber to the tailor to whom I must give my skirt to reduce as my waistline has shrunk enormously in recent weeks. I enjoy seeing this tailor and his assistants every week and I realize that my trips to cobblers, tailors, and barbers have been a constant source of calm throughout my life from New York to Bogotá to Delhi to Beirut to Bologna. There is a certain familiarity in maintaining contact with people whose presence you can count on as micro-moments to touch base, to realize another person's reality vis a vis a discussion about a zipper which turns into a dialogue about the recent election, or the work another shows you in the form of a long-sleeved, pin-striped deux-pièces which you kindly refuse because it is bright red and too hot for the Port-au-Prince heat. I practice my new Creole grammar and vocabulary on the guys and they teach me more about their language and culture. I fix my gaze on one of the largest trees in all of Petionville outside this tailor's shop and I think how I would like to stay there and learn how to properly design a pair of trousers and a winter jacket. But my obligations beckon my attention and I must head off to Café des Arts for meetings. I keep in the core of my thoughts this polemic of "development work" which in my third month as participant—and sometimes of participant observation—seems to be nothing other than a disaster. However, I maintain hope for this change as I compare notes with the only other unpaid volunteer I have met in Haiti, Rodrigo, who likewise feels the ups and downs of our collective energies.

I was at a party last Friday night, a birthday party of a MINUSTAH worker, and the party was frequented by those from NGOs, private firms and the usual UN crowd. The Minister of Culture attended as well and the dialogues were as diverse as the various levels of sobriety. I had just had what would be considered a disheartening day after hearing that UNICEF's Director of Child Protection had just told Myriam that child trafficking was no longer a priority of UNICEF. This struck me as both odd and deeply disturbing—odd because the number one human rights' issue in this country is child trafficking and the various forms that trafficking takes. Such a statement was even more deeply troubling simply because it takes an awful lot of chutzpah and/or corruption to utter these words openly with no demonstrable concern for repercussions.

Such audacity would indicate to me that this might very well be a policy being adopted by the world's premiere agency for child welfare and that UNICEF's new face of children's rights in Haiti is to do nothing. Hence, I arrived at the birthday party ready to drink nothing other than water since I am not one to "drown my sorrows." I remained quite alert as I collected stories from everyone at the party about their work in Haiti.

A UNPOL worker recounted how she does absolutely nothing all day long aside from making reports occasionally—reports based on previous mission reports, "All a waste of time," she announces.   "One day, a regional director came to the offices and our chief came in and said, 'Ok, you have to pretend to work now...just move around papers and type stuff!'" This UNPOL worker wants to leave her post and is finding it difficult to change missions given the political gravity of moving from one agency to another. Another worker in UNDP tells me that the UN ought to leave Haiti since it really does nothing for the country, adding: "Where are the jobs for Haitians?   We are called in and given lofty salaries to do really very little. We spend all day in meetings, or discussing the previous or next meeting and in the end, Haitians are still unemployed." The statistics do not speak well for the presence of MINUSTAH as the billions of dollars being spent here are producing foreign contracts and the list reads like a "Who's Who" from previous and current occupations if you consult our friends at the International Peace Operations Association.   If the business of mercenaries, capital, and neo-colonizing forces of the United Nations were not so tragic, it would actually be funny.

Perhaps this is why, during the entire party, I found it amusing as the only visibly non-drunk person, that an adjustor from Los Angeles kept calling me Maria the entire evening. I would correct him and he inevitably would try to remember my name, slipping back into calling me "Maria." But then it occurred to me while taking down people's stories, that Haiti was just another mission for these worker who came here to make money.   There was this idea, a subtext if you will, of "helping out" others and any risks— real or imagined—were rewarded with absurdly high salaries, contracts, and future promises of employment.   I even wondered if the heavy drinking I witnessed in Haiti might not be, at least in part, a result of this disconnect between doing the right thing and doing its antithesis.

I went back to see the UNPOL worker rather saddened by the state of the missions at MINUSTAH and I got a feeling that this person really did want to help out and not contribute to the scandalous non-action of this agency. Yet the only way to stop the flow of money from the UN to *everyone but Haitians* is to stop participating in the development circus. It was clear that MINUSTAH, initially slotted to leave Haiti in 2008, has only stayed on with the ostensible task of training the corrupt police force. The UNPOL officer asked my advice as to what she should. I responded, "Quit."

After several months here, I have seen one reason after another all which demonstrate why development work is an oxymoron. If anything, the work being done here is "underdevelopment work."   There could be no better formula for how to completely render helpless and dependent a nation:

implant 10,000 military and administrative personnel, spend over US $600 million per year on this infrastructure, double the annual budget of the Haitian government, and direct almost all the money towards feeding this "development" monster with its huge salaries whilst the Haitian people are still left jobless, penniless. People are eager to get their lives back and it is clear the answer will not come through any of the UN programs. The IDP Camps are a temporary solution and clearly long-term solutions are direly needed. Discussions in transport since the earthquake has focussed on education and how Papa Duvalier at least got that part right—"We were educated, you didn't see delinquency, you didn't see kids running around cleaning cars and begging for money," a MINUSTAH driver told me that day. "We need a real man as president and Préval is that man." Everyone shares their ideas about what is best for Haiti as those with jobs at the MINUSTAH are often on temporary contracts of three to six months. They realize that their time to join the masses on the streets is counted.

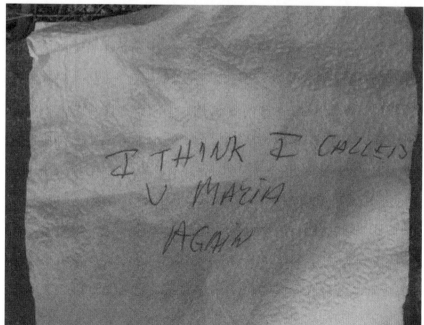

The adjustor came back to me towards the end of the night and asked me questions about my work in Kenscoff in the coming days. I return to my discussion with the person from UNPOL and am interrupted just moments later as the drunk adjustor from Los Angeles returns to hand me a paper napkin upon which he has scrawled a message. I read it and laughed realizing that this indiscriminate mixture of alcohol, sadness, stories of contracts and "development work in Haiti" made even less sense.

There is something entirely poetic about this cross-over of identity between Don Johnson, the harsh, gritty reality of Port-au-Prince, and the nonsensical nature of how alcohol will simply render surreal the manner in which we forget someone's name. These are moments of slippage, of remembering, of inventing, and then of forgetting again. And from this selfhood emerges filling in the fissures. The twelve-year old Don Johnson resembles nothing of the sleek, adult *Miami Vice* reference and my presence as Maria at this incredibly opulent party could have been the scene for any organized crime family or corrupt collection for whom the good and bad forces are difficult to discern. The powers of "good" and "evil" are recast through the pseudo-legitimizing forces of MINUSTAH and the United Nations for whom one type of evil is replaced by another as millions of dollars are paid each month in foreign salaries alone. The irony, of course, is that Haitians are the recipients of aid in donor reports

and in newspaper articles, while in reality the money goes to the foreign mission workers, not to Haitians. What is missing from this scene is the spirit of *Miami Vice*'s focus on its own legitimacy as this television show actually narrates various stories of police corruption as Sonny Crockett would occasionally go undercover as drug dealer, Sonny Burnett, to reveal the his very own police department's malfeasance along with other criminal entanglements. There is a sense in *Miami Vice*, albeit fictive, that there is a spirit of collaboration and transparency that is long absent from this theater of MINUSTAH and its associated agencies.

Burn Out

I thought of writing a stream of clichés from that which insinuates the lining of the silver cloud to knowledge as being power. Perhaps these are truisms and modalities for the atheist to explain one's existence outside the discourse of a godlike figure or for the erudite to dispel the existential crisis of the everyday. Regardless, I wanted to run a series of clichés together simply because I haven't the strength to describe the weight of what I have learned this past week. I am exhausted, shocked, despondent, but mostly I am conflicted.

I remember the first time I was explained slavery and the Holocaust. It was inconceivable to my young, innocent mind that humans could own other humans and that humans could plan and execute mass murder. I still do not understand these historical acts aside from their theoretical considerations, similar to photosynthesis. I know what both processes are about, but I cannot familiarize myself with either to the point of truly understanding as in, "I can relate to them as ." I truthfully cannot relate to either as the constructs of chemical connections and triggers might be memorizable and regurgitable for a chemistry exam as my undergraduate studies demonstrated; however, I cannot truly relate to these mechanisms any more than I can understand the desire to conquer, pillage or wipe out humans for the sake of racial purity or separation. These actions will simply remain incomprehensible to me as will other similar acts of depravity.

In North America, when we are taught about wars we are handed data to memorize: generals and presidents, treaties and dates, bombardments and lines of defense. We are taught that there are people with power and people without and thus when wars are undertaken it is usually the people in power ordering about poorer others (whom we wrongly believe to be entirely powerless) to suit up for the cause and to brave the winds of death. While there is resistance to the commands of insanity, these moments of resistance are rare. Many humans across the planet do not question the calls to violence in formalized acts of war. The masses enact mass murder either through uniformed practices of armed conflict against others or those who "stay home" participate in the economic backing that funds the carnage. Through armed conflict or through working and paying taxes, citizens inevitably contribute towards various acts of murder which our media carefully filters into justified deaths or murder. We are fed the language of "our heros," we are told of the "insane" enemy who is jealous of our freedoms, and "they" come inevitably to represent a terrorist other.

Acts of violence are coded through language—armed aggression, insurgence, terrorism, and war—which occludes an aporia for discussing violence and our collective and individual implications therein.

In the west, we have created institutions which ostensibly establish bodies for overseeing crises, economic functions, and peacetime politics. The United Nations is one such organization which purportedly operates as a "world body," while paradoxically the majority of the decision making power rests in the hands of the five security council member states. There is little ambiguity about the disproportionate distribution of power in the United Nations and the enormous veto powers given to these five member countries, especially in votes related to anything that would suggest that the state of Israel denies Palestinians their human rights, much last exercises a de facto Apartheid state.

I did not come to Haiti thinking that I would learn anything new about the United Nations, but in truth I have learned quite a bit about this institution, much of which was positive.   This organization hires the brightest and best and I have rarely met any one person in its employ who is not incredibly gifted in various modalities—linguistically, theoretically and analytically. The people I have met here in Haiti are without a doubt some of the smartest and these individuals certainly made me rethink my relationship to academia.   Every person I have encountered and worked with has been astute in her critique of the MINUSTAH underscoring that this organization is in quite a difficult position since it must function in support of the government of Haiti, even at the risk of being unable to unveil every instance of corruption.   From those who work with IDP camps, many are realizing that the immediate crisis is over and long-term plans need to be taken up, money for no longer needed projects needs to be returned, and future residences need to be seriously thought out and developed.   For those in human rights, the situation is trickier as many wonder why certain human rights issues are still unpronounced by the government or reflected in law. Some even wonder if the United Nations has remained silent for too long about certain human rights issues, suggesting that its position of support for and collaboration with the Haitian government detrimental to human rights. Child trafficking remains one such issue for many human rights workers and there are many who have left their missions disgusted and others who have sought out other NGOs and financial backers to continue the work which they perceive as hindered by the United Nations and UNICEF. Others still are distraught over the similarities of what they have seen in Haiti, Sri Lanka and Liberia.

I have been working inside this system and likewise as an agent between various ministries, as undercover investigating orphanages and as a researcher looking at the entire spectrum of child trafficking from the situation of orphans, child abandonment, *restavèk*, and both national and international adoption.   I have seen the fissures in these systems, I witnessed grave acts of dishonesty, and I was quick to perceive where corruption lay because it is simply not that difficult to spot.   Within my first week in Haiti I was able to put my finger on one of the most important actors in child trafficking who herself remains in a rather high position in the government, Madame Jeanne Bernard Pierre, the head of Haiti's Social Services. Apparently, after my suspecting Madame Pierre of illicit dealings after my infamous meeting with her, I was to learn from that this is the open secret in child protection in Haiti.   The UN does not want to make a statement, nor does UNICEF, nor do the Canadian, United States or French ambassadors who have been briefed on this woman. These agencies do not want to alienate the government in Haiti and so a major child trafficker remains in the Haitian government and there is nothing anyone can or will do.

None of this, however, prepared me for what I would learn from a series of NGO and UN workers which would implicate the United Nations as having knowledge of war crimes and doing nothing to stop these crimes in the final year of the conflict in Sri Lanka.   It has been a hard two weeks, hence my writing has diminished.   I have been given information that has essentially pointed to the United Nations High Commission for Refugees in Sri Lanka as having refused to speak out against the forced starvation, displacement, illegal shelling of schools and hospitals, and the murder of many Sri Lankans. Most UN workers are citing 20,000 deaths in the final months.   The United Nations had the obligation to speak out and from all that I have been told, the United Nations made a tactical move not to risk its position in the country, for fear of being kicked out, and it remained silent in the face of human rights abuses. How familiar this was to me after the months of attempting to have Madame Pierre's participation in child trafficking made public.

I have spent many days collecting testimonies from these UN and other NGO workers in order to publish an account of these actions.   It has been most difficult and I can only say that I am still unable to process it all. Then suddenly I was forced to leave Haiti after having my life threatened by the Russian mafia in Port-au-Prince which is quite active in the business of child trafficking.   In response to this threat I went to the safe harbor of friends in Santo Domingo. My friend, Nancy, defends Trujillo to me last night, "He was not perfect, but we had a central government, a strong economy and people had jobs! There is no government in the world where murder does not form part of their political power. Where you have rich, you have poor; where you have life you have death." I am thinking of the greater good these days and wondering if the United Nation's silence in Sri Lanka or in Haiti are acts that can be considered diplomacy or merely cowardly.

In the mean time, I remain unable to comprehend these tangled politics of development which would have us all believe that silence is a means of mediation and where the lifeless bodies left over from massacre could be worth the price of saying nothing. In the end I am left to ask myself if the political presence of the United Nations is so important that this body must rest in every geographical conflict to the detriment of the human rights for those it ostensibly protects? There is this constant maneuvering of the United Nations that I witness here which rests in a dance of indecision: to speak up or to support the government. These are not complimentary acts but they can be engaged in concert. To speak out about corruption and mismanagement of resources is not necessarily in antagonism to governmental support. In my months in Haiti, I have seen one agency after another continue to do nothing in the face of human rights, while children's lives in Haiti remain in peril. The United Nations represents the final word regarding human rights in this country and yet this organization is doing little to effect change, policy or law. I have learned that this agency is more invested in continuing its presence in the country and as such it must behave in a manner which will not have it "disinvited" from the scene. Hence the treatments of child protection officers like Myriam who are discouraged from actually carrying out their mandate and who are disciplined for carrying out their profession and actually establishing safe spaces for Haitian children or who instigate much needed studies which search for the links between international adoption and child trafficking.

I am burned out and numbed by all that I have learned recently. I will return with a report on this and other matters when my brain cells heal.

Biogas and Self Sustainability

As someone who has witnessed the results of "development work" since the late 1980's, I am quite disturbed by what are nostalgically called "development projects." Within this phrase is the presumption that everyone is on board with a monolithic notion of "development" that replicates the colonial modus operandi of "discovery" and "civilizing" that was at the heart of nineteenth and twentieth century domination of non-western spaces. The results of such colonial expansions were not pretty as the good people of Gaza and the West Bank can attest as can the disenfranchised miners of Oruro and Potosí. The Christian good will of spreading the word ended with an exchange of land for Bibles as the lovely Desmond Tutu describes: "When the missionaries came to Africa they had the Bible and we had the land. They said 'Let us pray.' We closed our eyes. When we opened them we had the Bible and they had the land."

The humanitarianism of neo-liberal religious policies grew into social and political policies throughout the twentieth century from the involvement of women in the early twentieth century during the war effort in Europe as volunteer nurses to the creation of goodwill missions such as the Peace Corps and Médecins Sans Frontiers in the post-war era. Good will was no longer a domain of the religiously inclined and has become over the past sixty years part of a political pragmatism which lends a hand to the economic facets of neoliberalism. In the 1950s, the Communist "scare" in the United States was a political weapon both domestically and internationally. As such this "scare" brought about increased foreign interest—primarily US—in the region of Central America and the Caribbean in which brutal dictatorships were propped up and given support while popular movements were entirely discouraged if not put asunder through massacre. The United Fruit Company (UFCO) was an American business formed in 1899 which traded tropical fruit grown on plantations in this region and then sold in North America and Europe. The company was formed as a result of a merger between Minor C. Keith's banana trade and Andrew W. Preston's Boston Fruit Company. UFCO flourished in the early and mid-20th century and quickly gained control of vast territories and transportation networks in Central America, the Caribbean coast of Colombia, Ecuador, and the Caribbean island nations. Competing with the Standard Fruit Company, the United Fruit Company had a virtual monopoly in certain regions, some of which came to be called, thanks to the literacy craftsmanship of O. Henry, "Banana Republics." Aside from the fruit trade, the United Fruit Company also created a radio station

(Tropical Radio) and Telegraph Company which earned them even more visibility and dominance in both the banana trade and the means for attaining information about local and national politics. The UFCO ensured market dominance by controlling land distribution to the peasants, and agrarian reform which was supported by the people and by many governments soon fell into abuse as the UFCO would claim that damage to the land from storms and disease would mean that land would be kept from government hands to redistribute to the people. The long term effects of such abuses are felt today in countries like Nicaragua, Guatemala, Honduras and Haiti where land rights tend to be the one factor dominating discussions for those working on the issues of ecology, housing and agriculture.

In 1954, the democratically elected Guatemalan government of Colonel Jacobo Arbenz Guzmán was ousted from power in no small thanks to US-backed forces lead by Colonel Carlos Castillo Armas, invading from Honduras. This military opposition was armed, trained and organized by the U.S. Central Intelligence Agency (Operation PBSUCCESS) and ordered by the Eisenhower administration. The directors of United Fruit Company (UFCO) had lobbied the US government to convince the Truman and Eisenhower administrations that Colonel Arbenz would align Guatemala with the Soviet Bloc. More disappointing for UFCO was that the Arbenz government was working steadily on agrarian reform legislation and a new labor code which was to give workers better working conditions, higher salaries and more rights. The Arbenz government's land reform proposed to expropriate approximately 40% of UFCO land yet there were already existing conflicts of interest between private corporations and the US government: American Secretary of State John Foster Dulles's law firm Sullivan and Cromwell had represented United Fruit, Allen Dulles, his brother, was a board member of United Fruit and the director of the CIA, Eisenhower's personal secretary was married to former UFCO president. It was clear in what direction US corporate and political interests lie. There were political ties between the United Fruit Company, the US government and various foreign governments in their struggle to maintain market sector interests, from Trujillo through contemporary issues of workers' rights in El Salvador. In 1970 United Fruit become the United Brands Company which later became Chiquita Brands International.

The moral of this story is that neoliberalism is a policy that is "market driven," an approach to economic and social policy based on neoclassical theories of economics that maximize the role of the private sector in order to control the political and economic priorities of the state. The use of the term "neoliberalism" also implies a shift of responsibility from governments and corporations onto individuals. This thinking since the 1950s has gradually been extended to a kind of market logic which is reflected in social and affective relationships. In the 1970s many Latin American economists began using *neoliberalismo* to designate programs for market-oriented reforms. By the 1990s, the term "neoliberalism" had become a pejorative term to pigeonhole liberal thinkers, who dismissed it as a catchphrase coined by radicals to denigrate the ideas of neoliberal economic architects, Milton Friedman and Friedrich von Hayek.

This mini-history here on the marriage between private market interests and government involvement in national economies and political processes is not meant to bore, but is intended to illustrate some of the numerous examples of how recent models of development have functioned—usually the development of transnational businesses and not the local economies or structures. Hence you might begin to understand, for those readers who have not ventured out of your countries to places such as Haiti, the utter theatre of development. Everything is rhetoric and real change and action are virtually invisible. Long-term sustainability for any enterprise remains a keyword for those development or humanitarian teams which utter phrases such as "the five Ps" (ie. prevention, protection, press, policing and prosecution) but for whom any realization or continuance of projects remains in the hands of those much higher and more powerful.

I attend various cluster meetings at the MINUSTAH and have noticed how these spaces become arenas for presenting projects from the private sector in need of funding—from various ecological stoves to solar panels to groups who promise to patrol a border that even Haiti's national police force is incapable of patrolling. Many—not all—of those in attendance are in search of hefty contracts such as the million dollar contract recently given by UNICEF to Heartland Alliance despite the fact that Heartland Alliance does not possess the experience in border patrol and trafficking as do a handful of other NGOs specialized in this field currently in Haiti. Hunting season is open and the bastard cousins of Halliburton and Bechtel arrive in Haiti salivating over the news that UN money is up for grabs. This entire business of development must be put into question from both larger institutional levels to cultural and ethical dimensions. We need to ask simply this: what is development and who decides what needs to be developed? After all development is relative as I come from a culture which drugs its children for "hyperactivity" and which throws people into prison for problems or possession of "illegal drugs." The contradictions are almost funny (if they were not so tragic) and the level of depravity shocking as governments base their economies upon the inequality of salaries coupled with cheap overseas factories whose conditions would be illegal were these factories to exist in Trenton, NJ. Western notions of development tend toward a colonial model of ex-appropriation and market reform that dismisses local capacity, culture and know-how.

Anyone who live here in Haiti knows the scene of "cash for work" schemes where fourteen people watch two or three people work. It is easy to say, "Haitians don't like to work" as I heard from a UNPOL (United Nations Police) officer from Nepal yesterday. But why would anyone feel motivated to do a job that they will hold for a maximum of 21 days? I have held really horrid jobs in my life when younger, but while wearing that brown polyester uniform I always thought about my future and hoped—with a reasonable amount of empirical proof to back up my hopes—despite all my work of filling a salad bar and chopping iceberg lettuce in a shredder which extruded perfectly-shaped one-inch-square pieces of lettuce, that I would not forever be working at that salad bar. Conditions of life and work inflect one another in the west and the "food for work" and "cash for work" programs have resulted in a literal and psychological dependency of many Haitians towards foreign bodies. In short, Haitians hold little hope for bettering their current or future realities.

Since beginning work on ecological projects and education and entering into the world of permaculture, I have been focussing communities on non-dependency, on becoming viable and self-sustaining without the injection of foreign capital. I am putting many agronomists into contact with NGOs which do not give out monies but instead which offer tools, seeds and seedlings.[12] Likewise I am working to keep grassroots communications and collaborations open while also encouraging individual and group enterprises which will allow Haitians to engage in jobs that they create and that they want. While the banana republic model of the early and mid-twentieth century seems far away and morally untenable, in reality such models flourish in the desire to "help" and model the other in the image of "us." What many call "development" is refused by most Haitians as they see through the multi-national head-hunting schemes that put at the helm wealthy, foreign subjects who have too little knowledge about the country and its people. "Why bring in foreign engineers when we have our own?" one Haitian tells me. Haitians in the MINUSTAH drive cars, clean bathrooms and repair motorcycles—few are to be seen heading any cluster or agency meetings. Hence, my collaboration in Haiti is inspired somewhat by those NGOs whose work tends towards business models of self-empowerment such as Tearfund or grassroots structures that attempt to build on local needs and participation such as AMURT, Trees for the Future and Seeds for Haiti. I cannot comment on each and every project of these organizations, but what I have noticed in working with some of these agencies is that these NGOs tend to work better than most others because labor tends to be sustained, self-determined and constructive. Moreover, in a city such as Port-au-Prince where ecological disaster renders life extremely precarious, ecologically conscious projects are a must.

Hence, for many months I have been trying to get involved in Viva Rio's project on biogas in the Bel Air section of Port-au-Prince. Finally, I had time yesterday to visit the project in what would be the beginning of my collaboration with this project. Ollrich greeted me and showed me around Viva Rio's project beginning with the lovely nursery which houses 30,000 seedlings with future plans to create another million in coming years.

The farmers were welcoming and generously showed me around their nursery as we discussed methods of creating revenue from reproducing plant life through relatively easy methods (ie. cuttings and seed collection) and how sales might in part sustain reforestation and agriculture. After all, how can Haitian rice compete with the very low price of US rice which has flooded their market? How can people invest in reforestation when land issues are one of Haiti's top problems as land often belongs to two different people since inheritance law demands that land be divided amongst all offspring for generations on end. Thus land titles remain

---

[12] To specify, donated seeds that are neither hybrid or GMO as in the recent case of Monsanto. Check back soon for my recent statement on what I termed the "anti-Christ of agriculture" and my impending meeting with the Minister of Agriculture on Monday.

caught up in legal battles.

Then the agronomists brought me to one of their colleagues who was having a nap and asked me to snap a shot of him. I did and they all giggled.

Ollrich took me from the nursery to Viva Rio's amazing biogas facility, a engineering project that is in use around the world with are more than 200 biodigesters in Brazil alone with many in Nicaragua and Spain.

Viv Rio brought in specialists who created a collection and treatment center called a biodigester. The system transforms human waste into methane gas. This "biodigester" is a pilot project in this poor neighborhood in Port-au-Prince which is making methane gas for electricity and cooking, using human waste from public toilets. The project provides an alternative to wood charcoal and can help the country overcome its massive environmental problems linked to deforestation (currently only 2% of Haiti's forests remain). Providing public toilets for an inferior price to the current model of chemical toilets which cost more works to offer a service for about a penny while creating green energy. Aside from the biodigester already in place in Bel Air, there is another in the IDP camp, Kay Nou, where this project flourishes since the earthquake of 12 January, 2010. Engineers with Viva Rio, the Brazilian NGO that runs the project, built this large underground reaction tank called a biodigester. Inside it are bacteria that are transforming human waste into methane gas a biofuel that can be used as a powerful, and virtually free, source of energy. Valmir Fachini, Viva Rio Project Coordinator, describes the biogas project to me. First he brings me to the biogas tanks which are almost completed construction, built of cement and set into the ground.

This photo above is from an ongoing construction of the tank where the feces will be stored and below shows the hole upon which a toilet will be installed. Everything from this container goes to a reaction tank.

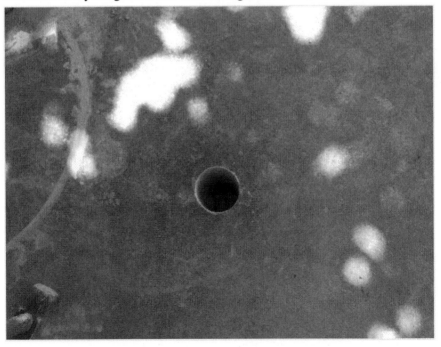

The reaction tank starts the fermentation process which produces the biogas that is stored in these cement tanks above. Biogas has various uses such as can be seen below with the cooker in Viva Rio's pilot kitchen.

Valmir Fachini then describes the production of biogas: "The first process is hydrolysis. The second process is a combination of acidogenesis and acetogenesis. Following this is methanogenesis which involves taking microbes (anaerobic bacteria) and producing a methane known as methanogens. The scission and the production of biogas starts, but because the biogas is lighter than air it rises to the top of the system in the biodigester and can be taken out right away to be used."

The gas crosses a column of water, and comes to rest at the top of the tank. This biogas can be used for cooking, heating and electricity among many other uses. The fermentation inside the biodigester also enriches the roots of the surrounding foliage, which act as a filter for liquid waste.

The reactor at Viva Rio has a capacity to produce fifty cubic meters of biogas per day. This will generate 3000 watts of electricity per twenty four hours. Biogas is cheap and easy to produce. If the project is replicated, it could give Haitians permanent green alternatives to charcoal fuel. This would combat deforestation, the underlying cause of the country's massive environmental problems, and deal with the issues of the transport of waste. The filtered water coming out of the biodigester is also rich in nutrients and can support many forms of plant and animal life.   There are hydroponic gardens surrounding the biodigesters to include an elevated garden which holds hundreds of plants and fruit trees. The water also provides for various levels of habitat survival: ducks feed on insect larvae

and fish prosper here.   With proper care this pond will become a
fishery, creating food and jobs in the neighborhood. In these tanks, the
water becomes rich with nutrients. The sunlight permits the production of

algae which are the primary food source for the fish. Additionally this excess water can be used to water plants in outlying gardens which supplements the soil with nitrogen and phosphorus.

To recap, the biodigesters' anaerobic microorganisms include acetic acid-forming bacteria (acetogens) and methane-forming archaea (methanogens). These microorganisms digest carbon through the process of breaking down organic matter as carbon is absorbed through the bacteria's cell membrane where it combines with oxygen and is released as CO_2. The biodigester's enzymes break down the complex carbon bonds making these materials easier to digest for the bacteria. This first stage is hydrolysis which break down of organics leads to the creation of simple sugars, amino acids and fatty acids.   The next stage is acidogenesis which breaks down the fermantative bacteria. The anaerobic digestion is the acetogenesis where molecules created in acidogenesis are further digested to produce acetic acid and carbon dioxide and hydrogen.   The last stage is methanogenesis whereby methanogens use the products of all three previous stages and use them to convert into methane, carbon dioxide and water.

A chemical equation for this process looks something like this:

$$C_6H_{12}O_6 \rightarrow 3CO_2 + 3CH_4$$

Viva Rio is running the one pilot project in Port-au-Prince which is helping an underserved neighborhood to produce green energy and improve sanitation while providing employment for many Haitians.

And just as a motorcycle showed up to bring me across town, another NGO representative arrived with an ethanol stove which costs $50 to be produced but which can be sold for $2 with the ethanol pro-rated within the production costs. This way the ecological stove could be sold to Haitians at an affordable price with the ethanol costing less than their current sources of natural gas and charcoal from fallen tress. The gas stove representative lit the stove and I was off.

A Day in the Life

I have been in Haiti for several months and I simply cannot imagine leaving. As I write these words I am being bitten by mosquitos, I smell terribly and have smelled this way since about seven o'clock this morning. I am also getting a whiff of that not so sweet smell of the nightly trash incineration nearby. There are objectively many reasons not to love Haiti but there are surely more reasons, which I cannot even explain to myself, why I remain.

In my meeting with the director of Fonkoze, a micro-finance company, Carine Roenen told me, "I think people stay here because we all have hope ultimately." I have suspected this regarding my own motives but could not put this into words. Her story resonates with me as I reflect upon the incredibly rich experiences I have each and every day in Haiti. Yet, here I sit writing at 19h30 after a day of meetings with the Early Recovery Cluster which is taking most seriously the task of creating employment for Haitians. After which I met with someone from MINUSTAH regarding the child trafficking sub-cluster and my work in the field which I execute every day between child trafficking and permaculture projects spread across four different parts of the city, followed by a a meeting with a Haitian agronomist from an American NGO, Trees for the Future, where we discussed the problems of hybrid seeds, the economic sustainability of reforestation projects in Haiti, and how the ecological disaster is feeding the problems of rainfall and erosion. It would perhaps be boring, tedious for me to run through my days, but they are peppered with surreal moments such that a cluster meeting, even if boring, is bookended by events that would not be believable. I even laugh at some of the odd moments because they are such in stark contrast to my life in Montreal with the exception of the eventful last few months. What is shocking to me is that no matter how hard things can be here, other things are terribly simple.

Just a few days ago, I was in need of a telephone in Santo Domingo and I grew nostalgic for the red vested young Haitian men of Digicel who roam the streets with their portable phones. At that moment I realized how development functions for this sort of commodity is untenable in New York as well—there is no communal phone which you pay five gourdes for a minute or two, there is only the individual telephone, selfishly possessed and rarely shared. In fact, many events in Haiti make me realize that the valences of underdevelopment are tones painted by the brush of a discrete authoritarianism: we are wealthy and hence "developed." The rest is simply other.

While coming to the MINUSTAH today I had a flash of an image for a development project I would like to perform back home. After all, we in wealthier nations need "development" as well. How I would love to see a development project that would rid the Christian Right from US politics! Would it not be great to see the Haitian, Iranian and Norwegian NGOs distributing t-shirts that attempt to develop the souls of these American religious zealots through cheap slogans? The ever so cliché t-shirts such as "FBI: Federal Body Inspector" or more lascivious ones such as "Honk if you're horny!" How to begin to develop the wholly *verklempt* and morally equivocated.

So, while I do not have the ability to order photos of such length on my iPhone from where I am writing 80% of these articles, I have decided to share what are pieces—even brief fragments—of my last few days in Haiti through the chance happenings and people I encountered in my daily life in and around Port-au-Prince.

Here is my lovely family's courtyard with the aunt cleaning dishes with a neighboring child helping her out. I sat here for several minutes before heading out to the street to wait for the car from the MINUSTAH. The aunt of this family is single and has never been married. She is devoted to helping out her family, Frantz, Johny and Poussin and their families. She also goes to church every single day and often she will stay and sleep over at her church for the entire night. She is always asking me to come with her to the church to spend the night. I hope to have one day free when I am not working 18 hour days.

I climbed up to the road to wait for the MINUSTAH car only to find Johny repairing his motorcycle. As I was observing Johny, a woman passed by me and suddenly stopped. She spun around, looked at me and said, "Take a picture of me!" I looked at her in disbelief since I generally do not take pictures of people like this, nor am I accustomed to people asking me for pictures. She insisted so much despite the fact I had no desire to take a picture, I pulled out my iPhone and obliged here. Here is her photo.

I wondered why she was so insistent that I take her picture given she hadn't gone to the effort to pose and smile as had Farah in her modelesque pose as if for a Milano 2010 fashion week spread. In fact, this woman above looked absolutely matter-of-fact about her life, her situation. There she was in her butterfly button up shirt, a knee-length skirt and plastic sandals that she had stretched to the limits of their life. It felt as if I had returned to the poem entitled "Theatre," as this woman wanted me to chronicle her life, her presence right then, before me as if to say that she was alive and I was a witness to this fact.

I spoke with this woman for several minutes to learn of her *goudou goudou* story and her tale of survival. Then she announced that she had to get back home to help prepare food for the day. And just as I was putting my telephone in my bag one of many Port-au-Prince's vitamin salesmen walked by. In all the months I have been in Haiti, I never really had the time to take many pictures of individuals. The vitamin salesman was one of the top professions I had wanted to photograph along with the construction worker and plumber who typically carry two or three tools in their hands on their way to a job. So, having my camera already out I stopped this gentleman and asked for his photo.

On the way to the Ministry of Education we came across a curious, if not altogether inventive, form of hitchhiking. These forms of travel are commonplace in most countries around the world; yet those who come

from western nations might be alarmed at such precarious travel methods. One day on the way to the Ministry of Education while stuck in a *blocus,* the driver of my car, Lucien, showed me photos of his fractured house indicating the two inch dent in his head, proud of his luck for having survived. He recounts, "The *goudou goudou* started and I shouted at my family to get out—my children got out first, then my wife and I ran out together. Just as we had passed the threshold of our front door, the entire house collapsed and I was only injured a bit." He points to his head. Later in the conversation he proudly presented me his national identity card.

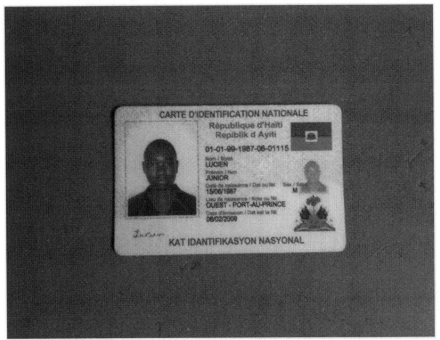

After procuring hundreds of literacy books for children at a nearby camp where I was doing permaculture work, I went to MINUSTAH to see a doctor for what I announced to the doctor as "stage two lung cancer." The young doctor from the Philippines rightfully laughed at me. My hyperbolic excess was due to my recent experimentation with smoking. When I arrived in Haiti I was virulently anti-smoking; yet in recent weeks I began to understand why so many foreign workers smoke. There is a sense of community in crises which often leave you feeling hopeless and isolated.

On my way to the UN clinic, I came across the Bangladeshi armed forces. I so loved their uniforms of purple and blue that I asked to take a photo of them. The officer in charge on the left, Akthar, agreed. I told her that her name meant "more" in Arabic and we discussed life in South Asia. I went to the doctor a few minutes later to find out that I did not have bronchitis, but the kind doctor did say that if I was to pick up smoking I ought to smoke much more than just a few cigarettes for a week.

On my way back home from Log Base, I realized I had left my telephone

in the offices of IOM and was told that my vehicle would be leaving in five minutes. I could not possibly go from dispatch to IOM and back in five minutes, nor did I wish to wait for what would be at least another hour if not two to get home. So I ran into the main road in the UN compound and found a truck of Pakistani soldiers who generously brought me to IOM and back in time for my ride home. I jumped in the back of the truck as we proceeded across Log Base and the soldier sitting in front of me wanted my photo so I acquiesced and he returned the service. During our trip across the Log Base and back we shared family stories of the 1947 partition of India and Pakistan as my family is Gujarati from India and his is Gujarati from Pakistan.

And here is my a tap tap driver to Kenscoff who, after being stopped by the police running verifications of drivers' license, had to leave all of us passengers at the side of the road, his truck parked, while he literally ran home to find his papers least he pay a huge fine and have his truck taken away. Forty minutes later he showed up sweating and smiling flashing his document for me to see. I love the way people here remain proud of their identity be it their driver's license, their citizenship card, and photos of their house, albeit demolished. On the one hand Haitians have every reason not to have hope, not to trust, and yet they surprise me over and over, such as this gentleman who sprinted home to find a document he rarely needed to carry with him only to proudly display it to me.

On my way to Kenscoff, I admired the tap tap's side mirror décor. And I thoroughly was entranced by the 1970's blue tinted treatment to the glass at the top on the windshield.

Datura stramonium, my friend Guy informs me, is a hallucinogen. I love its trumpet-like form and quietude amidst its neighbors. And I continued

snapping more of these amazing flowers in Guy's garden. It was a misty morning in Kenscoff and flowers of every form were in in abundance.

On a visit to a nursery outside Kenscoff, I study the terrain, seedlings and the grounds which house a former school's ruins, the newer structures of the school and reforestation project to include two different nursery sites. I went to assist these young farmers with their nursery as their needs for seed

propagation were beyond their capacity. I worked with them for several months on a seed-saving and seedling project which incorporated many of the principles of permaculture given that there was little good use of the leaves and humanure in the area. I worked with these farmers to establish composting and humanure toilets despite the fact that an NGO had recently spent tens of thousands of dollars on a new toilet facility which made no attempt to take into consideration the need for ecological methods. With many of the farmers, we ran workshops in this area to educate people about the importance of recycling, composting, avoiding the use of plastics and the dangers of burning garbage, a common practice in Haiti.

Here is part of the school which was badly damaged from the earthquake just thirty meters from the nursery due to the fact that the foundation which was set, as many buildings are in this region, on land that is prone to erosion due to the lack of plants to protect the earth. The foundation fell down the hill and the building followed. These bricks were constructed in

the more traditional method of rammed earth. Today many builders wish to return to his practice as these structures built on firm foundations are some of the most stable in the region. What has caused the greatest trouble in Haiti has been the use of cement in buildings, mostly due to the quality of the materials used, but also the lack of awareness in taking into account topographical and ecological changes for which rammed earth and other traditional building methods are better suited.

On my way back to Kenscoff I find a peach, jelly and liquor salesperson.

And another kilometer down the road is a tree whose roots are exposed.

A new friend whose body was covered with flies, unhappy with his two-meter-long roped freedom.

I recently returned from the Dominican Republic whose border with

Haiti reveals the stark differences of rich and poor separated by an imaginary line and very real political practices. The hundreds of meters of corrugated aluminum roofs reveal a poverty rarely discussed in the Dominican Republic. This is the often flooded marketplace at the border with Jimaní where children are commonly trafficked. After this area the Dominican Republic immediately changes in landscape and beauty: there is more green, more flowers and people are living in poverty, but not in misery. There is a notable difference.

I had a migraine for almost four days in Santo Domingo—in part due to the stress of the work which I was doing, in large part due to the Russian mafia threat which followed me to Santo Domingo. I was with my friend, Claude, and he was driving me back to my friend's home and a motorcycle came up to us and waved us over. We thought something was wrong with the car. The gentleman dismounted his motorcycle, walked up to our car and said, "I think you should know that someone has been following you." He described the vehicle and it had apparently turned off the road. I was not surprised, but a bit rattled by the dangerous implications of the work I had been undertaking.

The next day I had the most surreal experience as I awoke with yet another migraine. Outside of Nancy's house was parked this bright pink Kotex car and the pinkly dressed Kotex pushers giving away free samples to all in the neighborhood. "How many women are in your home?" the twenty-something man asks me. Being in a semi-migraneous state at the moment and moreso, shocked by the Pink invasion, I just stared at him. He smiled as I attempted to sense embarrassment in his gestures or words. There was none and he handed me five huge sanitary napkins with a smile. I thanked him. I then ran upstairs for my iPhone and chased the Kotex people down the street for a photo or three.

While these photos do not do justice to my existence here: the *studium* of my interpretation does not really violate any sacred truth. Likewise, the *punctum* of each image denotes the *blessure* (wound), encapsulating the very personal detail of each experience that I was able to photograph. The

experience is never the same and my ordering is also wrong. Though I really dislike the candid snapshot, I found myself lately bombarded by others' desires to be photographed and I allowed myself this infection. In this photo being "out of order" in this narratological time line and far from "how it really was," I find my experiences already transformed here. This photographic representation is nonetheless these two people's and my shared participation via technological reproduction and narration of the Kotexmobile.

Theaters of Masculinity

A couple of weeks ago, I learned that Twitter helped save lives in at least three separate emergencies at the Petionville Club IDP Camp: once to find a rabies vaccine, another incident involving needing to find an oxygen tank super quickly, and more recently in alerting emergency teams to what one nurse describes as the most horrific car accident she had ever seen.

Therefore, I was not surprised to learn that the World Cup would bring in much needed revenue for vendors in Port-au-Prince. Indeed, I have seen many a motorcycle brandishing their preferred team and several times a motorcycle was completely made up from seat cover to handlebar protection in a certain team's colors. Did I mention that here in Haiti there are only two teams to be considered in the world cup? Brazil and Argentina are the only flags sported by Haitians. This is both understandable—for who does not like near certainty—and odd since I would expect a bit more playfulness in selecting one's favorite team. Is the World Cup as intractably binaried in Haiti as political parties are in the United States?

Upon closer analysis I realized that this recurrent allegiance to both teams is not really that surprising and fits right in with some of the socio-political dynamics I have witnessed while living here. For instance, when I told one of the agronomists with whom I met last week, Timothé, of how I used to be afraid of lizards, he responded with "Why is it that girls are always afraid of animals?" I objected to this and said it was not a problem of sex but rather of culture. I reminded him that I was raised in a geography where children often did not know the word for lizard because it held no relevance. And after moving to the deep south, I was confronted with a new language, culture and zoology. It was not uncommon to fear creatures that one has not seen—especially when they jump around and onto you when as a child you are given the task of watering a neighbor-botonanist's expansive greenhouse for the entirety of the summer holidays. Were it not for my brother helping me out, Dr. Midget's greenhouse would have become a desert since my only defense against the lizards to run into the greenhouse with the water nozzle open screaming. I reminded Timothé that were he to come to Canada he would encounter animals such as dogs the size of small ponies which would frighten him to death.

Sexual difference, like football in Haiti negates the existence of alternatives and focusses upon the repeated patterns of history, of slavery, indentured servitude, *restavèk*, and the unfortunate manner in which many middle and upper class Haitians abuse their "servants" (Haitians still use this word) by underpaying, overworking and/or abusing them mentally, physically and sexually. Indeed, many Haitians have told me that they had no idea that the system of household servants was abusive until they lived abroad.   Yet, this practice flourishes with the pretext that it provides employment, or with no pretext whatsoever.   Why question what is tradition when "it's always been that way" seems to be the constant fallback for those under scrutiny for their practices. Meanwhile, there are no economic, labor or human rights protections for these workers, most of whom are women, many of whom likewise do not realize their own rights to freedom.

In the first moments after meeting Timothé, I heard his warnings of the oncoming car in the UN car park. "Attention," he would repeat each time a car passed at 2 kph, both of us safe out of the cars' passing. After about the third time that Timothé warned me, I turned to him and said, "Are you aware that I have ears and eyes?" His response was typical as I hear it often here in Haiti: "But we men must protect you women." [Yawn] I reminded him that this was the very same justification used to justify conditions of slavery, to which he objected. Well I ought not to be surprised since the Obama and Clinton race to the primaries demonstrated how certain forms of racism are surveilled in the United States while conterminously manifesting how myriad forms of sexism are readily available, a veritable prêt-à-porter for the liberal minded and uncorkable for any occasion. Even our entertainment industry is full of the images of women's gowns on the red carpet of the Tony and Oscar Awards. Women are still judged by their looks and access to posh clothing in much of the world, so why should Haiti be any different? More sadly, as many of us have experienced, sexual harassment or sexism in the workplace is often carried out by other women. As such the binarisms of sexual division continue and I wonder how Haitian women deal with these attitudes and behaviors constantly.

"A lot of women become lesbians," one UN driver tells me. Between a series of stops and an almost three hour drive I learned about how Haitian women deal with the men here. Many do not. But let me be fair—not all men here are thuggish brutes.   Even Timothé is a sweetheart who was raised by people who taught him to reify women, and ultimately to reify themselves in the process. Another agronomist with whom I collaborate, Sardou, tells me he has always cleaned his own clothes and room because he does not want someone to do what he should be doing. Many young men in Haiti are aware of the paradox of economic development and the servants both "willing" and the *restavèk* in the cities and in the fields. So some Haitians do make the connection between the abuse of *restavèk* and the mistreatment of women here, but not enough to enact real social change.   Most men are worried about their livelihood and put first and foremost their having a job, not asking their girlfriend or wife if she might like to pursue a career. I scratch the surface of these men's masculinity and realize that it is likely augmented—just as the *draggeurs* of Rabat who line certain streets—by the lack of a job or profession, the desire and need for employment. Conversely, such explanations do not reveal the workings of men who refuse to participate in the domestic activities of cooking and cleaning. Might there be an intractability to redefine the role of men in Haitian society in this double-bind to both "honor" and "oppress" women (just as in the rest of the world).   These farmers in Furcy showed me nothing but kindness and gentleness as we shared coffee Saturday morning.

And yet while watching the World Cup, I am reminded from its opening as to how effeminate this sport really is. And yes, I am putting a gender onto gesticulations—the player who writhes in agony while the presumably offending player has his arms up in the air to indicate that he has no fault in the other player's injury.   And when you see the scene replayed you wonder how anyone could be in such pain from a tiny fall—much of the writhing in pain seems rehearsed and recalls to me children playing on a field, inventing rules as they go along, nothing is truly clear. So, of course I am struck by the contrast of the male "warrior" as I see match after match whose highlights are men writhing in pain on the field. Is masculinity more about injury than goals, more about suffering and dramatizing this pain in the context of hyper-machismo discourses of strength, speed, precision and agility?   Perhaps the substance of masculinity is *its mystification as that which it is not*—for we are constantly given symbols of the player with the ball at his feet, screaming over a goal just realized, or

merely running during FIFA publicity.   In these advertisements we are never shown the head butts or players writhing in pain dramatically pointing to the culprit or faking an injury so as to disadvantage the opposing team.   Sports is a fetish of sexual division and isolation which reduces the multiplicity of identity into binarisms—strong/weak, foreign/ domestic and winner/loser. These binarisms are long-established and have been transformed over the years into various discourses, none of which evokes the injured body specifically. Many choose to think of football as a sport of "real men" who dominate the "losing men", just as many Haitian men see women as needing their protection.   There is a slippage here, a point in which certain theaters of strength are utter fictions, especially in a country where women carry the weights of both social oppression and of economic responsibility.

It came as no surprise to me that most every bank and finance company in Haiti, only lends money to women—Fonkoze included. This practice has become become more common in recent years with women making up seventy-five percent of all microcredit recipients internationally.[13] Statistics show that women pay back loans where men do not. One must ask who protects who in Haiti when lending and finance is definitely the small business owner's path out of poverty and the only ones entrusted by institutions to such monies are the allegedly "weaker sex," women? Or who maintains the economy when most of those working—even doing the heavy work of carrying kilos of food on one's head from Kenscoff to Petionville's market—are women? The choices of World Cup victors and gender clichés need serious reconsideration in Haiti as in much of the world. What such divisions offer are neat little packages for rendering static the relationship between strong and weak which fictionally posits a further correlative binary between men and women, all serving as mastheads for a fictional social structure and narrative of gender. What if there were no differences between the two aside from the socially constructed ones?

So while we are left with two teams upon whom to bet or for whom to root here in Haiti, I think the binarisms of choice needs to be broken down. We need to allow ourselves other team colors and favorite players. Clearly I am a dilettante at sports for I do not have a preferred team. During the last World Cup I was in Italy and Armenia and I joined my friends in their team's glory. But this year given that Haiti does not have a team in the competition I have decided that I would like a country that has never before won the World Cup to win. I will skip over the head-clutching and agonizing screams of my fellows here at the MINUSTAH and of the players on the field who have still no goals scored with seconds left on overtime, but many a bruise to be coddled. Let us focus upon the reality of this sporting event which offers a polyphony of possible winners. As the Ivory Coast just missed out on several goals during overtime, let us hope that maybe we can at least move beyond Brazil and Argentina. Or better yet, let us try to move beyond the notion of winning and losing, stronger and weaker, and instead let's just enjoy the "show", life.

---

[13] Armendariz, Beatriz. *The Economics of Microfinance*. Cambridge: The MIT Press, 2005.

"J.C. Duvalier, Bon Retour!"

A graffiti inscription which crossed my path—quite literally—in the Delmas region of Port-au-Prince yesterday read, "J.C. Duvalier, Bon retour!" A series of electric poles set up in the middle of a road suddenly block all circulation. Upon one of the cement blocks from which these poles spring is this anachronistic and curious wish for Duvalier's return. Admittedly, this desire for a Duvalier type of dictator is often mentioned by Haitians; yet Haitians do not wish for the return of Jean Claude Duvalier. Instead many Haitians recall how "good things were" under his father, François Duvalier, whom he succeeded after his father's death in 1971. Understandably, I was perplexed by this odd welcome for someone who is everything but loved by Haitians as Baby Doc's reign was that which destabilized Haiti economically until he was ousted from power in 1986. So why this confusing graffiti which seems not to recognize Haiti's history or, at the very least, which fails to employ any sort of critique?

"Francois Duvalier was a man's man!" I heard recently. These days I hear many Haitians these days declare more frequently the need for a dictator. A Haitian economist tells me, "Where is Préval? We have barely seen him since the earthquake?" She holds no hope for this president and as much as she hates to say it, she believes the country needs a dictator. I have to confess that there are moments when I cannot disagree.

In western Europe and North America the word "dictator" conjures up radical images as if through word association images of Hitler, Mussolini, or Hussein are the only references for such a term. In the west, generally speaking, we are educated to think that: a) our political systems work better than every other outside the west and b) that we are freer in our democracies than those who are led by unelected leaders. These are fallacies I would argue. Certainly as I had been reproached by a gay couple in a Toronto's uber-posh Queen Street neighborhood dinner party for saying that I did not fancy Celine Dion eighteen months ago, I wondered to what degree our democracy allows us certain freedoms to include fomenting individual ideas of taste and their expression or as is more common today the rigid policing of thought and dialogue endemic to neoliberalism. The need to convey one's "betterness" or eliteness is an extension of colonial thought and part of a larger pathology of those who are brainwashed about their country's superiority, usually accompanied by a large dose of historical ignorance. So while these two members of the Céline Dion fan club admonished me for daring to question "my country" (their words) because of my dislike of Céline Dion and my critique of a recent taser death at the hands of the Vancouver Police Department, this same couple had no embarrassment in referring to their neighborhood in Toronto as a "gayborhood" with the same ease in which they declared Canada's superiority over the rest of the world, a country whose Parliament had been prorogued just weeks earlier by Stephen Harper on 4 December, 2008.

Dare I say that I have never in my life felt my freedoms so trampled as in the nation of Canada where my right to physical protection was denied me by the state. In fact, I cannot think of any country where I have lived where my right to physical security was put into jeopardy by the state directly on so many instances from my witnessing police brutality, to being a vicim of it, to the manners in which civil law in Canada does not protect scholars from harassment or defamation. So the notion of dictatorship means very little to someone like me who has lived under a constitutional monarchy, a parliamentary system, an authoritarian regime, a federal presidential republic and a federal constitutional government. Most of these systems are or have been dictatorships in everything but name only. What matters to the individual is not what her government is called, but what her government does for and against her and how a government might nurture and create freedoms while diminishing violences. Names like "democracy" or "dictatorship" mean very little to those who live at the other end of political choices and disempowerment. What Haitians recall about their past leaders is best elucidated by an older gentleman with whom I spoke recently as we awaited a tap tap: "When François Duvalier was president, children went to school, they were educated, people had jobs, and there was no crime—there was none of this wearing your underwear outside your trousers!"

Haitians who harbor such ideals of François Duvalier forget the political murders estimated to be approximately 30,000 in the very same amnesia that dismisses the general climate of political repression. Many Haitians smoothly elide the fact that Papa Doc began Haiti's economic decline. It is so easy to wait for the most radical change when perhaps what one really wants is a benevolent dictatorship, the Duvaliers excepted. Can Haitians recognize—much less remember—the difference? Of course, I do not mean that Haitians are literally unaware of many of the problems the Duvalier regimes brought to this country. But there is a conscious elision to fully integrate what Papa Doc did for Haiti beyond the strict functioning of government, the economy and schools. There is a desire amongst Haitians to have a leader who, even if a ruthless despot, at least knows how to lay down the law. Yet in none of their expressions for a new dictator is present the sentiment that some violence might be necessary to invoke change.

Last weekend in Kenscoff a farmer selling seeds shows me three gourdes worth of carrot seeds and he turns back around to show me more of his stock.   His hands are shaking, he is frail, and he appears to be about seventy-five years of age.   From details he gives me, I do the math and figure that from his sales this gentleman is barely able to eat each day. Given recent events, perhaps a Duvalier is preferable to a USAID which is leaving more and more farmers desperate. USAID is regarded as an Angel of Death here which is leading Haitian agronomists to confront the likes of Monsanto whose wares we are already seeing peddled and whose products will augment the amount of poverty in the country if history is any indicator of the future.

So why on earth put up a graffiti welcoming a much maligned dictator in an era of ostensible recovery from disaster? Let me revisit the staging of this sign: it is erected on a cement pylon which is situated in the middle of a major street of Port-au-Prince, Delmas, obstructing the flow of traffic as this same pylon holds up an electric line which functions only a few hours a day. One could not dream of a more ironic setting for this graffiti than this. The pylon serves as its own social commentary on corruption upon more corruption upon idiocy. But then one might wonder why irony is used in this political gesture rather than direct critique which might serve to direct Haitians' voices in a clear denouncement of the current occupation of their country. After all, there are frequent manifestations at the university and on the streets in *centreville* about both the government and colonial presence of MINUSTAH. Haitians are not shy to express their political dissatisfaction in manners that are direct even if infrequently at times taking to more aggressive tones.

This morning before my meeting at the MINUSTAH Log Base, I went to write and check email in the deck café where the World Cup match between South Korea and Argentina was being aired. In front of the many television screens were no less than thirty Koreans cheering for their team. I was rather shocked by how calm the Haitians in the café watching this match were every time Argentina scored each of their four goals. There was a reverence of sorts for the Koreans' allegiance and not a cheer was to be heard after any of the goals by Argentina. People just looked politely as if an accident had happened...pretending it had not. I was curious after all the weeks of visual indoctrination to this event in the form of banners, flags and murals in support of either Brazil or Argentina to discover that there could be such docility at the actual event and no evidence of Haitian support for Argentina in this match. Football is usually about the spectators cathartically taking over the role of the sports figures on the screen as they cheer and antagonize in the hopes these performances will help their team win. But this was not the case today.

I can certainly not make any argument against the catharsis of sporting events, for this is very much a similar process to the catharsis of theatre. Moreso, such exchanges lead to certain realizations that bring out reflection and often change. But I was confused by all this energy—and money—invested in a month-long sporting event wherein material production screams commodity fetishism yet the performatives of team solidarity (at least today's) was gentle, even absent. The Koreans stood up and cheered each and every time their players got anywhere near the opposition's goal. After each goal by Argentina I witnessed the Koreans in the MINUSTAH café express slight disappointment, but mostly they were still hopeful and smiling, anticipating their team would score again. Today's match at the United Nations' Log Base was not at all about football despite the final goal of 4:1 in Argentina's favor—today's match was really about both the Haitian and Korean spectators. And what a paradox to be in Haiti at the UN Log Base watching this World Cup football match with nobody visibly or audibly cheering for what is one of Haiti's two favorite teams. Every so often I would hear a Haitian whisper to her neighbor, "That was a brilliant goal!" but never more than a discrete comment delicately whispered. It was as if Haitians were playing a politics of diplomacy at the UN Log Base through the surrogate of football, the only political power afforded them in the context of the UN.

Of all the possible modalities of celebratory and critical speech the graffiti in the middle of a road in Delmas does not function any differently than the polite silence of Haitians during the South Korea/Argentina game. There is a sense of anger and indignation as theft and violence are on the rise as are demonstrations against the government and the UN and more recently denouncements of the people against Monsanto and its hybrid seed "donations." Social and political actions in Haiti vacillate between a conciliatory politesse or an explosive and seemingly uncontrollable violence. Here I am reminded of Hannah Arendt's criticism of Frantz Fanon which elucidates the difficulties of normative and descriptive theory of violence in politics as she articulated in *On Violence*. To put Fanon's and Arendt's respective accounts of politics and violence into a wider context of thought and theory, it is imperative to understand that violence and politics are inextricably intertwined for many theorists while for others they are wholly unrelated. In the former understanding of politics and violence, political power is about domination—think Machiavelli, Hobbes and Weber here. These three thinkers examine politics from the point of view of state domination and hence many political theories of resistance are likewise dominated by actions of violence in order to overthrow the established order. And there are many thinkers who have worked through the stages of progressive violence for freedom versus repressive violence of domination, notably Fanon, Sartre, Merleau-Ponty and de Beauvoir. Violence is central to the philosophy of existentialism inasmuch as human life is defined by freedom and violence to achieve freedom is necessarily part of this process. As a result the political actors end up being tragic figures of violence to some (Weber) while others work through the impossibility of coupling power with violence since power depends upon the numbers of people and violence realized upon a few people (Arendt). In essence, Arendt sees violence as instrumentality and power in her analysis and therefore she views violence never a means to an end but rather as a condition that enables people to think through action. She likewise makes room for two types of permissible violence—that which responds to injustice and that which opens up the space for politics. She also admits that non-violence will not always be an effective tool, such as in the struggle against anti-political regimes such as Nazi Germany.

However, violence for Fanon is physical and it retains its power both in its threat to inflict and in its actual undertaking. Both forms of violence pervade every aspect of the world today, most especially those influenced by colonial and neo-colonial traditions. Fanon argues that the only response to structured violence is violence given that the reactions and actions of colonized people in response to power makes violence inevitable. In essence, it is important here to understand that Fanon elucidates violence as inevitable because he opens up the discourse of violence to include symbolic, economic and elitist violences which are not ordinarily realized through the word. And the contemporary problem of discussing violence in the case of Palestinian suicide bombers or of Somali pirates often lies in the discrepancies between its intended and its actual outcomes or effects and even the media representations which frame certain acts as more violent than others. Certainly one cannot easily argue against the idea that violence is in danger of destroying the purposes for which it was originally employed. In this way Arendt's argument against violence is quite persuasive. Yet Fanon's strength in arguing for violence is that he distinguishes between *violence as doing* and *violence as being*. Fanon recognizes that violence plays a structuring role in the ways individual and collective actors are produced and reproduced in both private and public domains of power. To analyze *violence as being* brings to the fore the necessary analysis of violence which is omnipresent and not a device one can simply pick up, engage and put back down. For Fanon violence is structural and his theories fit right into the politics of resistance which address the   greater structural violences of colonialism and neo-colonialism today.

The use of violence against Haitians today is as pervasive as it is back home where the notifications on the subway for what I call the "Jihad alert" underscore a growing Islamophobia in the U.S.A. Through the New York City subway system are yellow, black and white signs, "See Something, Say Something," a campaign which is still running strong as is a similar campaign on the London tube. This too is violence whose ethos is to foment fear, distrust and eventually outing of who is or might be a terrorist. In Haiti poverty and 1,7 million displaced still living under tarps, bed sheets and pieces of found wood and metal is another type of violence.

A pylon in the middle of a major road in Delmas stops the driver, forcing him to slow to accommodate the oncoming vehicles. This structure is quite violent and acts as a roadblock, demanding immediate reaction. Only then does the traffic accommodate this surprising and imposing structure by simply moving around it. Clearly, the only sort of resistance to such a monstrosity is either to hit it, an outright destruction of the edifice, or to engulf it in graffiti. Both are violences. *Violence as being* enacted through creativity is exemplified by this graffiti and will probably not oust Préval or force him to make a long-awaited public statement to the people. However, the discourse of absurdly welcoming the most unpopular of Haitian presidents in recent history upon a mass of cement suggests that *violence as being* might just have an enduring political legacy over *doing* violence.

Resisting the Hand of God

One system which functions extremely well in Haiti is the entire mechanism of social and economic segregation. One sees this in the fact that most every Haitian with lighter skin color in Haiti will likely not be poor, hence the popularity of François Duvalier. Duvalier latched onto Pan-Africanism, a movement which was popular in the the Caribbean and much of west and central Africa for much of the 20th century. His early political success was largely driven by the fact that he brought darker skinned Haitians into the political and economic folds of power and promised to topple the domination of light-skinned Haitians. Likewise, one easily notices myriad inequality in the interactions between foreigners and Haitians—and by this, I do not mean to imply a merely unidirectional inequality. Haitian property owners have increased the price of dwellings in places like Petionville such that the going price since the earthquake is inaccessible to most employed Haitians and foreigners are usually paying more for their flats here than they would in their native countries; foreigners are regularly charged five times (at least) the going rate for services such as motorcycle rides to domestic help; and foreigners of all backgrounds from Bangladesh to Peru, from the United States to the Ivory Coast, have the thrill of hearing "blanc, blanc, blanc" chanted to them by men and young, curious children who mistakenly believe this to be a salutation that will receive positive results. Of course, other inequalities are also recognizable: national staff at the MINUSTAH is paid far less than the foreign staff, after the earthquake national staff were each paid $2,500 and foreign staff $3,000 to help defray the costs of any damage (Mandatory Duty Relocation), the chances that a foreigner walking down the street in Haiti is unemployed is far less common than the average unemployed Haitian walking down the same street, and most Haitians equate foreign bodies with wealth because they have no reason to believe otherwise. Paradoxically, this practice of charging more for certain services while believing that these very foreign workers are somehow better equipped to develop this country's political, social and economic structures plays an important role in the psychological structure of Haitian society. It likewise reveals a blind trust for that which is foreign without any logical reason to trust these people who know very little about this society and, more importantly, who are barely familiar with the very long history of development programs which have failed. There is a definite tautology of dependence in Haiti and it seems nobody is willing to say "stop."

In the past few weeks, I have heard more and more Haitians critiquing this type of dependence and other problems they see in their society: "We will never change our society until we change our ways of doing things," "We Haitians are lazy—we want everything for nothing," and "Until we change our social inequalities, nothing will change economically here." Haitians are frustrated and find that it is not enough to critique an absentee president or his silent partners within the MINUSTAH. Haitians are hitting the brick wall of understanding that now as foreign programs are shutting down, now that as NGO monies are not flowing as they were four months ago, they see it is time to change gears. My driver this morning tells me that 1 July the dispatch is letting go of 10 out of the 18 staff drivers—he does not know if he is one of the lucky or unlucky as yet. He is 33 and is supporting his wife, his seven year old child, his parents and extended family. He is paid $1,000 US per month and this money is needed to support over a dozen people.

I cannot claim that Haitians want power, but they do want jobs which translates to a very useful arm of power. I have heard from shop owners, a franchise manager, and a restaurant owner how difficult it is to train Haitian staff to do their job, even to show up for work. "If Haitians had to work in Marseilles, where I studied and worked, they would starve to death!" one man tells me. I hear stories of how, within MINUSTAH, it is impossible to fire Haitians who are sometimes found sleeping in tents. The response is to make the tents off-limits, so Haitian workers are left to bake in the hot sun since these workers have few tasks assigned to them for the hours they work. I have also been told, "Haitians want to make money, they don't want to work!" at least four times in the past week by other Haitian business owners. I ask one such owner, "How do you plan to train your staff?" "It is hard," she tells me, "You have to repeat each and every time the same thing: 'Sweep and don't put the garbage in the street,'...And they never remember even though I have already told them this. It is really tiring to have to babysit people in a job they do every single day for over a year!"

I hear their frustrations as I have been working on permaculture projects in several areas in and around Port-au-Prince and find that people are more than happy to have the visiting foreigner come to help them set up reforestation and communal agriculture, but most simply do not follow through on simple tasks that are needed for regional NGOs to supply seeds, seedlings and tools. I explain to a horticulturist, also a university student, who asks me for assistance in writing a grant proposal that he needs to write one paragraph explaining the history of his project, a second paragraph explaining the future of the project, and finally a list of what he needs to do complete his mission. I offer to help him proofread his drafts and to give feedback. I am still waiting to hear back from him and it was clear to me from our interactions that he wanted me to write the grant and produce the funds. It is frustrating to undertake grassroots work where it is quite clear from the beginning that people like the language of solidarity much more than the actions thereof. I am struggling with my mission here because I have no intention on buttressing an already toxic scene of co-dependency and I am beginning to realize that it will perhaps take as many years of resisting the traditional structures of development that have led to dependency here—both physical and psychological dependency—as it has taken to develop the social fabric which presumes that foreigners can and will do most everything.

My objective is to work with already existing grassroots structures to help disadvantaged communities become more auto-sufficient and to help provide these communities their own nourishment through their direct participation and ecological practices (ie. human compost toilets, recycling, local sustainable farming) which will keep farming in harmony with their waste. I have been involved in education, communication and organizing people around these efforts. I have also been acting as an agent between various NGOs that can supply seeds and provisions to these communities, educating the communities about the fact that after the first year of their project they will need to collect seeds, produce cuttings and to save roots to reproduce their agriculture without depending upon these same NGOs. I attempted to make clear to those with whom I collaborate that I will not procure money for them and that these projects are about subsistence farming and communal empowerment. In essence, I try to educate Haitians in these communities that they do not actually need to be supplied seeds each year—that they ought to be self sufficient after a year, emphasizing that they take advantage of the free supplies for the first year and then learn how to harvest seeds without the intervention from external aid. There are agronomists involved in these projects and all the means are present—from free land (usually Haitians live and farm on borrowed land) to free supplies. Sadly, I am finding that many people say they want to volunteer, but they actually want to be paid to be part of this project despite the fact that they are gaining direct benefits from the supply of free fruits and vegetables. What might seem like a simple and obvious concept of saving money from grocery bills becomes difficult to sell when many Haitians believe an NGO will offer them a job to be a driver, a cook, a cleaner. Words say one thing here, but the actions are usually in conflict with the reality on the ground. In short, it is difficult to get through notions of self-reliance and non-dependency when many Haitians have lived through three generations of politics and NGO programs that nurture this dependency. I think of the words from a Haitian social activist the other day who told me, "Everyone is looking out for number one here and nobody wants to collaborate."

Certainly, the contradictions within the social structures of Haiti are similar to those of my own society. The major difference between these two cultures, however, is how these contradictions function. In the United States there is an embrace—even perversely so—of such contradictions where pedophilia is a much mediatized social issue and yet, the propulsion of young girls into beauty pageants is not at all questioned as parents push their seven-year-olds to prance around in a swimsuit competition. Or take the many instances in my country where one right-winged, homophobic politician after another is revealed to have a proclivity for bathroom sex with other men. Haiti is light years away from such postmodern irony in all its perverse destructions and beautiful creations that such contradictions produce. Conversely, Haitians tend to accept silently certain practices (ie. marijuana, homosexuality) while avoiding serious social problems of physical abuse against women and children. As such, the more serious social abuses remain muted and these subjects are simply not discussed. There is a structural parallel between the inability of a society to discuss its dark problems of violence towards women, for instance, and a society's desire to tolerate the existence of homosexuals, non-religious Haitians or even Rastafarians. I have to confess that I am tempted to start an NGO in name only called "Atheists for Haiti," just to balance the energies up a bit given all the Christian NGOs who aspire to bring "God" to Haiti. Oppression in Haiti is multiple and I cannot say that the economic and sexual oppressions are at all separable. The valences of "tolerance and invisibility" together with the massive human rights violations directed at the weakest of this society are inextricably linked. How is it that the real, very dire problems of economic and physical violences in Haiti are pushed aside with more ferocity than the non-problems of "alternative lifestyles," both paradigms which are rendered invisible, both problematically tolerated?

Twice in the past two weeks I have discussed with two MINUSTAH employees the scene of homosexuality today in Haiti. Both tell me that scores of Haitian women are leaving men for other women because, as one related, "Men are extremely abusive towards women here." Last week, a MINUSTAH employee tells me how she is married and has only lesbian friends, as she flirts with me. She is clearly afraid to discuss her own life, but I got the message and I politely declined her offer. Yesterday, another woman at MINUSTAH tells me how "macho the men are here and how they are never happy with just one woman." I told her from my observations and interactions with men here, that Haiti would turn me into a bona fide lesbian. She asks, "Do you like homosexuals?" I reply, "I am half-homosexual." She confesses, "Me too." She then pours her heart out to me about her girlfriend and her break-up ten days prior. "What did you do to make her leave you?" I chided her. "Nothing," she replies silently almost embarrassed. I rephrased my question teasing her slightly, "Did you cheat on her?" "Well, yes...sort of..." she answers, "It was only with one woman." I continue to tease her and I say, "So you are just like the Haitian men then!" She became very silent and so it was then that I tried to cheer her up. She told me of all the gay spaces in Petionville and we exchanged numbers making indefinite plans to go out for a drink together. She told me of her 18 year old daughter, a university student, who is totally aware and supportive of her sexuality. These are many of the stories we do not hear about "Haitian society" and the contradictions are neatly tucked away, out of earshot such that the fragmentary nature of this society allows for people to create their own pockets of existence. What is important she highlights is that nobody is offended, of course. So one is free to live her sexuality as long as it eschews the optics and cognitive grasp of the masses.

I notice a pattern emerging in my discussions with Haitians about this discourse of "Haitian culture": this ostensible monolith of "Haitian culture" is based on very convenient reversals of reality. I have observed that men are certainly not the primary protectors, providers or leaders of their families and communities (women tend to be); that child labor is pervasive in this society and is likewise utilized by both the poor and the rich (whilst the wealthier Haitians claim not to participate in this practice); and that the physical and sexual abuse of women and children goes unpunished and mostly covered up on all levels of society despite the recent laws against rape and physical abuses (2005, updated in 2010). This was the focus of the conversation over watermelon this morning with my housemates.

Hence, for every constructed "truth" of Haitian culture it is not uncommon to find Haitians arguing about where this alleged truth actually reaches, or if there is a singular truth at all. There is a superficial consensus about Haitian society on many levels—just as there is about the subject of identity in most countries. When Haitians begin to discuss certain "givens," they are quick to deconstruct most of these presuppositions. Or, when an outsider (ie. me) points out the absence or exclusion of certain margins, Haitians are quite open-minded in admitting this absence and they tend to re-evaluate their presuppositions of their society or "Haitian culture." In Haiti language and action function in contradistinction to one another. The "unnatural" of homosexuality, for instance, is accepted in action but never in public discourse. Likewise, the absolutely abhorrent practices of human slavery is underlined as part of the historical discourses of a Haiti which ostensibly freed itself of slavery in 1804. However, the present-day practices of slavery from women to children are still widely exercised. This is a society of etiquette and these mannerisms, unlike those of North America, do not begin and end at table manners—they extend to every level of social interaction and reveal the way power is acceded and exchanged.

An extremely large part of the cultural fabric here are the daily greetings— the forced, quotidian "bonjours" that many a time seems more aggressive than welcoming. The subject who does not say "bonjour" because she is reading or on the phone is reproached, given a stern gaze, as is the person who asks the waiter for a drink. The other night a drunken man, after I asked the female waiter for a lemonade, says to me, "You have to excuse yourself for interrupting me...I was talking to the waitress." Language is not so much about politeness as it is about recognizing power. How I long for the lengthy salutations of Morocco and Algeria where greeting someone begins five meters before the physical crossing of paths and continues another five meters thereafter, as both subjects continue to speak heading in opposite directions no longer seeing the other's face as their salutations prolong. However, I realized that night as the man poked his finger into me, pushing me for having dared to order a drink from a waiter with whom he was speaking, that he felt ignored despite the fact that people in Haiti order drinks all the time in bars and do not have to "ask permission" or excuse themselves to do so. I represented the "rich foreigner" and when I asked him to take his hands off of me, he replied,

"Yes, I should—I am getting my hands very dirty." Language in Haiti is often about being recognized as a subject since subjectivity is in constant peril here and often language is the only manifestation of power in the absence of material symbols and titles within society. Since I had "hurt" him by not recognizing his person, he was out to hurt me physically and through direct, verbal insult. As the language of aggression explodes onto the scene, words and action of violence were finally in synchrony.

Sunday's ride to and from the beach with new friends created a field of traveling zen for me. I love traveling by land and I dislike talking while so doing; hence, music, the sound of the wind from open windows and the hiss of pavement under the tires warms my spirit as I can spend hours doing nothing other than watching the road, the skies and the passing scenes of people, buildings and grazing animals. As Claude put Iggy Pop into the cd player, he announced a much-needed change from *kompa*. While listening to Iggy sing, I shot a video of the road, his lyrics framing what I imagine to be exactly what I and the driver are feeling as "The Passenger" played. There was this sense that the stranger driving and I were in the same mood and Iggy Pop set the relaxing pace for the day as the soundtrack for the Haitian landscapes, rain, and then soon thereafter, the sun. It was a magical journey, in part, because I did not know Claude until that morning over breakfast, and also because we both intuited that the other just wanted to travel in silence and meditation during the 90 minute ride to the beach. The first car led the way and Claude and I followed, in gentle pursuit of a breeze, the view of the sea, a series of IDP Camps near Corail, and the many villages nearby. I felt on vacation for these 90 minutes for this was a break from having to narrate myself, to explain where I am from and what I do, or to detail what mission I am on as is usually the case in many of my interactions here. This journey was a fragile relief for me where I was literally and in lyrical form, "the passenger" who "sees things from under glass."

Being a passenger means you do not need to make decisions, that you are free to observe and passively soak in the visions, that you are not really a subject in the frame of travel. Being a passenger means that you are a not responsible for directions or the state of the latest oil change or tire pressure. You are free of responsibility as a passenger and life is a series of following what another person's decision-making leads you to. Being a passenger is a lovely release from the chore of driving, of decision making. Likewise, it is a solid metaphor for the political passenger who can passively take in the scenery and observe without interacting, without speaking out, assuming someone else will do so simply because it is not your role. Even everyday language takes on the trope of the passenger—"How are you?" "Fine Thanks," "It looks like it is going to rain" "Yes it does"—and human interactions seem more based on roles rather than true feeling or committed involvement. We often speak as if on auto-pilot and the results of this pattern of speaking are to create more patterns. I engage these shapes simply because my existence would be unbearable if I were to role play what many people here (and elsewhere) project onto me. Hence in the ongoing discourse of identity, I push back as

I repel questions of origin daily—"Let's talk about something more interesting," I answer when I am too tired to narrate my origins. Haitians, curious of course, are ready to hear some morsel of information as if my saying that I am American will actually reveal something particular about me. So often when they ask me where I am from, I often throw back the question to them: "Moun ki bò ou ye?" "Haiti," they respond quite reluctantly, curious about why I would ask where they were from since the answer (to them) is patently obvious. As I refuse to fall into the role of the passenger in my daily life here or elsewhere, I took the opportunity to embrace this role to and from the beach on Sunday.

The resistance to patterns is necessary in order to break from the present in both our political and personal lives. Psychoanalysis has evidenced the difficulty of breaking from these patterns established within childhood through its study of language and narration and the problematic relationship between symbol and human relationships.   History demonstrates a similar dynamics of action and reaction. It is with this decolonizing spirit that I approach this year's World Cup as I inevitably learn the history behind football and study rivalries that date back to very specific matches, as if wars or slaughters, from which deep resentments are created and through which present games hold great historical meaning. It is never just Argentina and Greece—it is also the spectator's nationality at play and how she sees this frame of action. There is little forgiveness in sports and the passion of this theatre is both understandable and allegorical in relation to our collective human history.

So yesterday, while watching the Argentina vs. Greece match with two men, one Dutch and the other Belgian, I found myself defending Diego Maradona when the Belgian insulted him, "Once a drug addict, always a drug addict." Mistaking this person's dislike of Maradona for a dislike of drug-addicts, I reminded him that we all make mistakes and that Maradona seems rehabilitated enough to lead Argentina this far.   The Dutch gentleman said to me, "It is not about that really—" The Belgian interrupted him, "All the children look up to him and he fucked up his life and now look at him! He's an asshole with no brain and he does nothing! And look at his face, he is still doing drugs!" The Dutchman laughed and turns to me, "It really has nothing to do with that." Indicating the angry gentleman, he continued, "He is Belgian..." And the Belgian interjected again mentioning Maradona's arrogance over the infamous "hand of God" goal and the Dutchman said, "You have to understand, we will never push for Argentina. Don't forget 1978 for us, and 1986 for Belgium." Previous defeats defined the battlefield of today and I realize that sports is a field of emotional and physical play that does not embrace the passive passenger, but demands of the spectator to stand up, scream, cheer, and even cry. It demands both emotion and some form of action. I came to understand these men's dislike of Maradona, not because they allied themselves with their home country team, but rather because they resisted following the adulating media attention given to someone who claimed that God had a hand in his goal (illegally made with his hand, but missed as a penalty by the referee) and who— after years of self-destructive obesity and drug use—had the nerve to criticize Pelé saying "he should go back to the museum." The criticism of Pelé was clearly the "nail in the coffin" for these gentlemen and their refusal to adore (or forgive) Maradona was, in turn, their resistance to a pattern of sports adulation which ceased questioning the validity of one of football's most central and controversial figures.

There is catharsis in the theatre of football and the screams of support are the spectators' inclusion as actor, such that even a vibrant hatred for a team—or player—is more political life than the silence of indifference or the assumption that someone else will hate or act for you. Can Haitians bring football to the spirit of their social and political life? Can there be an establishment of political discussion and critique that might lead to more Haitians involving themselves in the uncomfortable and necessary dialogues about their social problems and their very participation in these social ills? This is a question that can only be answered by those passengers who wish to learn to drive and to rename the "hand of God" as it really is: an illegal move.

Goudou Goudou

Something you will hear all over Haiti these months is *"goudou goudou."* It is the term that people gave to this January's earthquake: "It is the sound the earth made during the earthquake, hence we call it *goudou goudou*, that loud bang of the earth," a UNFPA (UN Population Fund) worker tells me. This expression is an onomatopoeia of that which killed hundreds of thousands (now estimated to be 300,000), which has left, according to the latest figures, 1,7 million people in IDP Camps between Port-au-Prince and Léogane.   The sound of that which is ominous takes on a meaning that invokes history and tragedy, that itself seems a lilting expression that might have just as well been invented by children. *Goudou goudou* rolls off the tongue with a haunting effect of that is not at all light or joyous, as in the fairy tales of the Grimm brothers. A word which seems so beautiful and playful, harbors a deeply embedded mechanism of fear and death.   This word converts the unspeakable, the unevocable and it names that moment of death. For it was a moment—four seconds according to many—where you might have been saved if you were standing here and not there, moving like this and not like that.   Those four seconds of time literally separated space, and space cruelly selected who would be toppled by walls, who would receive scratches, and who would watch this destruction from a distance, helpless. Those four seconds of the *goudou goudou* distinguished the living from the dead.

I have two friends leaving at the end of this week: Cinzia and Julia. They are two UN Volunteers who have lived in Haiti three and two years of their lives respectively. Both are highly intelligent and capable in their fields and command admiration from all their colleagues as they excel at their professions—Cinzia, (Swiss-Italian) working in Human Rights, and Julia (French) in intelligence. Both were here during the *goudou goudou*, both lost many friends and colleagues. Cinzia invited me to her house the other night for dinner and she pulled out the pictures she had of the Christopher Hotel where the MINUSTAH offices were housed since 2004, showing me pictures of this five story hotel before and after the collapse. She pointed to where she would go to get coffee each morning, now covered by the rubble and no longer visible. She showed me where she would enter and leave the building, all the memories she had there. All five stories were in rubble and there was only the imagination to render space lively and I did my best to follow having only a heap of rubble upon which to imagine this storyline. She pointed to where her office was located and indicated the pool which always remained empty as she described the scene of the earthquake to me. It was clear that Cinzia was alive through a stroke of luck—her building also collapsed, but she was in the meeting room, the only part of her building that did not fall. The *goudou goudou* took the lives of two of her colleagues, injuring several others.

I came to know Cinzia through our collaboration in the Child Trafficking Cluster and she demonstrated courage in the face of corruption and dishonesty. I remember one day during a meeting when UNICEF's head of Child Protection refused to reveal the location of children who were rescued from a rather large trafficking operation. Cinzia stepped up to the task and gracefully but affirmatively let Caroline Bakker know that she was complicit in obfuscating information that is to be shared amongst all the child protection agencies. I wanted to jump across the table and hug her for she showed courage when others averted their gaze due to the mounting cases of harassment I witnessed and heard about. Then, one day several weeks ago, a UNPOL officer bellowed across the MINUSTAH cafeteria, "That woman there is a hero! What she did after the earthquake I have never seen another person do—she is my hero!" Curious as to what he was referring, I asked Cinzia what she did and she immediately withdrew and became shy, embarrassed even. She said she did not like to talk about it—but she had worked with the various rescue teams to identify the bodies in the first days after the quake. This was personal, not professional and I understood her reticence to discuss this subject, or to underline what she did. She said, "It was not work, these were human lives. These were my colleagues, some of them my friends." She did not feel that the discourse of "hero" fit anyone since all the survivors— Haitians and ex-pats—did what they had to do, what anyone would do. Her act was that of survival and solidarity, the only possible human retort to *goudou goudou* which breathed life into a time of profound loss.

I heard Julia's story of where she was during the earthquake over dinner a few weeks ago. She was working and realized straightaway an earthquake was occurring and so she immediately dove under her desk and yelled out to her colleagues to do the same. She mentioned how her building was next to the main Christopher Hotel and that her building— and not the Christopher—had been recently tagged as dangerous for earthquake conditions. In fact, they had been expecting a specialist to come on 13 January to do an evaluation on the state of the building. So if an earthquake were to occur, her building was expected to fall. Instead, the Christopher Hotel which was thought to be resistant fell and as Julia cried out to her colleagues to dive under their desks, her colleagues had different reactions at various cognitive speeds. Daniel, her boss and our friend, told me recently, "I was just walking towards the printer to get a document I had printed and I had no idea there was an earthquake until I saw the cement floor beneath me rolling as if waves of water and not cement. And the wall in front of me cracked and was opening and closing, opening and closing."

Julia and her colleagues all survived the *goudou goudou* and immediately exited the building helping colleagues from the other floors and departments descend windows by ladders. "I didn't even know the Christopher had fallen, I was in a daze just working automatically and helping my colleagues. It wasn't until some time later that I realized the Christopher had fallen." She worked for four days straight on no sleep, with Daniel and another colleague. These three were the only ones from MINUSTAH who travelled in Port-au-Prince immediately after the earthquake to do reconnaissance, attempting to learn about the areas of destruction, mobility and to attempt to communicate this information. They travelled in a UN vehicle during a gas shortage, keeping the volume of the radio very low so that it would last as long as possible. They passed the dead even though UN security prohibited them from helping, "We passed the body of a small child in the road and we couldn't even take it off the road," Julia tells me. I asked Daniel this morning about the sights he saw on the roads in the days following the quake, about the mourning, those crying. "No, nobody cried," he told me, "I didn't see one person cry. People were moving around on foot, lifeless, listless, in a state of shock." Last night Julia tells Daniel, "I will never forget the garbage truck." "What about the garbage truck?" I ask. "It was dawn," she begins, "and just in front of us was a garbage truck into which was being put bodies, and we saw the truck crush the bodies. You could smell the bodies, we could see everything, the shoe—Daniel, you remember the shoe, don't you? And it was the one time that they let us smoke in the car, smoke was better for them than the smell of the bodies. I will never forget the smell of the dead—it is not just a smell, it is a taste."

Julia's going away party was held in a graveled passage between the JMAC (Joint Mission Analysis Centre) offices yesterday evening. I met many of the intelligence officers with whom Julia has worked over these past years and I saw nothing but love and respect between everyone present. I was in shock given that I have just left a professional environment that was, quite frankly, the opposite. Every single person was beaming over this thirty-year old woman who apparently made their professional lives a joy. The collegial support was self-evident. This was not a theatre for the one-off party, for I had been in their offices before and frankly I even sought out signs of discord, given my previous experience in academia. Toasts were made, tears shed. This party made me think of the end of the "reign of terror" when my former head of department who had been harassing several professors for years had to step down to make way for the new chair. I also remember there being a lunch to commemorate this tyrant's exit from her post at a small café-restaurant near the university and it was painfully clear that my colleagues and I showed up for this luncheon out of politeness, not out of respect. At that "party" there were no words of esteem, no love, nothing. It was one of the most pathetic moments of an unscripted performance of non-appreciation I had witnessed in my life—only it wasn't a Mexican telenovela. It was real life in all its discomfort, unhappiness, and denigration.

Julia told me last night, "In those first days after the earthquake, we were able to distinguish those who were with us and those who were not. Those days revealed who was a caring human and who simply wasn't." The *goudou goudou* make painfully clear various levels of humanity.

[commercial break]

I have learned an enormous amount of things in my life from all people and professionally, I have tended to learn more from my students than from my colleagues. This is not an insult to my former colleagues, many of whom are brilliant in their own right, this is just a matter of fact reflecting the true nature of academia and intellectual engagement today. Scholars are hired to teach classes and in recent years we are often instructed to lighten the load since the students (literally called "clients" in Université de Montréal correspondence) are commanding the future of academia— "Welcome to McDonalds, may I take your order?" As such we are given courses to teach, students to direct, we attend committee meetings, we sit on doctoral and masters student exams and thesis committees, we produce scholarly work, we write grant proposals, attend conferences and we are led to believe we are to offer excellence. However recent changes in many universities' policies across North American demonstrate that professors ought not to challenge the students, that learning is now a capitalist enterprise with classes stuffed with students, and that we ought to avoid reflecting on institutional politics such that we offer neither quality nor rigor. What remains are cliches such as websites which proudly proclaim "one of the best universities in the world," when in fact this just translates to "over 2,000,000 served."

In essence, the university structure today is often based on a corporate model of downsizing, where education is no longer a process but instead a product, and where scholars are rarely able to dedicate themselves to the furthering of knowledge due to the Taylorized model of higher education. Quantity tends to count more and more these days over quality and rare are the discussions of intellectual endeavors amongst colleagues. The divisive politics of tenure and promotion do not help such that if you are not prepared to dawn your paper hat and step up to the microphone to take orders from the client, your tenure will be put into question. And what is most paradoxical, although we work on completely different topics in any given department, there is so much competition and division that one can only wonder about the mental stability of most everyone in academia. Certainly, academia can be a really lovely job if the environment is supportive the individual scholar and innovative teaching practices. This, sadly, was not my experience in my eight years at the Université de Montréal. I will never forget the departmental meetings I attended with colleagues most of whom were lovely, where the atmosphere was poisoned by discomfort, a palpable fear of two colleagues who rendered all communication toxic in addition to, over time, another two sycophants. I would note incongruencies in communications by the then head of department and I discovered that we were collectively being lied to in an effort to coerce us to vote a specific way on various departmental policies. Nothing seemed beyond the "pale" and I spent eight years in a professional pale, with the economic freedom to do my work. I spent eight years of my life harassed as graduate students were told not to work with me, a defamatory document was circulated about my person with character assassinations against my editors and universities where I had previously taught, my professional qualifications were put into question, I was the object of anti-Semitic comments and sexual harassment for which the university never once proceeded to investigate, and the ongoing harassment of myself and two other colleagues was essentially swept under the carpet. I raised my voice and this act of speaking out resulted in a concerted effort to marginalize and silence as is typical of institutions whose mandate is to maintain the status quo. Ultimately, my experience in this particular department at the Université de Montréal was bitter-sweet. I reached out to former professors only to hear of their past horror stories and then learned of a colleague who is experiencing similar tactics of defamation by certain members of his department at the American University in Cairo. One can only wonder how such unprofessional, sickening behavior is not only tolerated, but because of the lack of disciplinary measures, such behavior is inevitably encouraged. *The Lord of the Flies* is by comparison quite tame.

I am thankful for those colleagues who remained supportive throughout this "ordeal." In all sincerity, the only words of advice I can leave my colleagues would come in the form of a citation—but not from Derrida or Levi-Strauss, but rather from that brilliant horror film, *When a Stranger Calls*: "Get out of the house! We've traced the call and it's coming from upstairs!" I left happily, unwilling to waste one more blood cell carrying oxygen to my body over this affair. Mostly I am thankful for my students who taught me to have a load of fun on the sinking Titanic. What a beautiful last few months I had thanks to these students, down to the graffiti underneath a table that was soon to belong to Marc-André Grondin. I truly love these wonderful people who ought to be teaching certain of my former colleagues lessons on integrity and scholarship through praxis.

I am please to announce that as of today I am out of this toxic structure and I am free. الـحـمـد لله I am an independent scholar, filmmaker, artist, vagabond and I am more than happy with these titles. In the end eight years of harassment by two colleagues led me to Haiti and in most respects it was one of the best tragedies to befall me.

[Ultra Naté's "Free" streams into this commercial break]

> *Oh we are strangers*
> *does anyone really care deep down*
> *we're all the same*
> *try to take out our pain*
> *you think you could never trust another*
> *cos they're all lost to pleasure*
> *never trust another*
> *we've got to live in this world together*
> *open up our hearts*
> *love can finally start*
> *c'mon and try (Now's the time)*
> *cos you're free to do*
> *what you want to do*
> *you've gotta live a your life*
> *do what you want to do...*

[And now back to our scheduled programming...]

Julia indicated she wanted a beer but her colleagues kept approaching her and covering her with hugs and kisses. Realizing at this rate she would never get her drink, I went to the cooler and searched out a beer and brought it to her. When I returned I found Julia with Jens Kristensen. Julia had spoken to me previously about Jens. For five days he was trapped in the rubble and presumed dead with only his tobacco to comfort him. She joked, "He was already so skinny that five days without food was no big deal for him...He just curled up and was protected by the mere fact that his body was so small." Returning with the beer, I accidentally heard words they exchanged, and I will not repeat them. Needless to say that I was in awe of the level of professional respect and sheer human love I accidentally witnessed in those moments. The *goudou goudou* had destroyed many lives, but it brought as many together. What I have witnessed amongst professional staff in my months here is the precise opposite to the world of "professionalism" with which I was inflicted the last eight years at the Université de Montréal. I realized last night that all professional environments are indeed not necessarily toxic.

Like love affairs where we are hurt and find it hard to move on, so too are the lessons of the professional field where a Nazi and a Midget can indefinitely transform the human soul of someone whose only crime was to excel at what she does. Bitter jealousies, departmental meetings with colleagues who hurl insults, character assassination and defamation—none of these actions were to be found in any of my meetings at any of the UN offices and it was rare to find any sort of animosity. It is clear that for all the experiences of Julia and Cinzia, that they will leave Haiti and their work with the United Nations with a smile. What the *goudou goudou* took away on 12 January, these people gave back exponentially to those around them and they converted the *goudou goudou* into actions of caring, respect, professional rigor and sheer love. Julia, Cinzia, Anne and Eric are leaving Haiti on Saturday and they will take their experiences and memories in all their polyvalent tones and emotions outside and beyond this rich and lively country. Their experiences in Haiti are as much a reflection of their personal formations and characters as they are a demonstration of the institution which, although quite blemished and flawed by the undertows of a colonial past, has at least the professional integrity to support their work, allowing these individuals the space to grow and validate one another.

I will miss both Julia and Cinzia because of who they are as individuals and for what they have taught me about their work at MINUSTAH and about life. It is a testament to their strength of character that these two beautiful people remain positive, courageous and loving in their efforts to make sense of their years in Haiti, their professional work, and more poignantly their emotions surrounding the *goudou goudou*. The *goudou goudou* which ate life in four seconds, indiscriminately ending the lives of almost 300,000 brought me enormous clarity. Despite my critiques of the system of "development", I have learned from these twenty and thirty-something professionals to include the sort of pragmatism involved in some of these UN jobs. Let's be honest here, life is really quite a pragmatic theatre. For most professions outside of my own and very few others, pragmatism is professionalism and it is integral to the rationale and the execution of tasks. Theory and meditation are luxuries for those with four extra seconds. What I have learned from the analytical astuteness and dialogues with these women will stay with me. That they are able to translate the *goudou goudou* into a rich fabric of community, professionalism and communication makes my heart stop. I thank them for inspiring me to make the definite choice to leave academia and to move towards life, leaving behind my personal and far less tragic *goudou goudou.*

Saturday was Daniel's birthday party and the atmosphere was vibrant and full of warmth. There were three parties that day and Julia and I were to attend the others in due time. We went up to the apartment to get ready and Julia dawned a dress and shoes which she had bought on her recent trip to San Francisco: "$35 at the Gap she points to the dress." She pointed to her shoes, "Aren't these great? $35!!!" I loved her attitude as it was the first time I saw Julia dressed up and I was thrilled to see her extreme beauty. She continued, "These are the first clothes I bought since the earthquake. I lost almost everything—all my clothes—in the earthquake and what I didn't lose I gave away." I reached into my back pocket for my iPhone and said, "Let's take a picture."

Hope, Death and Football

A MINUSTAH intelligence officer informed me yesterday morning that after Brazil's loss to Holland on Friday, there were 13 violence-related injuries in Port-au-Prince and 5 suicides, one man throwing himself under a moving vehicle on Delmas. When I asked if any such thing happened in 2006 when Brazil and Argentina were disqualified from the the World Cup, the answer was a clear no. Watching the World Cup Saturday with this information of the precedent day's events was simply saddening. I have been maintaining to my friends here that we need to get behind the underdog in this sporting event and that we must stop supporting those teams which have already won quite a few times: Brazil (5) and Argentina (2). I look around and I see a Ayiti ("Haiti" in Creole) with so much cultural richness and love, but with no strong affirmation of its own presence in the world. Instead the surrogate for Haitian pride is Argentina or Brazil. (Robin proudly reported to having seen a Dutch flag last week.)

So I show up to the matches to sit with my new mates—Michele, Robin and Ghislain—to watch the games as I learn an enormous amount from these three men. I have a new respect for the act of watching sports on television after these past few weeks given that the dialogues I have had with these three humans have been illuminating, inspiring much of what I write, informing my spectatorship of these games, and educating me about the drama and catharsis of sport. Indeed, we have replaced the gladiator arena of killing, the animal maulings and the public participation in death with a far kinder spectacle involving human dexterity, speed, and intellect. In football, life-threatening bloodshed is infrequent while the tools of performative engagement resemble those of the past with flags, uniforms, horns, and chanting spurring on the action with the public arena—the common goal for each side is to win.

However, what does this winning really imply? For today, the match does not end in misery, one party does not die, nor is the loser subject to the audience's control of his future life or death. Losing a match is, in relative terms, not at all a tragedy. Losing a match of any sport is just not a "tragedy"—and this is the way the notion of game is conceived today. Certainly, the tragic elements are all there: emotions are high, players scream for joy jumping onto their teammates and they are essentially given a pass on homoerotic behavior in uniform, while other men cry their eyes out on the field as they hit the turf and continue weeping. At the end of each match, players and spectators alike must come face to face with either the realization of their hopes or the death thereof. You either win or or you lose the match and there is absolutely nothing in between these two valences.

Is it that these Haitians who took their own lives were uniquely upset about Brazil's loss? As I learned during my conversation Saturday afternoon with Daniel, a Uruguayan MINUSTAH staff, "I knew the guy who threw himself under a truck on Delmas Saturday. He was crazy." But what is this "craziness" precisely? Why in 2010 and not 2006 are these suicides after the World Cup an alarming presence for Ayiti? One cannot deny that the power of hope since January is salient in this country— people hope so they can move forward, wake up in the morning, take care of the children and the ill parent. People hope because it is the only way to get through the misery here. As a friend reminded me last week, "We need to root for a likely winning team because we need to celebrate, to forget about our devastation, and each passing day that our team has the chance to win the World Cup is another happy day of celebrations. This is why we support Brazil or Argentina." I felt a bit badly for supporting all the underdog teams during this year's World Cup; yet, I made my argument that at least some Haitians should be happy that a team which has never won the World Cup could actually win it, that there is more joy in an underdog winning than in going with the "usual suspects," passing through the clichés of victory.

There is little self-construction of culture in Haiti and all identity is constructed and modeled after others cultures: from the United States to France and from Brazil to Argentina. Economic and social models are idealized while others collide and Haitians do not invest themselves into any new investment of themselves. In general, Haitians just know what they want to resemble and then cling onto that symbol—Argentina or Brazil—which, now eliminated, are empty symbols of success. These symbols of success no longer symbolize winning (for Haiti) and in that ushering out of meaning this past weekend, Haitians simply do not have another team in which to invest their emotions, their hope. Nor have they made a backup plan for such. Even the streets are less jubilant, the motorcycles of blue and white and green and yellow are gone, the banners down. People are sad and for the naive outsider one can say, "But it is only a game." Football this year in Haiti, however, is not just a game. This is the sports equivalent of psychological transference whereby Haitians have redirected their hope for their country's reconstruction, for their personal and familial economic condition, to a new object—the World Cup victor. Haitians put their marbles in one basket—they bet and they lost. Hope was held out for many over the past six months and now hope has ended, the World Cup is the pretext. The real motive however, it is not.

Many of my friends who experienced the *goudou goudou* did not mourn the loss of people, did not really fully conceive or feel these losses, for several months.   Having myself suffered from post-traumatic stress disorder after the loss of my son, I realized these symptoms: people operate on auto-pilot, they move fast and hard, and they everything non-stop.   Stopping would mean that reflection could possibly enter the equation and that is definitely not an option for the victim of trauma. Hope is manifested in the actions of looking for loved ones, of waiting all night for family members to return home, of not eating for weeks thinking that starvation will punish the body of reality enough such that you are given your sister back to life, and working non-stop confers that movement, action of all nature, keeps the reality from sinking in. We must finish the task at hand to get to the next task and so forth. Continuity into the future is the *trompe l'oeil* of progress, much like the elaborately painted stucco buildings of Genova, Italy where one cannot tell if the wall is painted as brick or if it *really* is brick. And then, does it matter as the subject gazes onward?

When I last watched the World Cup in 2006 I was elatedly pregnant, surrounded by friends, lecturing all over Europe and the Middle East with a brief pause in Liguria and another pause in Naples for more research and writing. I saw this life form which I called my *girino* (tadpole), my little child curled up at 14 weeks. Life was entirely about hope and possibility and we are lucky subjects those of us who have a salary every fortnight, those of us who do not make choices between school for our children or food. We are a spoiled lot and we are the ones who must understand the white and the blue, the green and the yellow, ever more attentively. For when my little boy died, I lost all hope. The only time in my life I thought of taking my own life simply because hope was out of sight, not under a bitter discord with a colleague, not hidden under a momentary souring of a recent divorce, not even what I deem (by comparison) to be the easy loss of one's house to earthquake or fire. Oh, how I wanted to burn my own house down when my child died. Life simply made far less sense than I could have ever imagined. I spent two weeks rolling cigarettes and smoking with Martin, the only person with whom I entrusted my child when I would go shopping. He was the only person I could stand to see, the only person I really wanted to see. All the rest could fuck off. I spent ten days on Central Park West with my son's ashes sitting in my friend's apartment contemplating when I would go down to Florida to bury his ashes at sea. It was then that I discovered the "healing properties" of television and I checked out.

I am now quite well-versed in television language and have learned that there is now good television out there since my childhood of *Dynasty* and *Little House on the Prairie*. Nothing gave me hope and I resented those who tried to inspire it: "Think of your career," "Think of your books," "Think of your films" and all I could think of was death itself. I did not want what they wanted as my muse for continuing to breath on this planet. I wanted my son back and it was my daily role to go back over his death and try to remember things I could not remember. Amnesia as a result of my trauma and hope were my realities while also the very concepts which I scorned. I did not want hope and part of me still resists it. Hope is for movies, hope is Scarlett-fucking-O'Hara and her rhetoric of "Tomorrow is another day" and or Mrs. Skeffington's conversion at the end of her life. Hope was all that shit that I did not believe because to have hope you have to believe in something and in order to believe in something you have to have something else that is *actually believable*. Alas, even belief is a form of transference.

So on I went throughout 2007 obsessing over where little Madeleine McCann was and in my sick mind I actually thought that should she be found, my little child might come back to life. I even contemplated cryogenizing my son and imagined him hanging next to the Walt Disney of Jean Baudrillard's narrative. I obsessed over George W Bush and grew upset that the gods of this earth, those horrid monsters that kill would allow that terrorist-murderer to live and not die after choking on a pretzel, yet I had to live day in and day out the word SIDS, a syndrome that nobody seems to know anything about. "But hey, there was nothing you could do, Madame," I was told. Hope comes from the knowledge that something can actually happen *as a result of* or *concomitant to* the act of hoping. When there is no parallel or conterminous action that brings to life the "dream," then there is simply no reason to hope.

So when the World Cup schedule was announced and I was aware that I would be in the middle of a mania in Port-au-Prince, I realized it was time to take a vacation or grin and bear the memories of my pregnancy and of my loss. I watched the first few minutes of the first match with tears in my eyes for much of it, South Africa v. Mexico. I had to leave for it was too painful for me to return to what came to epitomize for me a time of hope—parents who are expecting children are quite simply *expecting*. And what we expect are good things—we do not wish to think our child can be born sick, that we can have a miscarriage, that our child will develop a serious illness or that our child will die. We expect out of life—especially those of use from wealthy nations—and we resist all knowledge of things that are not "up" or "bubbly" or "positive." How I now dislike that word "positive," because those who announce how positive they are tend to be those who simply cannot handle the very genuine and sad realities that life imports us all.   So I cried in the bathroom at the MINUSTAH one afternoon realizing that something I never really cared for, football, represented the end to my hope and I did not think I could stay in Haiti for the entirety of the World Cup.

Then came my "angels," Michele, Robin and Ghislain (and "now they work for me"). I end up watching many matches with these men as I learn the history of the sport, the rivalries, the excellent and absurd plays and the democracy of judgement that goes on during each match as the video contradicts a referee's call. And then we discuss. I never in my life thought I would watch football this way because four years ago it was a different type of watching—many more people singing karaoke in between matches and a lot of personal discussions amongst friends obfuscating the serious nature of the sport.   Neither was better, but this year's World Cup is especially healing for me as I had to confront this symbol of "hope failed" and sit with it day by day. These men, unbeknownst to them, have helped me get over this hurdle as we laugh and make fun of everything surrounding the game.   Just on Friday the game started promptly at 9h00 and it was the horrid ESPN with a British announcer who put everyone to sleep.   Then suddenly the men started to scream out after certain plays either "¡caramba!" for a bad play, or "¡sabroso!" for an excellent play. They were upset by the commentator and expressed their desire for the

Spanish Univision channel which this cafe usually puts on, despite neither Robin nor Ghislain having any comprehension of Spanish whatsoever.

What these men loved about the Spanish commentator was how he delivered the play by play action with passion, joy and energy. Anyone who has heard a goal being scored in Spanish knows that the space between English and Spanish commentary are light years apart. And so there I was with these beautiful men screaming out "¡caramba!" and "¡sabroso!" until the cafe finally changed the channel to Univision where we were given the treat of a commentator who would fill in the slow-paced scenes with sponsorhsip commentary on home mosquito repellent and other products. Those who understood Spanish were laughing until they cried and others of us translated. It was then that I realized that I was having the time of my life. Unexpectedly the World Cup had become a joyous space of celebration and hope for me simply because these individuals reminded me that personal tragedies do not necessarily repeat themselves and that there is hope for the future, be it personal or sports. The World Cup has come to be invigorated with hope, not just for the countries and players involved, but for myself personally. I have been given this renewed sense of life simply because stories created in and around these matches, personal and political, breathe hope and life into the present. I can have hope because when I am in western nations, for instance, I look around and see a million stories of hope and my life's trajectory is one I create, simply because I have the luxury to make choices and move freely. I can stop or go at any given time and this is the greatest luxury of all.

So when I look around me here in Port-au-Prince for the stories of hope, there are few. The rhetoric of hope is thick, "Ansamn nap rive pi lwen" says the Voila telephone company sign ("Together we can go further"). But the concrete reality of hope remains pure rhetoric—it has resonance as a sentiment and is vacant as a lived reality here. There is no reason to see an *ansamn* (together) here in Haiti, for there is little collaboration within and amongst communities, government agencies and all the organizations here who clearly invested in putting their projects out with heightened visibility as their NGO slogan occupies a sleeve or pocket. Much of the work being done here is wasteful, uninformed and comes down to getting individual NGOs recognized and funded. Relief and development work is an industry like any other and it is rarely discussed in the media or amongst the very agencies creating this business. All Haitians know this fact and they know what is in their future with this almost $10 billion pledged in aid to Haiti. They know that jobs will not be developed, nor housing, nor help with transportation, or their children's education will come of this money. They know that they are in another theatre: that of international benevolence with less than half the funds promised that have actually been received. Haitians know the score because they have been in the middle of the western pity-fest before when hurricanes and deposed leaders become the stuff of Wikipedia's entry on Haiti or the "click to donate" button for those who want to "help" without being at all informed as to the psychological complexities that donating money does to these people, their systems, and their perceptions of the world.

This is the beginning of the end, these are the overtures to the continuation of a system that eats the brains of Haitians: the best of the educated have been long gone having been offered scholarships and passports to countries far away, and the young just want to leave.   Of course they want out and frankly, who can blame them.   There are a few dozen wealthy families in this country who control the politics and economy and there is no hope for the millions who will remain homeless, penniless, and jobless. Tellingly *nap rive* ("we will go further") is a fiction whose value on a huge billboard on the Pan American Route means nothing other than more "blah blah blah."   Haitians know this is bullshit and they have no reason to have hope for $10 billion which is never coming their way, but will instead pave the way for multinational companies, contracts, and their government officials who feed off this cycle of dependency.

My way of watching the World Cup was reinvigorated with hope because I was fortunate to be able to take breaks with a group of men who nurtured me, engaged me in political and sports dialogues, and who taught me a lot about both their work and football. I had the luxury to support an underdog because I had a task at hand to occupy my every day here in Haiti, I had a reason to wake up in the morning, I had a future to which I could look forward with my research, writing and films, my new and old friends, and the knowledge that Thursday salsa at Quartier Latin would give me the mental break in what are generally 15 to 18 hour days.

I have hope on a personal level even now because I hope to have a family and I can think this way simply because I have the economic and political means that allow me to think this way. Haitians have no reason to have hope and hence Argentina and Brazil became these surrogates of hope and likewise these nations became the stand-ins for Haitians' own country. Nowhere do we see hope expressed directly for Haiti—instead I witness the daily hope for Haiti through damaging surrogates: international NGOs, the United Nations, and all that is in the form of a foreign body. Argentina and Brazil *were Haiti* simply because dreaming "pi lwen" was impossible—you can only dream further if there is space for a "further" to reach. Here, today, at this moment, there is absolutely no hope. I wish I could say differently but the evidence is here before our eyes: almost six months after the *goudou goudou*, nothing has fundamentally changed.

The shock of the earthquake is suddenly affecting everyone now. Haitians who suspended judgement about the many NGOs and their own government started to grow frustrated by the absolute inadequacy and absence of the social and political structures. Needless to say that there is an increase in the incidents of rocks being thrown at UN vehicles and petty theft. However, security is not an issue here—I am told by people working in security at the UN that crime in the Dominican Republic and Jamaica is much higher (ie. sixty murders took place in Jamaica three weeks ago). Haitians were placated by the World Cup and the growing security sector noted this change as well with NGOs increasing their curfews recently from 18h00 to 23h00. The World Cup represented a pause in the student manifestations and the civil unrest, but now that both of the favored teams have lost, one noticed as early as noon Saturday, the traffic *blocus* returning and the people were again depressed. This was not what I had hoped for when I had discussed getting behind a team that had never won. I falsely believed that Haitians were in this World Cup for the sport. They were not. Haitians wanted their teams to win to prove themselves the winners. They didn't want to get behind Ghana or Mexico because those are not the models of football success that Haitians envisage.

Sadly, the cultural notion of success comes from believing that the same people always will win simply because in reality, in Haiti, that is precisely what happens. For the impossibility of giving the 1,7 million of Haitians made homeless a hectare of land is also rooted in Haiti's deepest crisis: land titles which will remain in legal contestation for decades to come if the government does not intervene. Approximately twelve families own this country and not even the government which has the power to expropriate land is doing anything to change it. So why not root for those who have won in the past? After all, they were the political subjects most likely to win and they are today those with the houses, jobs, servants, drivers, and swimming pools.

Haitians are still in line for jobs at the UN and NGOs—the two sources for decently paid work in the city. They are beginning only now to feel the longterm effects of the January quake. Aid workers are returning home, people are finishing their UN contracts and many are confessing that the earthquake is only hitting them now. Clearly for these Haitians who have survived far worse than the loss of Brazil and Argentina at the World Cup, the discourse of football has come to represent the hope that people hold for the future. Many of the development projects at hand are failing and many are cynically designed for six months at most; hence this country is a social laboratory for ex-patriots to come and tinker about. As I look around Haiti, I see one huge colonial workplace for highly—and dare I say overpaid—individuals to come in and flood the already skill-filled country with specialists created for various industries that are engaged in making money off poverty.

The bets on the post-colonial political subjects of the World Cup (ie. Cameroon and Mexico) have failed and it looks as if the only team playing which has not before won the World Cup that also has a chance of winning is Holland. Perhaps Haitians might get behind this team to imagine that Holland, which has never won the World Cup, might indeed win and that we can all say "¡sabroso!" together, welcoming a new winner to the fore. More importantly, let us hope that Haitians might begin to see themselves as social subjects such that choosing a World Cup team does not constitute the exclusive extent of their political and personal choices, where the only real decision that the Haitian subject can make is between hope (Argentina and Brazil) or death.

Mwen Renmen Ayiti

Last night Sophie, a photographer from New York, told me, "People in the camps are extremely organized—within weeks the people here created beauty salons, stores, and food stands. There is Internet in this camp out front [Place Boyer]." Sophie added, "Can you believe that on February 29th I went and had a manicure in one of the IDP camps? 10 Haitian dollars!"

We were seated in the Quartier Latin, a bistro where main courses run between $12 and $22 USD. In front of this posh restaurant is an IDP camp. The juxtaposition is surreal, disturbing at the very least; but it is also a fact of life as Haitians living in this camp are as used to watching from across the street those who can afford to enter the gates. Likewise, those of us who enter are accustomed to Haitians camping outside. But what is the reality of these people? Who are the camp dwellers? And who are those whose job it is to solve the problem of 1,7 million people in camps living in precarious shelter made of fragile tarp, plastic, found wood, metal and even bedsheets?

Before entering the Quartier Latin yesterday afternoon, I noticed two men standing outside their tents—Sanson and Paul, neighbors. They were looking at me. I was coming to the Quartier Latin to work and later that night to go salsa dancing. I crossed over to speak with these men. Paul lives in a tiny tent which we would use for camping in North America—it was big enough to sleep two. Sanson lives in a tent/house—a structure made of various materials from found wood to canvas to plastic with a proper door to lead into the 8'x10' space. After introducing myself, the first question I asked was: "Are you being supplied water?" They said they were given water every two or three days for bathing. I asked how their food supply was—they said, they had none. Both are unemployed as most Haitians are and their days consist of waiting for news of their hopeful transfer to a camp where they would not be baking under the sun. The heat has been unbearable this week in Port-au-Prince (40 degrees Celsius) and hearing their stories I immediately felt guilty about complaining about my experience with heat which was nothing like these men's and their families' hardships. Paul's tent was directly on cement and was a cheap tent that would not last many months longer. Sanson's house was a heat box with the only advantage of being tall enough to stand up in it. They said the real water problem was not to bathe but to drink—no potable water was supplied to them and they were worried. I wanted to make the situation right for these men, for the entire camp, but I knew there was nothing I could do given that various NGOs are in charge of these camps and often have made the political—in some cases the necessary—decision to stop supplying food and water. I learned in my first weeks here that potable water was simply not supplied to people in any of the IDP camps, nor in the makeshift schools, nor anywhere. There are debates within many NGOs about the supplying of food and about the forced migration of people from camps elsewhere.

Indeed there are NGOs like ACTED which refuse to participate in any forced migration projects such as the forced migration of people to Corail where I am working on an agroforestry project with Viva Rio. Yet these men and their families want to be anywhere but that festering hot park. How can all these organizations make the right choices when 1,7 million humans are caught in the middle and when the thousands of organizations involved are struggling to balance the inaction of the invisible government with actions that might ethically solve the IDP camp problem? More pointedly, why is the government's power to expropriate land not being used judiciously to offer terrain to these 1,7 million displaced. My plan from the beginning was that the government should offer people 1 hectare of land and to employ agrarians and students of forestry and agriculture, giving them jobs advising 15 families at a time on the appropriate methods of farming. Guy, my farmer friend in Kenscoff had a similar plan to split up the $10 billion amongst all Haitians. The government has done little to advance a massive plan for taking care of 1,7 million people in tents. It is swelteringly hot, there are no jobs and Monday will not only mark the six month anniversary, it also marks the first day after the World Cup. The people will surely manifest their frustrations.

The theatre of development attempts to show that a lot is happening: see them working in the shirts emblazoned with x organization's logo, they are busily digging that ditch, cash for work and food for work and come Monday, on half year since the earthquake, very little has changed. Did I mention that there is no head of child protection at UNICEF and there is nobody expected for at least another six weeks? The situation is serious here and yet despite all the business of NGOs running about, so little actually happens. In part, it is a mammoth task to attempt to manage almost 2 million people in the absence of a governmental structure. In part, because there is simply no infrastructure in Haiti. Getting to work for most Haitians in Port-au-Prince involves two hours of travel each way in tap tap. For those fortunate enough to have a private car, this time can be cut in half. But overall, there is a subtle disjuncture between all the cluster meetings and the actions that would ostensibly grow from so much communication and inter-agency cooperation. It would seem that little is being done in certain agencies, and UNICEF seems to have won the prize in this domain. I constantly think of Govinda's reference to UNICEF as the organization which "moves the furniture around" and I am reminded that this, indeed, is still true months after my arrival. There is no massive campaign against child trafficking, there is no project on board to develop alternative educational methods, no campaign against *restavèk*, and there is pretty much an absolute silence concerning all things related to the trafficking of children. As unemployment is getting worse, the NGOs who came for emergency relief are now leaving taking along with them the jobs their NGOs had created for Haitians. Certainly, Haitians are growing upset by the lack of response to their needs and their government is conspicuously absent, invisible even.

So I was going to a meeting in the Quartier Latin and I told Sanson and Paul I would come to speak to them about their situation afterwards. Sanson said, "Do you want to see in my house?" I replied affirmatively and he opened his door to reveal a lace entry covering and then on a big bed, the entire family—seven members—facing me watching a television set just to the right of the entry. They all smiled and waved and I left so they could continue to watch their movie. This is how Haitians make it through the day—television from hijacked electric lines and familial support. This is certainly not ideal, but it gets these people through the day as they await transfer to a more livable abode, as they seek out work, as they struggle to find a means of sending their children to school, and more generally, as they make the most of a terrible situation.

I was informed by one person collaborating with USAID that each site that is excavated, there are on the average of 18 bodies found in the rubble. Sometimes the bodies are quite fresh as they have been so deeply buried in the rubble that the lack of oxygen and the cooler temperatures has preserved the bodies. One of her jobs is to order body bags. She spoke to me of how she finds dependency as one of the greatest problems here: "You just cannot give Haitians food. That is wrong, it creates a whole other set of social problems..." Most everyone I have met in the field echoes this sentiment as most are despondent about the emergency situation which, though not in the same state as in the first few months after the earthquake, is nonetheless critical. What is actually being done for the 1,7 million displaced Haitians living in IDP camps? And why are dependency models, despite the knowledge of the damages done, still being employed?

There is an irony here in that the very people organizing the domiciles of Haitians, the transfer of them from one IDP camp to their future homes in their old neighborhoods, or in new IDP Camps such as Corail, are themselves individuals who are generally out of place, never at home, often in antipathy with their country of origin. I include myself in this category as someone who has designated the heartless city of Montreal as "Schmontreal," for many years, putting the "schmo" back where it belongs. Of all the people who do development and humanitarian work whom I have met, most have not lived in their countries of origin, nor do they wish to. These are highly skilled, intelligent people who have found themselves out of place in their own countries of origin. That this is an irony, however, I do not find problematic. That humanitarian workers can relate to displacement lends to a certain comprehension of this reality, albeit a self-imposed migration is in many ways different than one forced upon the individual. How can these individuals resolve the grave problem of relocating 1,7 million people without forcibly migrating individuals who simply do not wish to live outside of Port-au-Prince?

My drink and dinner at Quartier Latin progressed to where I met yet another person who works with a French NGO, ACTED, who told me that Fort National, a district downtown, was totally destroyed and that those people are living in Champs de Mars, a large park in the center of Port-au-Prince.   There is currently taking place a reconstruction project, a pilot program initiated by President Préval for rehabilitation of this city quarter. It will take years for the project to be finished and in the meantime, Champs de Mars will remain the alternative living quarters.   The goal of many NGOs working in Haiti who refuse to collaborate with projects of mass migration (ie. IOM) is not to displace individuals.   This aid worker from ACTED told me that their collaboration in the project of Fort National offers the possibility of returning people to their communities by putting them in semi-permanent structures.   This project started at the beginning of the week.   The UN, USAID, CHF, ACTED and World Vision are implicated in this project and it is far from finished, but there seems to be an optimism amongst the people living in Champs de Mars that they will be able one day to return home.   However, I have noticed a trend with USAID sponsored projects from the Monsanto fiasco through various farming projects in Kenscoff: these projects tend to be cover operations that propose the enterprises for other private companies and their specifically targeted projects, contracting jobs for construction, development and the growing security industry here.   Between the projects of Corail I, II, and III and rehabilitation projects such as this at Fort National, I am still waiting to see results that are tangible.   More importantly, Haitians are awaiting these projects' completions so as to continue life in a domestic space that is minimally sanitary and safe.

Meanwhile, I stand at the entrance of Quartier Latin and take a 180 degree photo which reveals the surreal nature of wealth and poverty in Haiti: on the left and center, a posh restaurant, courtyard and paid managers and staff; on the right, a small IDP camp of several thousand unemployed, impoverished, malnourished Haitians.

People are clearly upset about the conscious underdevelopment of their country at the hands of those who claim to come and "help" and even "develop."   And since Argentina and Brazil were eliminated from the World Cup, the mood is demonstrably tenser on the streets.   The decisions to be made are difficult, yet nothing is evident.   For every person who says cash for work schemes are a failure, there will be those who disagree.   Or more tangibly, there will be a Haitian relieved to have some money for her family unaware how these schemes damage social and economic models of labor and how they render Haitians dependent upon schemes which rarely last beyond three weeks. The reality is that there is not one right decision to be made—but there are plenty of bad decisions already being made. The primal fact of Haiti is that informed decisions do need to be made and realized by those with their country's best interests at heart and that these antiquated neo-colonial measures for "developing" Haiti need to be abandoned immediately.

I am not giving Paul the octopus the decision-making power that many lent him during the World Cup of 2010. But since the leader of this country is clearly absent and every NGO and humanitarian agency has their knives sharpened reading to cut more portions of the $10 billion pie, we might as well let the fate of Haitians rest within Paul's tentacles until a saner, more humane commitment to critiquing and reversing the damage that neoliberal dependency models of "development" have engendered.

Bibliography

Agamben, Giorgio. *Homo Sacer: Sovereign Power and Bare Life.* Trans. Daniel Heller-Roazen. Stanford: Stanford University Press, 1998.

Armendáriz, Beatriz. *The Economics of Microfinance.* Cambridge: The MIT Press, 2005.

Fenton, Anthony. "Haiti: Private Contractors 'Like Vultures Coming to Grab the Loot.'" *Global Policy Forum.* 19 February, 2010.

Foucault, Michel. "The Birth of Biopolitics." in *The Essential Works of Michel Foucault 1954-1984.* Ed. Paul Rabinow and J.D. Faubion. New York: New Press, 1997.

"Haiti Ripe for Child Trafficking." *The New Zealand Herald.* 25 January, 2010.

Langer, Gary. "Voices From Iraq 2007: Ebbing Hope in a Landscape of Loss." ABC News. March 19, 2007.

Maohadjerin, Mashid. "Haiti's Orphan Industry." *The Wall Street Journal.* 26 February, 2010.

St. Fort, Nazaire and Jeb Sprague. "Haiti: Once-Vibrant Farming Sector in Dire Straits." *Inter Press Service News Agency.* 4 March, 2008.

UNICEF. "Statement on Intercountry Adoption." 31 July, 2014.

Yves Pierre-Louis and Kim Ives "Préval Nominates Michele Pierre-Louis for Prime Minister. " *Haitian Analysis.* 2 July, 2008.

Index

Printed in Great Britain
by Amazon

43051544R00149